Claiming Her Place
in Congress

Claiming Her Place in Congress

Women from American Political Families as Legislators

KATHERINE H. ADAMS

McFarland & Company, Inc., Publishers
Jefferson, North Carolina

ISBN (print) 978-1-4766-7718-7
ISBN (ebook) 978-1-4766-3717-4

LIBRARY OF CONGRESS AND BRITISH LIBRARY
CATALOGUING DATA ARE AVAILABLE

Library of Congress Control Number 2019943094

Front cover—top: seal of the United States Congress;
from left: official portrait of United States Representative
and Speaker of the House Nancy Pelosi (United States Congress),
116th Congress official portrait of Liz Cheney (United States
House Office of Photography), Jeannette Rankin, circa 1916
(Library of Congress); background: United States Capitol Building
photograph © 2019 Shutterstock/WeTakethePictures

Printed in the United States of America

McFarland & Company, Inc., Publishers
Box 611, Jefferson, North Carolina 28640
www.mcfarlandpub.com

For Leslie and Pam

Acknowledgments

This is the first book that I have written by myself in a long time. Michael L. Keene died in February 2018. He is sorely missed as my friend and as my co-author. I so appreciate our decades of work together.

As always when I write, I would like to thank the fine librarians of Loyola University, especially Pat Doran and Jim Hobbs. I would additionally like to thank both my previous and my current chair, John Biguenet and Hillary Eklund, for their kindness and their support, as well as my dean and my provost, Uriel Quesada and Maria Calzada.

I would also like to thank the politicians who allowed me to speak with them over the phone for this book. They include Mary Bono, Cynthia Hedge-Morrell, Kay Bailey Hutchison, Susan Molinari, Lisa Murkowski, Stephanie Herseth Sandlin, Sheila Simon, Kathleen Kennedy Townsend, Christine Whitman, Carol Williams, and Jeanne Zeidler. Their experience and insights have greatly enriched my research.

For the excellent images included here, I am indebted to the Photoshop skills and generosity of Willie Wax. I would also like to thank Heidi Braden for her help with processing these images.

I would also like to thank the fine editors at McFarland. I have been so fortunate to work with this publisher.

Table of Contents

Introduction

During the late nineteenth and early twentieth centuries, even before a federal suffrage amendment became law in 1920, a few women ran for office in both suffrage and non-suffrage states, often for positions related to education. In the 1860s and 1870s, male voters commonly elected women candidates to Massachusetts school committees; in 1906, eighteen women became county school superintendents (out of fifty-three) in South Dakota.[1] And in 1916, a year when women voted in twelve states, Jeannette Rankin entered the U.S. House of Representatives from Montana, the first woman elected to a national legislature.

After the federal amendment passed, a few more women entered state and federal office, but voting did not quickly lead to anything resembling parity in representation. In 1931, Emily N. Blair, a Missouri suffragist and a vice president of the Democratic National Committee, wrote of the two major political parties that "women were welcome to come in as workers but not as co-makers of the world. For all their numbers, they seldom rose to positions of responsibility or power. The few who did fitted into the system as they found it. All standards, all methods, all values, continued to be set by men."[2] Blair labeled the barriers to election as "almost insurmountable" since "the dominant political parties do not nominate women for political office if there is a real chance for winning."[3]

These trends from the 1920s did not change measurably for a long time, especially in regards to the U.S. Congress. Before 1950, fewer than a dozen women held seats in Congress at any one time. In 1961, there were only seventeen women in the House of Representatives and two in the Senate. As Ellen Malcolm and Craig Unger declared concerning the early 1980s, though women had successfully entered many other fields, "when it came to the United States as a representative democracy, half the population was still being ignored."[4]

It was not until 1992 that this trend showed any signs of change. Voters elected more women to Congress that year than ever before: twenty-four new representatives and four new senators, with Kay Bailey Hutchison joining them in June of 1993.[5] But even with these increases, the Senate had six women as members (6 percent), and the House forty-seven (10.8 percent). As Jennifer L. Lawless and Richard L. Fox argued in 2005, "The organs of government were designed by men, are operated by men, and continue to be controlled by men," and the low percentages of 1992 acquiring the label of the Year of the Woman substantiate their viewpoint.[6]

Although the numbers and percentages of women in Congress have risen since 1992, their participation certainly still does not approach women's percentage of the population: the 115th Congress, in session from 2017 to 2019, had twenty-one female senators out of a hundred (21 percent), one more than both the 113th and 114th Congresses, and an all-time high, and the House had eighty-four women (19.3 percent). In 1986, Ellen Goodman referred to American women's advances in public office as progress by the "drip method."[7] In 1989, the Center for American Women and Politics forecast that attainment of a fifty percent equivalency in Congress would take 410 years.[8] An estimate done in October 2016 put parity not so far away, but still at another hundred years.[9] Because of such slow progress, the United States has fallen behind other nations: we now rank ninety-eighth in the world in the percentage of women in the national legislature, down from fifty-ninth in 1998, just behind Kenya and Indonesia, and barely ahead of the United Arab Emirates.[10] As governor and ambassador Madeleine Kunin wrote of American politics, "The historic male model, while no longer idealized, has nonetheless become synonymous with a universally accepted definition of 'leadership.'"[11] Certainly progress occurred in the November 2018 elections for the 116th Congress, bringing the total to twenty-four women in the Senate (24 percent) and 105 in the House (24 percent), another highly publicized increase that may signal further movement toward parity.

Reasons for Slow Change

Given American electoral history and this data, it is not surprising that scholars have recently sought causes for both women's successes and failures in politics. Many variables have been studied repeatedly, if contradictorily, to determine reasons that so few women run and win, in both state and federal elections, and that so many don't.

Since the 1920s, as many scholars have noted, party officials have given lip service to inclusion, but often encouraged women to enter elections that they couldn't win.[12] By 1994, as Susan Carroll concluded, two-fifths to one-half of women running for office had opposed a powerful incumbent or had run in a state where the opposing party securely held the seat.[13] New Jersey Republican Christine Todd Whitman, who in 1990 ran a surprisingly close Senate race against Bill Bradley, the incumbent, believes that if the party had thought there was any chance of defeating Bradley, it would not have nominated a woman to run against him.[14] Recent studies, however, have pointed to change concerning the two major parties and women: Susan J. Carroll and Kira Sanbonmatsu in *More Women Can Run: Gender and Pathways to the State Legislatures* (2013) and Barbara Burrell in *Gender in Campaigns for the U.S. House of Representatives* (2014) maintain that especially the Democratic Party has recently become a positive force in encouraging women to run in competitive races.[15]

Beyond party affiliations, another variable, also changing over the decades, is the level of voter prejudice against women taking on political roles, especially the presidency but also membership in the Senate and House. In 1937, the Gallup organization asked a sexist question, in which gender seemed to be a "respect" that made a woman less qualified. In a national sample, in response to "Would you vote for a woman for President if she was qualified in every other respect?" 34 percent answered yes and 66 percent no. Favorable responses rose in each decade, to 48 percent in 1949; 76 percent in 1978; and 92 percent in 1999, with the altered ending of "if she were qualified and your party nominated her." But prejudices remain, especially concerning a woman's ability to oversee the military and insure national security. After 9/11, as survey data showed, voters were less likely to support women candidates, for all national offices, than they were in 1999. And in 2013, Kristina Horn Sheeler and Karrin Vasby Anderson declared that "the strategic frames of sports and war reinforce notions of heroic masculinity and rugged individualism that undermine a female candidate's ability to inhabit a presidential persona."[16] Although in 2014 the affirmative response to the Gallup question was 95 percent, doubts remained about a woman's ability to defend the country in wartime.[17] And according to a 2018 poll, while 63 percent of those who voted Republican in 2016 said they thought it was likely they would live to see a woman lead the country, only 40 percent actually wanted this to happen.[18]

While women might be dogged by judgments of their capacity to attain and succeed at the highest offices, they have also faced endless scrutiny of their appearance and private lives, what Diane Heith has called the "The Lipstick Watch," a form of discourse that might stall a candidacy or keep a woman from running.[19] Certainly, the fashion choices of politically active women have commonly been picked apart by the media.[20] For Hillary Clinton, famously, the physical critique has been unstinting. Sylvia Bashevkin also notes that women's romantic lives can be another unwanted subject of interest, rendering them less than serious to the public. As Senator Barbara Mikulski concludes concerning these judgments, "If you're married, you're neglecting the guy; if you're divorced, you couldn't keep him; if you're a widow, you killed him; if you're single, you couldn't get a man."[21] While candidates take this type of coverage seriously, some scholars have deemed it an outlier and downplayed its effect on election results. In 2009, using survey data, Deborah Jordan Brooks argued that party, ideology, and incumbency have a greater impact on election results than gender or gender stereotypes. In 2014, Kathleen Dolan employed a representative sample of 3,000 adults to conclude that voters are remarkably even-handed in judging male and female candidates, regardless of the commentary about women's hair and dresses that might appear in a few sites. After analyzing the 2010 and 2014 congressional elections, Danny Hayes and Jennifer L. Lawless concluded that female and male candidates for the U.S. House received similar coverage in their local press and garnered similar evaluations from voters in their districts.[22]

In a complex space, of judgments that may combine complexion and ability, some scholars maintain that another key factor is confidence. In 2012, when Lawless and Fox polled women and men in "feeder" careers (business, law, education and public service), they found that women were likely to have relevant experience equal to men. But when asked about whether they were qualified to run for office, only 57 percent of these women agreed, compared to 73 percent of men.[23]

Other analysts don't concentrate on parties or incumbency or confidence: they claim that few women seek to enter office, especially in the U.S. Congress, because of its contentiousness and even danger. Kathleen Hall Jamieson, for example, has depicted this negativity as name calling, vulgarity, hyperbole in attacking others, and non-cooperation or extreme partisanship.[24] In 2004, in the *Washington Post*, Dana Milbank and David S. Broder claimed that George W. Bush had promised to change the tone for the better, but had instead made it worse, with neither Democrats or Republicans interested in seeking common ground.[25] The civility called for after the shooting of Steve Scalise in the summer of 2017 appeared to some critics as yet another promise of change that did not lead to fruition, with the situation seeming to worsen during the presidency of Donald Trump.

As recent events have revealed, another factor that has discouraged women from entering Congress is not just the lack of civility but the danger. In the fall of 2017, Representative John Conyers of Michigan, accused of demanding sex from women in his office, was under investigation by the House Ethics Committee. Facing multiple allegations, he resigned in December. Other lawmakers, such as Senator Al Franken of Minnesota and candidate Roy Moore of Alabama, also stood accused: Moore lost in a special election campaign in December 2017; Franken resigned in January 2018. And such activity was not new, of course, having involved Anthony Weiner, Mark Foley, Eric Massa, Mark Souder, Vance McAllister, and others. Beyond these accusations, reports have concerned secret payments of taxpayer money to settle sexual harassment complaints, by Blake Farenthold, Pat Meehan, and Trent Franks, all evidence of a space that women might choose to avoid. Though these three have resigned, others who have been accused, such as Ruben Kihuen and Bobby Scott, remained in office.

In the fall of 2017, adding to what staffers asserted, women members of Congress began telling their own stories of harassment. Senator Claire McCaskill recalled vulgar suggestions made when she was a young legislator, about how a woman could get a bill passed in the Missouri House. Representative Jackie Speier posted a video sharing her experience of being forcibly kissed by a chief of staff while she was working in a congressional office in the 1970s. Representative Diana DeGette told MSNBC that former Representative Bob Filner tried to pin her against an elevator door and kiss her. Representative Linda Sánchez of California spoke about being sexually harassed by two male colleagues in the House. And Debbie Dingell spoke publicly about having been harassed by a high-level politician. She evoked a strong response especially among other women who had not spoken out because of their fear of losing a job or being labeled a troublemaker: "What people don't realize is there are still consequences for a lot of people [who come forward]," Dingell said. "Honestly, we're going to have to work very hard … to really change the culture. We've got to work together as men and women."[26]

In response to so many allegations, Representative Jackie Speier and Senator Kirsten Gillibrand introduced bipartisan legislation called the ME TOO Congress Act, to overhaul the current process available for reporting harassment, a bill that remained in committee in 2018.[27] The House and Senate mandated previously optional sexual harassment training for all lawmakers and Capitol Hill employees. While such responses have been helpful, prospective candidates may choose to fulfill their ambitions in less dangerous spaces.

Another Key Element Not Considered

In a complicated research space, of so many variables and forms of analysis, of disputes about why women run or don't run, about why they win or don't, one key element has not been thoroughly considered. Kira Sanbonmatsu and Susan J. Carroll, in "Women's Decisions to Run for Office," from 2017, consider ambition, incumbency, and party power, but when they turn to the impact of family, they just deal with domestic responsibilities of female and male candidates and the age of their children. What they don't consider, as have few studies, is the power of membership in a political family. In what Barbara C. Burrell has called "variation in opportunity structure," one of the most powerful forms of opportunity, which may engage significant liabilities as well, comes from the American tradition of politics as a family business.[28] Membership in a political family is here defined as having family members, by birth or by marriage, involved in government as officials, including legislators, judges, and sheriffs, or as party leaders. These family members—grandmothers, grandfathers, mothers, fathers, brothers, sisters, husbands, and partners—have all played a key role in the political careers of women.

In the history of democracies as well as other forms of government, leaders have often come from elite groups, generally engaging fathers and sons, not mothers and daughters. In *The Recruitment of Political Leaders*, Kenneth Prewitt describes three levels leading to power: the dominant social stratum, from which some members enter a politically active stratum, in which they learn "the ins and outs of the political game," and then a third level of actual candidacy. This model, historically engaging only the prestigious few, often involves the power of individual families: as Prewitt claims, "persons who control the pathways to public office tend to perpetuate their own kind."[29]

This prevalent tendency in the United States, of electing members in families, occurred from the beginning of the nation. In 1966, citing seven hundred families in his first study of American dynasties, Stephen Hess noted an "odd phenomenon, a democratic electorate's love affair with a political royalty," and he cited family names such as Rockefeller, Stevenson, Long, Kennedy, Byrd, and Talmadge. As Hess mentioned, these families traditionally involved fathers and sons and a wider network of relatives, as in the case of presidents John Adams and John Quincy Adams as well as cousin Samuel Adams, delegate to the Continental Congress from Massachusetts and later governor of the state—and at least twenty-one other elected officials. Similarly, the Calhoun family included in the early nineteenth century John E. Colhoun, a state representative and U.S. senator from South Carolina; John C. Calhoun, U.S. secretary of war and vice president of the United States; and Andrew Pickens, governor of South Carolina. Especially in the past, in this country, these elite family members were overwhelmingly male, white, Protestant, college-educated, in prestige occupations, with above average incomes, of Anglo-Saxon descent.[30] Hess claimed that it's not surprising that elite children seek to enter the career: "It's daddy's business. Lots of doctors' children go to medical school." What he finds more interesting is that Americans keep voting for them.[31]

Many of these families moved to prominence from a state or regional power base. The Long family, for example, is identified with Louisiana, the Harrisons and Lees with Virginia, the Roosevelts with New York, the Daleys with Illinois and more specifically Chicago, the Muhlenbergs with Pennsylvania, and the Tafts with Ohio. Other political families have been connected with more than one state. The Bush family entered politics in Connecticut, with Prescott Sheldon Bush serving as a U.S. senator from 1952 to 1963, but is now more closely identified with Texas and Florida. In a fourth generation, George Prescott Bush, the oldest child of former Florida governor Jeb Bush, has been twice elected as the commissioner of the Texas General Land Office. Members of the Rockefeller family have been elected in New York, West Virginia, and Arkansas. Kennedy family members have run for office in New York, Rhode Island, Connecticut, Maryland, and California, in addition to their primary base of Massachusetts. The Udall family first became prominent in Arizona but the most recent generation had three cousins simultaneously serving in the U.S. Senate, from Colorado, New Mexico, and Oregon.

Scholars like Hess have primarily documented the paths of men from political families. Indeed, in his updated study from 2016, Hess claims that "women had always been part of the shaping and motive force in politically active families, but essentially as wives and mothers." In a section on Hillary Clinton, he quickly refers to the widows who served in Congress as involved in a "noncontroversial placeholder technique"; the only female politician whom he credits as a role model for the current generation is Margaret Chase Smith.[32]

But Hess' judgments have left out a much fuller story. After the approval of suffrage, political families began to involve women not just as helpmates or party activists but as candidates.[33] Corinne Alsop Cole, for example, a great-granddaughter of James Monroe, a niece of Theodore Roosevelt, and a first cousin by marriage to Franklin Roosevelt, became a Connecticut state representative in 1925 and a delegate to the Republican national convention in 1936. Susan W. Fitzgerald, a Massachusetts state representative elected in 1923, was a descendent of Timothy Pickering, a member of the Massachusetts legislature in 1776, the U.S. secretary of state, and a U.S. senator from Massachusetts.

In the U.S. Congress, the presence of women from political families developed into a significant trend as soon as women could enter office. In the U.S. House, beginning with the election of Jeannette Rankin in 1916 through the 115th Congress of 2017–2019, 286 women have served; of them, 44 percent have come from these families, thirty-nine of them widows of the men whose seats they assumed, and eighty-seven from political families, these two possibilities thus 31 percent and 69 percent of the total. This trend, of women being elected to the House from political families, though now involving fewer widows, has not decreased in recent years. From 2001 to 2018, a period when only one widow, Doris Matsui, entered the House, 57 percent of those who were elected came from political families, a marked increase over the long-term percentage of 44 percent.

In the Senate, for which obtaining a six-year term perhaps requires more connections and fund-raising clout, 64 percent of the women elected through the 115th Congress came from such families, thirty-two of fifty, with eight from this group being widows (25 percent) and twenty-four being connected through other family ties (75 percent). Beginning in January 2001, there was a slight increase, to 65 percent, with only one member of this group, Jean Carnahan, entering as the widow of a senator. Of these fifteen senators serving from 2001 through 2019, 6 percent, indeed Carnahan, was a widow following her husband into office, and 94 percent were members of political families.[34]

Study of This Trend

Though women have entered office from these families from the beginning of women's suffrage, just a few writers have seriously considered this trend and its impact on opportunity and legislation. Beginning in 1980, Irwin Gertzog began writing about the widows who had entered office to replace their husbands.[35] A few other studies have noted the larger trend. In 1994, Linda Witt, Karen M. Paget, and Glenna Matthews in *Running as a Woman* commented that a political upbringing offered "a first-hand glimpse of politics," an opportunity that "seems to help daughters enter politics, regardless of whether their fathers support their ambition."[36] In 2010, when Jennifer Lawless and Richard Fox surveyed men and women with appropriate educational backgrounds for elected office, they found that the likelihood of considering a candidacy was nearly double for those with a political upbringing.[37] In 2013, in *Women and Congressional Elections*, Barbara Palmer and Dennis Simon devoted a short section to women from these families.[38] Though some attention has been paid to widows in office and to other members of political families, no study has looked thoroughly at this significant governmental presence and what it can teach about opportunities that enable outsiders to become insiders.

In 1992, when many women were running for office and would be elected in low but precedent-setting numbers, Pat Robertson claimed, employing hyperbole, one would hope, that women seeking political parity were engaged in "a socialist, anti-family political movement that encourages women to leave their husbands, kill their children, practice witchcraft, destroy capitalism and become lesbians."[39] Though this view deems women's entrance into office to be "anti-family," entering politics is in fact a family tradition. This variable stretches from some of the first candidates for office, such as Victoria Woodhull and her sister Tennie Claflin, to Jeannette Rankin in 1916, to Lindy Boggs, Margaret Chase Smith, and Nancy Landon Kassebaum, and to many women in office today, such as Linda Sánchez, Lisa Murkowski, and Susan Collins.

Though this study considers state officials as well as federal legislators who served through the 115th Congress, I finished writing it after the November 2018 elections. In January 2019, the largest group of women that had ever entered Congress, and especially the House of Representatives, would include legislators from these families, encountering the opportunities and criticism of earlier generations. But elections for the 116th Congress also engaged many women decidedly not from an elite background—not all wealthy, Christian, native-born, or white. That fall's elections seemed to involve for the first time a significant extension, through new and expanding organizations, of what only political families had provided in the past. As more women choose to run in the future, as they attempt to move from constituting a fourth of legislative bodies to half or more, the story of women from political families can provide instruction concerning what it takes to be elected and to become principled, independent legislators.

ONE

Forging Their Own Political Family

The Sisters Satan, Woodhull and Claflin

As Stephen Hess has noted, many family connections in politics have involved men, and especially fathers and sons. The first family encouragement for women would come from sisters and later brothers and sisters, siblings seemingly more open to promoting the political careers of women than were the scions of earlier generations.

One early family duo that broke with tradition, that formed a new path of political family power, was Victoria Woodhull and Tennessee (Tennie) Claflin, one who ran for president in 1872 and one who, if quickly, ran for the U.S. House from New York in 1871, even while coping with crazy and selfish relatives who certainly offered no assistance. Though neither was elected, and indeed they attempted to run for office long before women had the legal right to do so or even to vote, they provide a touchstone or harbinger, for the essentials of how an outsider might become insider. From this start came traditions important for forwarding the careers of women—involving family members willing to support each other and, with that backing, to make independent choices as legislators.

Woodhull and Claflin had to create a political family; they certainly did not come from one. Their father Buck Claflin and his wife Annie had ten children, two boys and eight girls, three of the girls dying young.[1] A "one-eyed snake oil salesman," he marketed his beautiful daughters as mediums, able to communicate with the dead, while he posed as an itinerant preacher, a doctor, and a lawyer, keeping the girls on the road, not in school, as he pursued money-making schemes: Woodhull attended elementary school for three years and Claflin for no more. While Buck forced his children into constant work and housed them in squalor, he assured their obedience through regular beatings. Their mother Annie, prone to religious fervors, to late-night frenzies and babbling in tongues, provided no protection or stability. Without any other safeguard, Woodhull became close to Claflin, seven years her junior and the last child born into the family, the two leaning on each other as they would also in adulthood within the hostile worlds of business and politics.[2]

In his wagon shows featuring his daughters, Buck was cashing in on a mania for Spiritualism crossing the country from the 1850s to the 1870s, spurred by the deceptions of two other sisters, Kate and Margaret Fox. In 1848, Kate, then twelve, and Margaret, fifteen, lived in Hydesville, New York, with their parents. The family became frightened by unexplained sounds that sounded like knocking or moving furniture. Thirty years later, Margaret would tell the actual story of these mysterious "rappings" that ultimately would get attention not just from her family but from the nation: "When we went to bed at night, we used to tie an apple to a string and move the string up and down, causing the apple to bump on the floor, or we would drop the apple on the floor, making a strange noise every time it would rebound. Mother listened to this for a time. She would not understand it and did not suspect us as being capable of a trick because we were so young."[3] For family and neighbors, the sisters claimed to be communicating with spirits, and they quickly developed a code, by which raps could signify yes or no in response to a question or could indicate letters of the alphabet. With an older sister Leah taking charge of their careers, Kate and Margaret enjoyed success as mediums for many years, staging séances at which hundreds of people might receive detailed "messages" from the dead.

These charismatic performances spurred the development of Spiritualism, a faith grounded in the belief that the spirits of the dead could speak about ethical truths and the nature of God as well as about the past. This positive religion provided an antidote to the hellfire and damnation expounded upon from so many Protestant pulpits, and, during and after the Civil War, a means of dealing with so much death. By 1897, eight million followers in the United States and other countries felt drawn to this faith lacking canonical texts and formal organization, which held adherents together through periodicals, camp meetings, and tours by accomplished mediums, many of them women and girls.[4]

Though Buck Claflin involved his family in Spiritualism as a popular and lucrative trend, charging whatever the market would bear for moral guidance and other-worldly communication, he could not hold onto the money that he made. Forced to leave the road in Homer, Ohio, Buck failed when he attempted to operate a gristmill; he then burnt his family's home and the mill and left town with five hundred dollars in insurance money. The local Presbyterian church held a fundraiser to enable Annie and the children to follow him, happy to help a destitute mother and to have them all go away. After the family moved on to Mount Gilead, Ohio, where Buck again found no means of subsistence, he insisted that his daughters spend much more time on the road, working from the wagon, his control cruel and seemingly absolute.

At age fifteen, in November of 1853, as a quickly plotted escape, Victoria married Canning Woodhull, age twenty-eight, a handsome doctor, practicing medicine in Ohio at a time when the state did not require formal medical education or licensing: she met this quasi-professional when he came to treat her for exhaustion. Instead of providing safety, Canning Woodhull, who was addicted to alcohol and morphine, soon revealed himself as unfaithful and violent, and increasingly more dangerous.[5]

After losing control over Victoria, Buck worked further at exploiting the talents of Tennie, booked as the Wonder Child, suddenly able not just to communicate with the dead but to cure ailments. Working long days in small towns across the Midwest, she sold hands-on cures along with Miss Tennessee's Magnetio Life Elixir. In a more dangerous iteration of this health scam, in Ottawa, Illinois, in 1863, Buck set up an infirmary in an old hotel, claiming to cure cancers and other serious diseases.[6] In June 1864, when he advertised that Tennie had cured a woman named Rebecca Howe, who was in fact dead from breast cancer, her suffering having been exacerbated by severe chemical burns and blindness caused by the infirmary's application of lye, the police indicted Claflin for manslaughter and Buck for medical fraud. Faced with these accusations, the family fled, abandoning the infirmary and the patients there, found to be dirty, malnourished, and dying from disease as well as the supposed treatments for it. Like her sister, Claflin then tried to escape through a hastily chosen marriage, which ended almost immediately and left her with no choice but to return to her parents.[7]

As Claflin sought independence, Woodhull kept trying to improve her own situation. After moving with her husband to Chicago, she gave birth to a boy, Byron, suffering from severe mental retardation, his presence increasing her sense of entrapment: if she left her husband, she would not be able to obtain custody. Under the common law of coverture, defining legal status in marriage and changing slowly through the nineteenth century, a married woman was legally one with her husband; she was not a legal person and could not own many forms of property, children being considered as assets over which their fathers had sole rights. Making the decision to stay with Canning, she moved with him to San Francisco to evade his debts. There Victoria attempted to stave off creditors by working as a tailor and as an actor, appearing in various melodramas, including Alexander Dumas' *Corsican Brothers.*[8]

Like Louis with his former conjoined twin Lucien in Dumas' tale, siblings with an indelible bond, Victoria believed that she could feel her sister's emotions, even at a distance in San Francisco. She decided that Tennie needed her—and she certainly needed to change her own life. Returning to Illinois, Woodhull gave birth to a healthy daughter, Zula Maud, and then obtained a divorce, promising to continue to support Canning so that he would allow her to maintain custody of her children. The sisters then ventured out together, first to Cincinnati, working as clairvoyants with Tennie supplementing their income through prostitution.[9] In St. Louis, Woodhull met Colonel James Harvey Blood, who had suffered five bullet wounds during the Civil War, a spiritualist himself, married and with children: he immediately left home for Woodhull. From there, Blood, Woodhull, and Claflin, sometimes free of other family and sometimes burdened with Buck and Annie, the Claflin siblings, and Canning Woodhull, went on to Pittsburgh and then to New York, where the sisters planned to expand their money-making potential while working for women's rights, the lack of which had left them constrained by fathers and husbands.

In New York, Cornelius Vanderbilt, running his empire of railroads and building the Grand Central Terminal, had been consulting spiritualists to communicate with his dead parents and wife, and he had been treated for heart and kidney troubles by faith healers. The sisters met him when Woodhull was thirty and Claflin twenty-two, and he was immediately taken by their skills and by Claflin's beauty. He called her his "little sparrow," and he began teaching both sisters how to succeed at the stock market.[10] In the summer of 1869, responding to family pressure, Vanderbilt married a staid cousin, but he continued to see Claflin and help the sisters. By the end of that year, they had grown wealthy, taking advantage of wild swings in stock prices, as occurred, for example, when Jay Gould attempted to corner the gold market in September. In February of 1870, they embarked, as sisters and business partners, on a new endeavor: opening a brokerage firm on Wall Street, the first women to do so.

From the beginning of this endeavor, Woodhull and Claflin carefully controlled the visuals that spelled success. They rented two rooms at the posh Hoffman House at 44 Broad Street, for the office of Woodhull, Claflin, & Company. A large crowd attended the opening, including Vanderbilt and many other businessmen as well as Walt Whitman. The sisters were so besieged by curious visitors that a hundred police officers came to keep order. Immediately and quite publicly, Vanderbilt and his cronies began trading with the sisters. They also marketed their services to women, with a separate entrance and office space: society wives and widows, teachers, small-business owners, actresses, and high-priced prostitutes sought out investment advice in their special space within the new firm. With profits coming in, Woodhull and Claflin rented an expensive apartment in Murray Hill. At work and in their home on visitation days, they wore matching outfits to emphasize their unity and independence: tailored, mannish jackets cut to the waist and daringly short skirts that came to the tops of their shoes, with no jewelry but instead brightly colored neckties.[11]

As they made their way in the world of high finance, the sisters attempted to construct a respectable family history: they repeatedly told false tales of being well educated, their father a respected attorney and not the swindler that Buck actually was.[12] Tennie described herself as married and began using the name Mrs. Claflin. The sisters made no mention to the newspapers of their history as spiritual healers or clairvoyants—and certainly not of the manslaughter charge that Claflin had evaded by fleeing from Ottawa, Illinois. They appeared in photographs and articles as well-coiffed, well-dressed, and well-educated women of Wall Street, a style of personal rhetoric with which they continued as they entered politics.

As the first and only women taking this form of business risk, and certainly looking beautiful as they did so, they quickly expanded their clientele through publicity provided by the New York press. Like the coverage of many women who would later enter politics, these articles combined body rhetoric with some attention to professional goals. The *New York Herald* hyperbolically lauded the sisters as the Queens of Finance and the Future Princesses of Erie while commenting on their beauty and short skirts, but also tied their efforts to the extension of women's rights and to women's ability to enter new fields. One article even quoted Claflin as she derided the public concern for what both sisters wore: "Were I to notice what is said by what is called 'society,' I could never leave my apartments except in fantastic walking dress or in ballroom costume." The article continued with Claflin's assertion that women were just as capable of earning a living as men, just as tough, though they often feigned being the "sickly, squeaming nondescript," what society preferred them to be.[13]

In the winter and spring of 1870, this story, of beautiful and determined financiers, appeared in newspapers beyond the city, these articles combining body rhetoric with general amazement along with some hints of seriousness. The Nashville *Tennessean* on April 1 included a portrait of "Vanderbilt's two protégés" in their brokerage house, the piece beginning dramatically with "enter, if you please." The writer reported the sisters' claims concerning women's equality while also posing a judgmental question about Woodhull: "Did ever tongue rattle as fast as this woman's?"[14] A long piece on February 8, in the *Reading* (PA) *Times*, claimed about Woodhull that "her features are full, and a continuous smile plays upon her countenance." But the interviewer also quoted her at length on women doing business: "I think a woman is just as capable of making a living as a man; and I have seen men so vain of their personal appearance and so effeminate that I would be sorry to compare my intellect with theirs. I don't care what society think; I have no time to care."[15] This publicity helped the brokerage firm, but it also brought Claflin unwelcome notice. In March 1870 several Illinois merchants swore that a woman who owed them money was she. A lawyer in New York took Claflin to court, representing Chicago grocer James Blake, who claimed that she had not paid him $125.70 for purchased "medicines," such as blood root, sherry, and morphine. She went to court, accompanied by her sister as was their wont, smiled at the judge, and claimed that she had never gone in Blake's store, but was required to pay.[16]

Beginning with these first articles, in which Woodhull and Claflin sought to extend their positive reputation as stock brokers and to overwhelm critics, they also portrayed themselves as social activists who sought political careers. Indeed, from the time that the sisters arrived in New York, they began establishing themselves in politics and in the suffrage movement as well as in high finance. In January 1869, Woodhull went to Washington to attend the National Female Suffrage Convention and made plans for joining in this effort crucial to the fuller rights that both sisters sought and knew the lack of—concerning marriage, divorce, and labor equality.

In 1870, newly acclaimed as women of Wall Street, the sisters received the attention they sought from suffrage leaders. Susan B. Anthony visited the brokerage office and then praised the sisters in her journal *Revolution*. Because of this unprecedented foray into high finance, Anthony wrote, Woodhull and Claflin were "destined not only to achieve position for themselves, but to stimulate the whole future of woman by their efforts and example." She continued by claiming that the sisters were "full of pluck, energy, and enterprise," while also praising the "sound sense, judgment, and clear-sightedness they show in financial matters."[17]

The sisters entered into the fight for suffrage at a fractious time for the campaign. After the Civil War, suffragists had divided over whether to support an extension of civil rights for African Americans and voting privileges for African American men, as would be achieved in the Fourteenth and Fifteenth Amendments, since no legislation was forthcoming to extend voting rights to women. They had also divided on whether to work for liberalized divorce and child custody laws as well as suffrage. Woodhull and Claflin came to believe that these debates only separated women, diluting their strength as a group, making them seem hysterical and petty.[18] They decided—as they had in eluding Buck's authority, moving to New York, and opening the brokerage house—to take independent action together.

On April 2, 1870, at age thirty-two, too young to seek the presidency even if as a woman she could have legally been elected, Woodhull declared that she was putting her name in nomination for this office.[19] With this announcement, the sisters argued that the Constitution did not actually bar women from voting or running for office. As Woodhull announced her candidacy in the sympathetic *New York Herald*, where she had established a relationship with reporter Stephen Pearl Andrews, she portrayed herself as required to take this step to strive against illegal restrictions and to move women forward, as suffrage organizations were not able to do.[20]

As Woodhull announced her candidacy, the oddity of the situation insured coverage, not generally respectful. A writer for the *Democrat and Chronicle* of Rochester, New York, for example, commented of Woodhull, a bit incredulously, that "she feels herself more than a match for all our statesmen" and added that she believes herself "abundantly able to grace any position except that of the contented matron and educator of the happy children of a devoted husband."[21] Such coverage, in this newspaper and elsewhere, emphasized that she had no right to run and no qualifications to do so, her quest unnatural for a woman. With a barrage of criticism descending, Tennie Claflin, as her sister's partner in business and politics, spoke at length to reporters about reasons that strong women like her sister needed to assume political power—to erase so many inequities. After reviewing this rhetorical support, the Jackson, Mississippi, *Clarion-Ledger* commented that Claflin "is Woodhull condensed, double distilled. She talks without period or comma, and seems to have an inexhaustible reservoir of breath."[22]

To assert their worthiness and secure more positive publicity for the campaign, the sisters launched *Woodhull & Claflin's Weekly*, in May of

1870, using funds from the brokerage house. That spring Susan B. Anthony and Elizabeth Cady Stanton had sold their journal, *Revolution*, because of financial problems, and the sisters intended to secure those readers and many more, as they reached toward a fuller program of activism. In the *Weekly*, the sisters advocated for a Woodhull presidency as well as for rights for women that they believed suffrage alone would not insure: for control over themselves in and out of marriage. In the journal, they also advocated for better regulation of Wall Street, an eight-hour workday, and laws ensuring workplace safety.[23]

Woodhull & Claflin's Weekly was, perhaps, the most notorious publication of the second half of the nineteenth century. At its height in 1872, this journal had a circulation of 20,000 while *Revolution* never exceeded 3,000.[24] As the *Weekly* argued for social and political change, it created strong public personas for both sisters, employing supposed letters from fans, dialogue, and key scenes to do so. On July 1, 1871, for example, a letter created the persona of a rural fan to praise Claflin:

> Letter from Hawk Nest Peak, NC, June 12, 1871:
>
> I am a wild old rover in the mountains of North Carolina. Very near I am to Tennessee, if not dear to Tennie C. Only a line divides us—I mean from *Tennessee*. I drop a line to see if it won't unite us—I refer to *Tennie C*.
>
> I saw your picture, beautiful as life, at Brady's the other day. I took a good absorbing look at it and brought it with me, in my mind's eye, down to these wilds; so I know to what manner of woman I am writing.

As the letter continues, it segues to Claflin's progressive political values securing positive attention even in the mountains of North Carolina as well as the response from men that she sought as enemies, their values contrasted with her own: "And now, today, descending from the crags and peaks to the nearest post town, I am surprised to find your paper strayed to this most unlikely part of the world, and all the young Ku Klux of the neighborhood warmly discussing and generally denouncing it."[25]

To further prepare to take on a leadership role in politics, in January of 1871 the sisters went to Washington and booked rooms at a center of influence, the Willard Hotel. Woodhull's powerful friend, Massachusetts senator Ben Butler, a suffrage supporter whom she had met when she went to Washington in January 1869 to attend a suffrage convention, told her that a suffrage plank would not make it out of the House Judiciary Committee. She asked him to allow her to speak there, as a presidential candidate, the first woman to petition Congress in person. Expanding on an argument she had made in the *Herald*, Woodhull spoke, with her sister accompanying her, on the rights of all citizens. She asserted that "women are the equals of men before the law, and are equal in all their rights," reminding those assembled that the Fourteenth Amendment begins by claiming that "all persons born or naturalized in the United States, and subject to the jurisdiction thereof, are citizens of the United States and of the state wherein they reside. No state shall make or enforce any law which shall abridge the privileges or immunities of citizens of the United States." She also noted that the Fifteenth Amendment states that "the right of citizens of the United States to vote shall not be denied or abridged by the United States or by any State on account of race, color, or previous condition of servitude." She thus claimed that women already possessed the right to vote.

Learning of Woodhull's planned address to the Judiciary Committee, suffrage leaders Susan B. Anthony, Elizabeth Cady Stanton, and Isabella Beecher Hooker postponed the opening of the National Woman Suffrage Association's (NWSA) convention in Washington in order to attend the hearings. Many newspapers reported on Woodhull's testimony and on these leaders' support: *Frank Leslie's Illustrated Newspaper*, for example, printed a full-page engraving of Woodhull delivering her remarks with suffragists at her side. The accompanying article claimed that she "led her

Victoria Woodhull speaking on women's suffrage at the House Judiciary Committee. "The Feminine Invasion of the Capitol," *Frank Leslie's Illustrated Newspaper* 801 (February 4, 1871), 349 (Library of Congress).

women-at-arms into the committee-room" and then launched into her "well-considered address" concerning the Constitution, making arguments never heard in that space before.[26]

But though Anthony and others attended, the NWSA group did not fully support this committee appearance, its members both pleased that the first woman had spoken to a congressional committee, and about suffrage, but dismayed that this key speaker was not one of them. After a contentious discussion, they ultimately asked Woodhull to speak at their convention. Before a packed hall, she read what she had said at the judicial committee. That night, over the objection of some suffragists, Anthony labeled Woodhull as "the spirit of the age," especially praising her argument that women already possessed the vote, and made a public commitment to release several thousand copies of the congressional statement.

A month later, again in Washington, this time introduced by her sister, Woodhull, as suffragist and presidential candidate, spoke at another suffrage meeting. Instead of just reading her committee speech, she advocated for the rights of working women and emphasized the inequity of women facing taxation without representation.[27] At many other venues, Woodhull continued to speak to large crowds, addressing political and business corruption and the rights of labor—to broaden her political base and move beyond suffrage squabbles. As she emphasized justice for all Americans, what drew the largest crowds and greatest response were her arguments concerning the rights of women to pursue happiness as they chose, to divorce if they sought to do so, to find their best partners and keep custody rights to their children, values labeled as "free love." As she argued, a woman should never be required to give up sexual choice:

> I make the claim boldly, that from the very moment woman is emancipated from the necessity of yielding the control of her sexual organs to man to insure a home, food and clothing, the doom of sexual demoralization will be sealed.... To woman, by nature, belongs the right of sexual determination. When the instinct is aroused in her, then and then only should commerce follow. When woman rises from sexual slavery to sexual freedom, into the ownership and control of her sexual organs, and man is obliged to respect this freedom, then will this instinct become pure and holy; then will woman be raised from the iniquity and morbidness in which she now wallows for existence, and the intensity and glory of her creative functions be increased a hundred-fold.[28]

In many speeches, she moved from these arguments to the controversial label: "Yes, I am a Free Lover. I have an inalienable, constitutional and natural right to love whom I may, to love as long or as short a period as I can; to change that love every day if I please, and with that right neither you nor any law you can frame have any right to interfere."[29]

While Woodhull's presidential candidacy involved controversial speeches, news articles, and relationships with suffragists, it also stirred up the Claflin family. In May 1871, Annie Claflin petitioned the New York courts, claiming that, with her daughter consumed by activism, Colonel Blood had taken the opportunity to kidnap her and attempt to kill her. The judge indicated that he would be willing to dismiss these allegations, but Blood insisted on a trial to clear his name, a decision that would harm Woodhull's reputation. This trial, to the delight of local newspapers, included details of fraudulent wagon shows and clinic cures; of Woodhull's involvement with both Blood and Canning Woodhull; and of Claflin's dalliance with Vanderbilt. The New York *Sun* and *Brooklyn Daily Eagle* provided detailed descriptions of the court testimony, almost too strange to be true.[30] Papers from afar, employing, for example, the article title of "Blood, Be-lud!!, S-Blood!!!," further emphasized all the details that "bid fair to increase their [the sisters'] notoriety, if not their reputation."[31] Both women also appeared in the sporting newspapers, like *The Days' Doings*, depicted in illustrations as tramps, fighting it out in low-necked dresses, the images linking aggressive, un-chaperoned women with free love and with all that was inappropriate or illegal.[32]

Along with this shift in reputation, the sisters lost both brokerage accounts and support from suffragists. To establish a new base and further Woodhull's quest for the presidency, in the spring of 1871 Woodhull and Claflin sought the backing of labor, joining Karl Marx's International Workingmen's Association (IWA). They took leadership roles in IWA Section 12, called the Yankee International, which began holding its meetings in the *Weekly* offices. On December 30, 1871, this journal became the first in the United States to publish Marx's "The Communist Manifesto" in English. At IWA meetings, the sisters argued not just for the rights of workers but for an extension of civil rights—for women, freed slaves, Native Americans, and immigrants. As they made this larger argument, they angered Marxist leaders who expected the local sections to advocate only for white male trade unions.

As Woodhull and Claflin came to seem more radical and untrustworthy, castigated for their family and for their radical allegiances, they decided to seek a little justice, or revenge. They centered their efforts on the Reverend Henry Ward Beecher, probably the best known minister in the country, whose vivid oratory had regularly berated the satanic sisters. Elizabeth Cady Stanton told Woodhull in July of 1870 that she had been at the home of Theodore Tilton, Beecher's assistant at his Brooklyn church, when Tilton and his wife argued loudly about her adultery. After running upstairs to Stanton, with her husband beating on the door, Elizabeth Tilton admitted that she had been sleeping with Beecher. As a means of revealing Beecher's hypocrisy, without the risk of a libel charge, in May 1871 Victoria sent a letter to the *World* and the *Times*, revealing the injustice of being repeatedly attacked by an unnamed teacher of religion who was living in concubinage with the wife of one of his colleagues: "I do not intend to be made the scapegoat of sacrifice, to be offered up as a victim to society by those who cover over the foulness of their lives and the feculence of their thoughts with hypocritical mouth of fair professions, and by diverting public attention from their own iniquity and pointing the finger at me."[33]

When Theodore Tilton came to see Woodhull and begged her not to reveal names and specifics, they became lovers, and he wrote a glowing, imaginative biography of her in his *Golden Age* magazine, concentrating on her quest of the presidency.[34] That summer and fall Tilton helped her energize her campaign, through an alliance that they formed of Spiritualists, labor activists, freed slaves, socialists, abolitionists, free lovers, and radical feminists. Woodhull tried to get Beecher's support for her candidacy by offering to stop accusing him; she asked him to introduce her at what would be a packed meeting at Steinway Hall in New York in November 1871, where she defended her character and spoke on marriage, divorce, and free love. That night, Victoria's sister Utica started screaming from the audience, stopping the speech and creating more family drama, but Beecher didn't come.[35]

In the summer of 1871, Victoria was not the only one of the sisters running for office. Tennie Claflin decided to run for the U.S. House, representing the primarily German Eighth District of New York. In the *Weekly* on July 8, 1871, as Claflin discussed her reasons for this choice, she spoke of her desire to second her sister's efforts as well as to effect "what my own genius can design and realize."[36]

As Claflin honed her position statements, she spoke for the same principles as her sister, but she argued less for the necessity of large changes in social mores: instead she maintained that the tipping point had already occurred. On August 5 in the *Weekly*, Claflin claimed, concerning the right of women to vote, that "the best interests of the country demand an immediate settlement of this great question." She wrote further that "the male citizens thereof, from their gallantry and courtesy, will as heartily and earnestly join with women to permit this settlement." She also stated her hope, concerning specifically the Eighth District's male voters thus complimented in her speech, that "I may suit their tastes or opinions, and be deemed to possess the proper personal characteristics, independent of sex." And she announced that, if she received a majority of the votes, her campaign would become a test case, leading to more women being elected to federal office, which, in her rhetoric, the Constitution already allowed and most Americans already approved.[37]

In all of her public statements, Claflin spoke of women as well as men as voters, reaching out to them at meetings that she planned along with her sister, without a party's support. To several hundred members of the German-American Progressive Society, as she announced her candidacy at Irving Plaza surrounded by German and American flags, she spoke in German, having been coached by Stephen Pearl Andrews, a master at languages.[38] She was introduced by Dr. S.T. Ehrenberg, president of the German American Progressive Association, who lauded her at length. In this speech and others in the district, for which Woodhull frequently introduced her, Claflin argued that in the wake of scandals, fomented by the Grant administration nationally and Tammany Hall locally, voters should try the experiment of trusting an unconnected woman: as independent citizens, women could move the state and nation away from corruption. She also spoke against temperance, as aimed at immigrants particularly who might choose to drink as a recreational and communal activity. And she always presented these points as what the audience already agreed with, as what sensible people would naturally believe.

In her essays in the *Weekly* and in her speeches, Claflin also talked about some of the most controversial rights needed by women, as ones about which more information would naturally change minds. A campaign to criminalize abortion accelerated in the late 1860s, through efforts of legislators and the American Medical Association; increasingly abortions occurred in unsanitary conditions, the death rate growing to thirty percent.[39] In a melodramatic tone, Claflin described women seduced by evil men and then left to die by back-alley abortionists, realities that had often provided entertainment for the worst of journalists: "Some woman has been found coffined in a trunk, her remorseful seducer has committed suicide, an abortionist has been arrested, another case occurs the next day, and, the next, a whole bevy of women are hunted to bay in a doctor's shop of that order. The newspaper men are delighted. There is an immense flutter of agitation and excitement. The public is treated to a wonderful feast of sensation in the morning and evening papers."

In this speech, reprinted in the *Weekly*, Claflin labeled these abortion practices as "one of the indicative symptoms of the ripening and the rottening of our prevalent state of society" and argued that only the wealthy had the wherewithal to obtain safe abortions. She also claimed that for many poor women, with no control within marriage and without the means to support their children, repeated abortions became the only choice: "Many women learn to practice it on themselves, and many of them have repeated it dozens of times.... Child-bearing is not a disease, but a beautiful office of nature. But to our faded-out, sickly, exhausted type of women, it is a fearful ordeal. Nearly every child born is an unwelcome guest. Abortion is the choice of evils for such women." Claflin's solutions, with which her audience would naturally agree, were for women to have access to safe abortions but also to learn about "the mechanisms and liabilities of their own systems," to gain the freedom to decide about sex in marriage, to be able to support themselves, and to advocate for their own rights.[40]

In the summer and fall of 1871, as Claflin attempted to run for office with her sister's help, New York newspapers reported her speeches, with emphasis on her sexuality and her inappropriateness as well as on her platform for change. A long article in the New York *Sun* concentrated on Claflin's dress and hair, on all her broker friends in attendance at her nomination meeting, the "American element" thus added to the German, and on her pleas for personal freedoms.[41] Across the country, the more negative coverage segued to witches and Satan. The *Athens* (PN) *Gleaner* referred to Claflin as the "sister of that innate dunce Mrs. Woodhull" and claimed dramatically that "these sisters, in the language attributed to Satan when speaking of his horns, are 'a pretty pair.'" *The Friends of Temperance* in Raleigh, on September 6, 1871, harangued Claflin for speaking up in support of beer and then declared that both sisters were "enemies to law and order," their free love "but a pretext to general prostitution." These "brazen enemies of divine institutions and social order," the article continued, should be burned at the stake like witches of another era.[42]

While attempting to cope with adverse press attention and the lack of party sponsorship, Claflin also faced a powerful incumbent, James Brooks, a member of the male educational and electoral elite as was his brother. A graduate of Waterville College (now Colby College) in 1831, James Brooks became an attorney and a Washington correspondent for the *Portland Advertiser* and then entered the Maine House in 1835. After he moved to New York City where he founded the *New York Daily Express*, he served in the state assembly as did his brother Erastus. Then James moved into a long career in national politics: serving in the U.S. Congress, as a Whig and then a Democrat, in office at various intervals between 1849 and 1875. Employed also as a director of the Union Pacific Railroad, this insider had nothing to fear from Tennie Claflin.[43]

Though she had no means of prevailing, Claflin had engaged in electoral politics and had involved both women and men in the district. And
that fall both Tennie and Victoria attempted to vote, a year before Susan
B. Anthony did so; they had been allowed to register but were turned away
on election day. Woodhull wrote a letter of protest in response, which
appeared in newspapers across the country, following up on arguments
that she had made to the House Judiciary Committee and in later speeches
about women's constitutional rights.[44]

In the late fall of 1871, the sisters kept their names before the public,
both positively and negatively. Together they continued their activism for
Section 13 of the IWA. Newspapers in many states and in London
reported, concerning an IWA parade in New York City on December 17,
that immense crowds had come out especially to see the "female Communists," walking in front of the marchers and carrying the flag for Section
13 along with a banner reading "Social and Political Equality for Both
Sexes." As one article noted, their presence "seemed to afford the boys
intense delight."[45] That same month the sisters were again infamously in
court over a widely reported family squabble. Using the article title "Her
Daddy and Mamma Bother Her," one Kansas newspaper reported that
Woodhull had gone to court in New York to claim that her parents had
created disturbances at the residences of both sisters, accusations that the
judge refused to consider.[46]

Into 1872, the presidential election year, both sisters remained in
demand as public speakers, famed for their matched appearances as well
as their radical views on the rights of labor, on marriage, and on sex. In
February 1872, Woodhull gave a rabble-rousing speech, entitled "Impend-
ing Revolution," at the Academy of Music in New York City, with 12,000
people in attendance, another 6,000 unable to get in. There she spoke
against the growing power of capitalists such as William Astor, and even
Vanderbilt, as well as for social change. That winter, the sisters' radical
speeches secured an increasingly vituperative public response. On February 17, 1872, Thomas Nast created a cartoon, published in *Harper's
Weekly*, to warn against their advocacy of free love and women's rights.
In this illustration, he depicts Woodhull as Satan incarnate. Here a poor
wife in the background spurns the evil temptations of free love, despite
carrying the heavy burden, of children and an alcoholic husband, up the
steep slope of life. The wife addresses Woodhull directly, quoted below
the picture: "I'd rather travel the hardest path of matrimony than follow
your footsteps." And in larger letters the cartoon features a tag line, aimed
at Woodhull: "Get Thee Behind Me, (Mrs.) Satan!"

As they entered the election season, the sisters tried to learn from Claflin's failed congressional run of the year before. Particularly they knew that they would need the support of a party: they couldn't change their ages; they wouldn't change their radical views; but they could attempt to secure this necessary base for a presidential run. At the May 1872 NWSA convention in Steinway Hall, Woodhull sought this group's nomination for the presidency, with some suffragists, including Elizabeth Cady Stanton, willing to back her. But Susan B. Anthony refused her access to the podium because free-love radicalism was taking emphasis away from the vote. When Woodhull rushed to the stage to urge suffragists to support her, Anthony had the lights turned off.[47]

Thomas Nast, "Get Thee Behind Me, (Mrs.) Satan," *Harper's Weekly*, February 17, 1872, a depiction of Victoria Woodhull (HarpWeek Images).

Without NWSA backing, Woodhull next sought to form and lead an Equal Rights Party, using the name of a disbanded group from the Civil War, which had involved suffragists and abolitionists. She endeavored to rally a reform coalition by focusing on the corruption of both the Ulysses Grant and Boss Tweed administrations as well as the urgent need to abolish monopolies, end war through international arbitration, suspend capital punishment, and draft a new national constitution establishing full suffrage and fuller civil rights for both women and men.

Much of the media discussion of Woodhull's platform came in long newspaper pieces about the nomination night. At Apollo Hall in New York City on May 10, 1872, for an audience of 600 delegates of whom 350 were women, twenty speakers introduced the platform of this amalgamated "party of principle." Reports in the *Cincinnati Commercial*, reprinted in the *Weekly*, commented on the enthusiastic crowd of both genders and of various classes attracted to new ideas: "There were large numbers of fashionable dressed ladies, and most of the gentlemen evidently belonged to the business and professional classes. There were also plenty of Reformers, and in fact, it was they who contributed the real genius of the assemblage."[48] Not everyone was so enthusiastic about the crowd: the usually supportive *New York Herald* referred to the women delegates as "the radical wing of the female shriekers" and "more homely in the face than as many nutmeg graters."[49]

At this meeting, Woodhull spoke for an hour, called to the stage over and over after she sat down, Claflin by her side as she claimed that the duo would campaign together and enter the White House together.[50] One article about the night, with the subhead, "Vic Says 'I Will Stump the States with Tennie C.,'" noted that they had entered the Apollo Hall similarly attired and planned to continue appearing in matching outfits as they campaigned.[51]

The *Weekly* reported on the choice of a vice president in especially dramatic terms:

> Then followed an hour's wrangle, with countless speeches as to the candidate for the Vice Presidency. The first nomination made was that of Frederick Douglass, who was eulogized by half a dozen speakers in succession, and opposed by two or three, on various grounds. We had the oppressed sex represented by Woodhull; we must have the oppressed race represented by Douglass. Other names followed: Ben. Wade, Theodore Tilton, Spotted Tail, Ben. Butler, Henry Ward Beecher, Robert Dale Owen, Governor Campbell, Wendell Phillips, Richard Trevellick, and others. Frederick Douglass, however, at last got the vote of the Convention. And was thus nominated for the second place on the Woodhull Presidential ticket—the Executive Committee being empowered to substitute another name in case of his refusal to accept.[52]

That night, Woodhull informed the press that she and her sister would be campaigning with Douglass, but he ignored the nomination and began instead to give supportive speeches for Ulysses S. Grant.

To extend the reach of their speeches and keep their names before the press, Claflin then made a much reported move involving the National Guard. In January 1872, after robber baron James Fisk, known as "Diamond Jim," was fatally shot, Claflin asked for his vacant seat as colonel of the Ninth Regiment of the National Guard in New York, a request much noted and mocked by the press. The men of the Ninth Regiment ignored her, but their commander Thomas J. Griffin invited her to apply for the colonelcy of the newly organized Eighty-Fifth, the only African American regiment in the state, and this group selected her as their colonel in June 1872. She had earned their respect through her advocacy of the rights of labor and through the nomination of Douglass. These guard members recognized that with her participation, they would gain greater notice, as a full and equal unit of the state command.

The reporting on this appointment did mention the unit's status— in articles that combined racism and sexism. The *New York Times* argued that these men would accept anybody who would provide them with uniforms; the new togs would have to be bright since "the colored race has a tropical fondness for brilliant colors." This article next turned to what length of uniform skirt Claflin might wear, where she would put the sword, and whether she would ride a horse astride like a man or to the side like her "former sex." But, in whatever manner she rode, the *Times* continued, to truly fit in she would need to "change the cosmetics of the Caucasian woman for the burnt cork of the pseudo African" since "she may rest assured that to this blackened complexion she must come at last."[53]

Many other newspapers across the nation stressed the humor in Claflin's association with the African American unit. The *Daily State Journal* of Alexandria, Virginia, compared "Miss Tennie Claflin's *corps de Afrique*" to Skiff and Gaylord's Minstels, a popular blackface vaudeville troupe. Illinois' *Sterling Standard* focused attention on Claflin as though she were engaged in some odd sort of battle: "Look at Tennie C. Claflin mounted on her briny steed, and flashing her new tin sword in the eyes of affrighted millions as she leads her colored regiment on to victory."[54]

In the summer and fall of 1872, because of the regiment, an inappropriate presidential bid involving an African American nominee for vice president, and repeated declarations on women's rights and free love, the sisters lost their remaining brokerage customers, and their creditors sued. They also lost much of their labor support: in the Hague in September, officials of the IWA leveled accusations at the sisters for diluting the message and strength of the group with non-union issues.[55] The sisters also dealt with repeated judgments of their morals, the barrage led by an old foe: from his pulpit, his accusations repeated in the national press, the Reverend Henry Ward Beecher stepped up his condemnation of the sinful duo and their brand of free love.[56]

Under so much pressure, the sisters again sought revenge against Beecher, this time naming him as the adulterer in the Tilton case. On

November 2, 1872, *Woodhull & Claflin's Weekly* published 100,000 copies of a special issue, with "The Beecher-Tilton Scandal Case" on the cover. The main article took the form of an interview between Victoria Woodhull and an unnamed reporter, with Woodhull providing salacious details of the affair between Beecher and Elizabeth Tilton. In the same issue, Claflin threatened revelations about other important men by printing a letter from an anonymous madame who promised to reveal the names and addresses of her clients: as a first revelation, the *Weekly* offered specifics concerning the seduction of a young girl by Wall Street trader Luther Challis.[57]

The Beecher story created a sensation. On the day of the *Weekly's* publication, Woodhull, Claflin, and Colonel Blood were arrested and charged with publishing an obscene newspaper and circulating it through the United States Postal Service. The sisters quite infamously spent the next few months in and out of jail as they faced obscenity charges brought by the vice crusader, Anthony Comstock. They sat in jail on election day, Woodhull receiving no electoral votes and an unknown (but minuscule) percentage of the popular vote. As another result of these accusations, Beecher stood trial in 1875 for adultery, a sensational public event that ended with a hung jury.

In the wake of that trial, the sisters left New York for England, returning just briefly for Woodhull to seek the presidential nomination in 1884 and in 1892. Establishing a residence at Bredon's Norton in the Cotswolds, they built a village school along with Zula Maud, becoming champions for English village schools that served the working class.

These sisters, teaming up to gain independence, affluence, and elected office, were certainly outsiders. They sought the right to run for national office as well as to speak their own truths, beyond the platform of established parties. Almost fifty years before women could vote, they moved forward with the strength and support of a political family, sisters being those family members willing to help other women in the 1870s. Along with the right to vote and run for office, Woodhull and Claflin faced other key deficits encountered by women candidates through the decades—a lack of financial backing and party support; a platform concerning women's rights that might prove unacceptable to male voters; a desire to speak about other issues, like the rights of labor, about which they might not be trusted. These sisters also recognized the difficulty of securing positive media representations, with so many reporters constructing them through body rhetoric and labeling them as unique or unnatural. To prevail, this pair attempted to ally themselves with other oppressed groups, of outsiders, as later women candidates would also. As Woodhull and Claflin worked together, with separate and combined strengths, weaknesses, and ambitions, they trod a complex path that women in more established political families would also embark upon.

Two

Brothers and Sisters
Jeannette Rankin,
Her Brother Wellington and
Women Candidates Before 1920

While Victoria Woodhull attempted to mount a second campaign for the presidency in 1884, Belva Ann Lockwood, the first female lawyer to argue a case before the U.S. Supreme Court, made a more substantial run for the office that year. She was nominated by a California contingency of the Equal Rights Party, which had loose affiliations to Woodhull's group from 1872. Lockwood advocated for women's suffrage and other reforms during a coast-to-coast campaign that received respectful coverage from at least some publications. She financed her campaign partly by charging admission to a series of well-attended speeches. That year major suffrage organizations endorsed the Republican candidate for president, James G. Blaine, instead of Lockwood or Woodhull, claiming that their impossible quests would not further the campaign for the vote.[1]

Into the twentieth century, before the federal granting of suffrage, twenty women ran for the U.S. Senate and House, nineteen of them not successfully. Their platforms bore some resemblance to Woodhull's and Claflin's: these women were generally more radical than male candidates, male voters, and many women voters. In these elections, knowing that they needed a base for campaigning and fundraising, most of these candidates attempted to secure support from a minority party, as had Woodhull and Lockwood; others sought nomination from one of the major parties, a more difficult goal to achieve. Like Woodhull and Claflin, these women often attempted to forge political families, generally involving brothers and sisters, as fathers were not yet helping to establish the careers of their daughters and there were few other sources of support for women in politics.[2]

31

Like Woodhull in 1872, most women candidates secured the opportunity to run for office through minor political parties, with little chance of victory. At its beginning in 1869, with women having launched the temperance campaign, the Prohibition Party became the first to accept women as members and to give them full delegate rights at conventions. As this party engaged successfully in getting communities and counties to outlaw alcohol, its ideology broadened to include many aspects of progressivism: better public education, safer urban spaces, and fairer treatment of workers. Through their activism in this party and on these issues, many women achieved the chance to secure nominations and support. Caroline M. Clark, who taught in Nebraska public schools and began writing newspaper articles about temperance in 1882, became a state university regent as a nominee of the party. In 1894, she was an unsuccessful Prohibition Party candidate for Congress. In 1900, Amanda M. Way, a Quaker minister, served as the Prohibition Party candidate for the U.S. House from Idaho. This nomination rewarded a long career of advocating for prohibition and for equal rights, activism that Way had curtailed only during the Civil War to work for the Union Army as a nurse, serving both in hospitals and on the battlefield.[3]

In 1902, Mary Burkhart was nominated on the Prohibition ticket for the U.S. House from Kentucky, well before women's suffrage came to the state. She ran on a platform of "Prohibition and the Golden Rule." An employee at her father's lumber yard, Burkhart gained attention in the race by launching a house-to-house canvass, "finding her way over the sparsely inhabited mountain counties on horseback," her voyage furthered, as the magazine *Public Opinion* stated, by "the chivalry of the blue-grass male."[4] Echoing Victoria Woodhull's logic, Burkhart claimed in a *New York Times* interview, reprinted around the nation, that if elected she intended to serve, "and there is not law to prevent me."[5] As another nominee of the Prohibition Party, in 1912 Helen M. Stoddard, involved in fighting against child labor and for temperance, announced her candidacy in California for the U.S. House. In 1914, two years after Kansas approved women's suffrage, Emma W. Grover became a Prohibition Party candidate for the U.S. House, unsuccessful as were other candidates from this minority party.[6]

Like the Prohibition Party, the Socialist Party, created in 1901 through a merger of older organizations, gave women some opportunity to run for office if not to be elected. In 1902, Ida Crouch Hazlett became a Socialist Party candidate for the House from Colorado. In 1906, Luella Twining, another Socialist Party activist, ran for the House from that state. She spoke in support of strikes undertaken that year by the Western Federation of Miners. Dr. Elizabeth Baer, active in the suffrage movement, secured the Socialist Party of Pennsylvania's nomination for election as congressman-at-large in 1916. She told reporters that "I know I will not be elected but nevertheless I shall put up an earnest sincere fight for every possible vote."[7] She promised if elected to pass laws to improve health care for women.

As some women ran for office from the Socialist Party before 1920, espousing progressive arguments as did Woodhull and Claflin, they encountered the sexual and body rhetoric that engulfed these sisters and that many women candidates have experienced since. Lena Morrow Lewis, born in Illinois, her father a Presbyterian minister, graduated from Presbyterian-affiliated Monmouth College in Illinois in 1892 and launched a career of activism. She took a post as a national lecturer for the Women's Christian Temperance Union and worked for women's suffrage in Illinois, South Dakota, and Oregon, her assignment to interact with labor union leaders and convince them of the importance of universal suffrage for the protection of workers.

Lena Lewis joined the Socialist Party in 1902 and soon became the first woman to serve on its executive committee, working from the San Francisco Bay area. She promoted the party as a national organizer, lecturer, and pamphlet writer, distributing 200,000 copies of her pamphlet, "The Socialist Party and Woman Suffrage," at various events. Like Woodhull and Claflin, she commonly spoke and wrote on love and gender equality, arguing that "true romantic love is a thing of the future. There can be no real love until woman is economically man's equal."[8]

Although Lewis planned to run for the U.S. House from California, she ultimately decided not to do so because of sexual shaming. Like Woodhull and Claflin, she faced public exaggeration of her free love philosophy. Then she became a target of scandal because of her supposed tryst with the Socialist Party's national executive secretary, J. Mahlon Barnes. In the summer of 1910, Thomas Morgan, a socialist lawyer in Chicago, accused Barnes of being an "adulterer, drunkard, and debauchee" and named, as an example of wonton behavior, an alleged affair with the party's sole female administrator, Lena Lewis. This accusation led a Christian wing of the party to launch a crusade against immorality within it, with Lewis' free love frequently mentioned as its cause. A party journal, the *Christian Socialist*, printed letters from its adherents that linked Lewis to an "assignation house" in San Francisco and labeled her as a "moral degenerate," supposed facts then repeated in other publications.[9]

In response to this scandal, Lewis moved to the Alaskan Territory where she continued to serve as a party organizer. In Juneau, she re-established herself, as editor of the *Sunday Morning Post* and then co-editor of the *Alaska Labor News*. Having weathered the allegations, she ran, unsuccessfully, for territorial delegate on the Socialist Party ticket in 1916.[10]

While securing some, albeit complex and limited, opportunities through the Prohibition and Socialist parties, women also ran for office without much chance for victory as members of the Progressive Party, formed in 1912 after Theodore Roosevelt lost the Republican Party nomination to his former protégé, William Howard Taft. In 1914, Eva Morley Murphy, of Goodland, Kansas, campaigned for the U.S. House as a Progressive Party candidate. Born in Illinois, she taught school for five years before becoming a leader in the state's temperance and women's suffrage campaigns. Murphy believed strongly that "mature women," finished with child rearing and accustomed to family and neighborhood leadership, should take on the "larger political responsibilities of the nation"; such concerned citizens, of whom she was one, could counteract the immoralities of men, a contrast that she stated succinctly: "I shall not spend one cent in cigars or candy to bribe voters."[11] In 1916, Cora Pattleton Wilson, an administrator with the Industrial Workers of the World, served as a Socialist Party candidate for the U.S. House from California.

In 1916 as before, the smaller party was not a means of securing election and was still the only means by which many women could attempt to do so. Given these difficulties, women began attempting to secure a power base in one of the two major parties, a more difficult task with few leaders encouraging them to take that step, as Emily N. Blair would note in the 1920s.

Those women seeking a U.S. House seat in 1916 as a Democrat or Republican found themselves in political situations that would occur frequently thereafter: serving as an attention-getting candidate, labeled as an unconventional first or as unique, recruited to run against a powerful incumbent, their suffrage rights thus recognized but with no real chance of being elected. In October 1916, Josephine Marshall Fernald became the Democratic candidate for San Francisco's congressional district. Born in Kentucky, she had studied at the Boston Conservatory of Music, and she continued to perform and teach music in California as she became involved in politics. Not surprisingly, she could not mount a serious challenge to longtime incumbent Julius Kahn, elected as a Republican to Congress from 1899 to 1903 and from 1905 until his death in 1924, the 1916 contest one in which the Democratic Party did not want to "waste" a stronger, presumably male, candidate.[12] Kahn's wife, Florence Prag Kahn, would follow him into office after his death, but no woman candidate would defeat him.

In other elections in 1916, the major parties encouraged women to run in primaries against establishment men, the goal to engage women voters and bring publicity to the state and party, not for these women to be nominated. Eva Harding secured this limited support of a major party for one U.S. House election. Raised in Lafayette, Indiana, and educated at Purdue University, she received a medical degree from Hahnemann Medical College in Chicago. She soon became known for providing medical care to the poor in Topeka, Kansas, where she set up her practice. She also advocated for better public education, for the creation of kindergartens, and for urban family spaces: she bought and donated the land for Topeka's Shimer, Children's, and Euclid parks. She also became an outspoken advocate for prohibition: in 1901, police in Topeka arrested Harding, along with Carrie Nation and six others, for defacing a saloon as they protested both liquor and the male violence that it incited.

In 1916, Harding did better than the party expected. In the Democratic primary, she ran her own campaign, backed primarily by her own funds, employing a platform of anti-militarism, prohibition, women's suffrage, and old-age and mothers' pensions. While a *New York Times* article emphasized the novelty of her having "shied her bonnet into the ring," local newspapers gave serious attention to her platform, her history of activism, and her medical career. Facing the Reverend H.J. Corwine, a parole agent and former chaplain of the state senate, she ultimately lost by just 337 votes; he failed to win in the general election.[13]

In 1916, when a few women from suffrage states represented either minority parties or major parties in weighted elections, two had the chance to come into a major party through the support of a political family, indeed with an establishment brother as family partner. These women's preparation—and these connections—enabled further movement into politics, beyond Victoria Woodhull and Tennie Claflin and beyond other candidates in 1916. While most women candidates would not prevail, even in the primaries, these two would secure government appointments and even win elections.

In one case in 1916, a relationship to the connected brother helped with access to a seat in a state House, if not in the U.S. Senate, and to an ongoing career in government. Frances Cleveland Axtell, from Sterling, Illinois, her father a rancher, earned a PhD at DePauw University in 1889 before moving to Bellingham, Washington. Her brother Frederick A.

Cleveland graduated from DePauw in 1890. He studied for the bar, but gave up his practice in 1896 to devote his attention to economics. After attending the University of Chicago, he became a professor at the University of Pennsylvania and then the New York University School of Commerce. In 1911, as an accounting expert and established author, he secured a position on President Taft's commission on economy and efficiency, a group of Republican Party stalwarts that drafted the federal budget. He was then appointed director of the federal Bureau of Municipal Research, which engaged both Republicans and Democrats in professionalizing civil service, a position he maintained when Democrat Woodrow Wilson came into office in 1913.[14]

That fall, in Bellingham, Frances C. Axtell ran as a Republican and was elected to the Washington House of Representatives, where she served until 1915. In her committee work and bills sponsored, Axtell focused on a ban on child labor, minimum wage legislation, workers' compensation, and pensions for the elderly, disabled, and widows. Though she had served her state well, Republican leaders encouraged her to try another party if she wanted to seek office again: she was not a major fundraiser among Republicans and her priorities differed from those of party regulars. In 1916, Axtell ran unsuccessfully for the U.S. Senate, as a Democrat in that election, a year in which Republicans maintained their allegiance to the ultimately victorious incumbent, Lindley H. Hadley, a lawyer who served in Congress until 1933. After this election, Axtell's prior service as well as her relationship with her brother brought her to the attention of President Wilson. In January 1917, he appointed her to the Federal Employees' Compensation Commission, on which she served until 1921, administering a compensation program for injured civil service employees, an effort that furthered her brother's priorities and her own.[15]

While Frances C. Axtell could not obtain federal elected office from the state of Washington, Jeannette Rankin would do so from Montana. Her candidacy presented a combination not seen before, one that would lead to the first woman elected to the U.S. House: a well-educated, well-connected woman, a leader in the suffrage movement, with a brother who also frequently ran for office and who could make a difference for her. In comparison with Wellington Rankin, Jeannette had superior campaigning skills while he had influence within the Republican Party and power in the state: together they created a more successful, connected version of Woodhull and Claflin or Axtell and Cleveland. As James J. Lopach and Jean A. Luckowski have noted concerning Jeannette Rankin, "There's a lot written about women in politics historically, and the barriers, and often it was a husband or a father who gave them a leg up, and in this case it was her brother. He helped her overcome the barriers."[16]

In 1870, Jeannette and Wellington Rankin's father John had emigrated from Canada and built a stamp mill at Unionville, Montana. Their mother Olive Pickering, who taught school in New Hampshire, had an uncle who spurred her desire to go west, and she took a job as a schoolteacher in Missoula in 1878, working there until her marriage. Living on a ranch and then in town, the Rankins had six girls and one boy: Jeannette the oldest and Wellington the third child. In a busy family, Jeannette helped to raise the younger children, her brother being the one with whom she was closest.

Although Jeannette and Wellington both had the chance to go to college, their genders would lead to different expectations and opportunities. Jeannette followed the requirements that a family made of a daughter, leaving home for new challenges but then returning to reassume household duties. She went to the new state university in Missoula, graduating in 1902. Afterwards she taught at a rural school in Grant Creek, near the family home, a respectable choice for an unmarried woman, but a taxing job that she did not enjoy. After teaching next in Whitehall, 150 miles away, she came back to Missoula to care for her siblings, as a dutiful daughter, while working at a dressmaker's shop. She found these requirements limiting: in her personal journal, she wrote to urge herself, "Go! Go! Go! It makes no difference where just so you go! go! go! Remember at the first opportunity go!"[17]

Jeannette Rankin and Wellington Rankin (Bettmann/Getty Images).

After beginning his college study in Missoula, Wellington went to Harvard. He was expected not to return to Montana when his father became ill but instead to continue his studies in Cambridge and prepare for a career in law and politics. When John Rankin died, Wellington came home to arrange for the management of the ranch and then quickly returned to college, from whence he went on to study at Oxford for a year and then to Harvard Law School.[18]

While Wellington pursued a steady course that would lead to power in his home state and a profitable profession, his equally intelligent and ambitious sister had a harder path to finding a meaningful future beyond the confines of teaching and sewing and home. When Wellington became ill in Cambridge after the death of his father, Jeannette embraced the opportunity to go tend him, extending the role of helpful sister and daughter, but in an exciting new venue. She accompanied him to Theodore Roosevelt's inaugural ball in March 1905 before she had to return home—to help with raising the two youngest girls.

In 1909, Wellington came home from Cambridge and began practicing law in Helena at the firm of Nolan and Walsh, and then after two years he established his own law office. After he went into business for himself, he represented cattle ranchers and other landowners, whose interests often collided with those of the powerful Anaconda Mining Company, a mammoth copper business, one of the nation's largest trusts, which controlled several state newspapers.

Throughout his career as a highly successful attorney, Wellington used his profits from his law office to acquire vast land holdings, and he also sought to enter politics. In 1912, representing Roosevelt's Bull Moose or Progressive Party, as had Eva Morley Murphy in Kansas in 1914, he secured only 6,000 of 80,000 votes when he ran for a seat in the U.S. House, challenging the state's major party, the Republicans, as an outsider. Returning to the Republican Party, Wellington ran for office eight more times, seeking election to the U.S. House and the U.S. Senate, as well as the governorship, but he had to settle for the elected position of attorney general of Montana, in 1920. In these campaigns, his opposition repeatedly stressed his corruption: as evidenced by his large fees as an attorney, his overgrazed ranches, his practice of having men from the penitentiary paroled to him to work as hired hands, and his overuse of water as the state's largest landowner. Though he won only one election, Wellington had access to political power: for many years he directed the state Republican Party, managed campaigns, and influenced governmental appointments. In 1924, Republican governor Joseph M. Dixon appointed him associate justice of the Supreme Court of Montana; in 1925, Calvin Coolidge appointed him U.S. attorney for Montana, with Herbert Hoover reappointing him in 1930.[19]

As Wellington was establishing his career and a power base in Montana, Jeannette was living in New York, the younger children no longer requiring her help. Looking for a meaningful involvement, in 1908 she began studying economic policy at the New York School of Philanthropy, where suffragist Alice Paul had enrolled in 1905. For the New York Woman Suffrage Party, Jeannette worked as a sidewalk campaigner, lobbyist, and field organizer in an ongoing and frustrating state campaign: suffrage would not pass in the state until 1917.

Seeking challenging work and self-definition, Jeannette returned to Missoula and then left for the west coast, employed at the Children's Home Societies in Spokane and Seattle and then at a settlement house in San Francisco. Like Alice Paul who did philanthropic work in New York and London, Jeannette soon found the lack of opportunities for women and children to be "suffocating": "I couldn't take it," she claimed. "I saw, that if we were to have decent laws for children, sanitary jails, and safe food supplies, women would have to vote."[20] Returning to Seattle, she joined the Washington state suffrage campaign, speaking on street corners, as she had in New York, and studying oral expression at the University of Washington to improve her skills. Her brother encouraged her to thus expand her education because he recognized the impact of forceful oral persuasion—in campaigning and in the courtroom. When Washington approved women's suffrage in 1910, Jeannette was part of that successful effort.

After the Washington state vote, Jeannette served as a field secretary for the National American Woman Suffrage Association (NAWSA), traveling across the country for this group formed in 1890 by joining NWSA with the American Woman Suffrage Association. Then to continue her involvement where she knew that she could make a difference, she went back home and took a leadership role in the Montana Equal Suffrage Association. On a visit at Christmas in 1910, she had realized that the state legislature was only bringing suffrage up pro forma, almost as a joke, a situation that had to change. In 1913, working from Missoula, she became involved in administering a reinvigorated state campaign, the effort also led by Belle Fligelman of Helena and Margaret Smith Hathaway of Stevensville.[21]

As would occur over and over in Jeannette's career, the successful trial attorney Wellington aided in the campaign, his advice both helping and not helping, as she noted about her public speaking: "I worked on a speech and Wellington helped me and fixed it up, and I'd go on working on it and every time he'd leave me, he'd say, 'Now this is a very important occasion,' and scare me to death." Their ongoing mutual critique helped her to become a "spellbinding orator" in the volatile space of campaign meetings while he excelled at the more controlled territory of the court-room.[22] As a result of a hard-fought campaign, in November 1914, a suf-frage bill secured a majority vote in the state legislature, and Montana men voted for women's suffrage in a state referendum.[23] Along with other organizers, Jeannette received praise from national suffrage leaders for this success.

After this victory, Jeannette felt that the next step was for women to run for office: the presence of the first victors would prepare the way for more. Some NAWSA leaders, like Carrie Chapman Catt, advised her to begin by seeking a minor post, not election to the U.S. House; Catt felt that a woman with a law degree and more civic experience would be better prepared to win. As had occurred with Victoria Woodhull, this negative reaction may have been motivated by Jeannette's criticism of suffrage movement tactics: in 1915 Jeannette had severed connections with NAWSA because this organization did not agree with her preference for a federal campaign instead of more frustrating state-by-state work. Jean-nette had reproached Catt for being narrow minded and had then joined the more radical National Woman's Party, led by Alice Paul. Like the suf-fragists who discouraged her, Republican Party officials scoffed at Jean-nette's candidacy, one of them advising Wellington to "keep Jeannette from making a fool of herself." Past U.S. senator and fellow Bull Moose supporter Joseph M. Dixon suggested that Wellington should refuse to "let" his sister run.[24]

But while Jeannette lacked support from some national suffrage lead-ers and from the Republican Party, she did have her brother's backing. He described to his sister what he judged to be the appalling difficulties that she would face as a woman candidate: "I am shocked at the prejudice that exists against a woman going to Congress.... The biggest campaign of edu-cation that is going to be required is to the effect that a woman can do the work there and should probably be sent there, rather than the question of you, individually, going.... The prejudice is substantial."[25] He argued that suffrage campaigning had been a good career move for entering pol-itics, better than her social work, but that the networks she had thus cre-ated would only help her if she acted right away.[26] And Wellington went further, claiming that he would help her regardless of what suffragists thought or did: "Well, now, you're going to run for Congress and I'm not very much interested in whether these women go along with you or not. I'll manage your campaign and you'll be elected."[27]

Aided by her friend Belle Fligelman, Jeannette opened her campaign headquarters in Wellington's law office. Following the plan that these three formed, she went to visit with prominent women, many of whom she had met during the suffrage campaign, thus becoming what Wellington labeled as the "best known person in the whole state" as she countered objections to her candidacy. She traveled by car and train, her sisters speaking along with her, while Wellington in Helena kept track of public sentiment. As Jeannette energized voters, she asked them to mail postcards to their friends, to make telephone calls, and to bring their neighbors to her speeches and small group meetings. Additionally, the siblings established the Jeannette Rankin for Congress Club, with units across the state. Given the control of state newspapers by the Anaconda Mining Company and the prejudices of the Republican Party, both Jeannette and Wellington recognized that a meeting-by-meeting approach would be their only means of securing positive public notice and votes.

In her speeches and campaign literature, Jeannette emphasized issues affecting women, forging a platform that her friend, journalist Mary O'Neill, described as "messianic maternalism."[28] Jeannette informed the *New York Times*, which also made claims about the quality of her needle-work, of her plans to improve women's economic and political situation: "I am going to Washington to represent the women and children of the West, to work for an eight hour day for women, and for laws providing that women shall receive the same wages as men for equal amounts of work" and certainly to fight for suffrage.[29]

This campaign highlighted the strengths of both siblings as well as their ability to understand and help each other. Jeannette demonstrated a level of concern and humility in her interactions with voters that Wellington would not be able to muster in his own campaigns.[30] She would caution him about the necessary connection to voters that he seemed to disdain: "I know your ideas and mine on campaigning are not the same, but I am thoroughly convinced you cannot win unless you go out among the people yourself and find out how they feel.... Your chances to win would increase tremendously if you would meet the people. Your aloofness is your greatest handicap."[31]

While Wellington lacked her sense of solidarity with state residents, he possessed greater knowledge of a range of issues. As he ran her head-quarters, he conducted research about the needs of men and women voters around the state and the best means of appealing to them. Wellington began the campaign knowing Missoula and the western part of the state well, and he immediately started studying the eastern section. As he wrote to his sister while she was traveling, he reminded her to speak about key issues engaging each community: "In Sheridan, Richland, and Dawson counties prohibition will be an excellent plan; in Billings you will be confronted with the tariff on wool, and you will have to bear in mind that the Republican Party has been based upon tariff issues chiefly, and in those sections where they are dependent upon a tariff on wool for prosperity they will not vote for anyone that does not favor protection."[32] In her campaign, in various vicinities as Wellington and Jeannette carefully planned, she spoke on local issues as well as for women's rights and against both the all powerful Anaconda Mining Company and possible involvement in the war in Europe.

As the sister and brother extended her reputation, employing Jeannette's campaigning skills along with Wellington's research and state-wide organization, he began to introduce her to the power brokers of the state's Republican Party. Wellington already knew the price of leaving the party to run in a minority group, as he had with the Bull Moose Party. They both recognized the power of being the nominee of a major party, and even though Jeannette was not a member, she sought this support that her brother helped her to obtain, as she later noted: "I was never a Republican. I ran on the Republican ticket."[33]

While meeting with influential groups and seeking party support, Jeannette and Wellington planned to take advantage of the legislative situation in their state. In 1916, Montanans would elect two representatives to the U.S. House, with both to be at-large members since no districts had yet been designated. Seven men and Jeannette formed a field of eight in the Republican primary, from which two would be selected to run against two Democratic candidates in November. To take advantage of this situation, the Rankins made a definite plan: at each campaign stop, Jeannette assured Republicans that they could choose any male candidate and still vote for her, thus making a traditional selection while honoring Jeannette's preparation for office and the right of women to participate in government.

By early August, just three weeks into the campaign, sister and brother had gained considerable momentum. Jeannette easily won the primary, with 22,549 votes against 15,429 for the next contender. Then, with two Democrats and two Republicans in the general election, including the Democratic incumbent John Evans, a lawyer who had been mayor of Missoula and would serve in the House from 1913 to 1921 and from 1923 to 1933, the siblings argued that Montanans could elect Jeannette Rankin and John Evans, with both parties and genders thus represented. Although on election night it looked like Jeannette might not prevail, two days later with all the returns in, she had won by 6300 votes.[34] Reviewing this campaign in *Flight of the Dove: The Story of Jeannette Rankin*, Kevin S. Giles recognized her formidable campaigning skills and her supportive network of activist women, but he also concluded that Wellington "had been a godsend in Jeannette's election to Congress, for without his political intuition and astute engineering she probably would not have won."[35]

Having achieved what no one but the two Rankins had at first thought that Jeannette could or should do, she quickly became a nationally prominent figure, interviewed and sought after for speaking engagements. Jeannette realized that some of this attention came from shock over a woman's election, as one journalist expressed the general opinion of the day: "Women policemen, yes; women doctors, yes; women lawyers, umm-m, yes: but women congress-'men'—appalling! Had Montana voters gone plumb crazy! What sort of joke were they putting over on the rest of the nation!"[36]

While noting the oddity of her election, many newspapers concentrated on Jeannette's looks and domesticity—she was "small, slight, with light brown hair" and she made her own clothes.[37] An article in the *Washington Times* noted that she would be driving a car from Montana to Washington, a surprising choice for a young woman.[38] In an article in the *Oregon Daily Journal*, with the positive title of "Jeannette Rankin Is Well Qualified to Serve in Congress," Bert Lennon mentioned that he went to Montana to interview her, expecting a six-shooter or a quasi-man, but instead found a surprisingly youthful woman with curly hair who could make her own clothes and cook.[39] Even the *Woman's Journal and Suffrage News*, which discussed her education and suffrage work, commented that "she dances well, makes her own hats and dresses, and has won fame among her friends for an especially fine kind of lemon pie."[40] As scholar Maria Braden noted in *Women Politicians and the Media*, Jeannette "became what we would now call a celebrity."[41]

Right after the election, both siblings found the press attention overwhelming, making Jeannette into something of a sideshow act. Even before the end of November 1916, Wellington had issued a request that "moving picture men and press photographers" stop attempting to make more appointments.[42] He spoke to many reporters for her, stressing that she was not an oddity but a real person, a good stump speaker, sympathetic and informed on key issues. Papers across the country, such as the *Charlotte Observer* and the *San Francisco Chronicle*, quoted him concerning his sister's priorities: "'Her life is devoted to the cause of mankind and good government, first, last and all the time.... The rich and the poor, the high and the low, will always get a square deal from my sister.'"[43] To enable Jeannette to reach the public without speaking to biased reporters, Wellington served as her agent as she signed three deals: to produce fifty articles for the Chicago *Sunday Herald*, to give talks for a New York speakers' bureau, and to write for women's magazines like the *Ladies' Home Journal*, her articles and speeches concerning an eight-hour work day, an end to child labor, fair wages for women, and the qualifications of women to be legislators.[44]

After Jeannette entered Congress in March of 1917, even though she wanted to work on so many issues, all of her focus had to concern war. She had been opposed to American entrance into this war since its beginning. Like many progressives, she felt that this European combat was about economic struggle, about using workers to fight for the territory and resources sought by the wealthy. In the *Literary Digest*, she said of her state's residents at the time of her election: "I judged the sentiment in Montana was overwhelmingly against war."[45]

Though Wellington had forwarded his sister's career, both in Montana and on the way to Washington, they did not agree about war—and her choices would damage his career as well as her own. While Jeannette was making up her mind, Wellington committed himself to American involvement in this conflict. He wanted her to decide on "a man's vote," for war as well as for her own ambition and future: she was on trial with America, he argued, and must make what would be deemed the patriotic choice.[46] "I knew she couldn't be elected again if she did vote against the war. I didn't want to see her destroy herself," he said later about their disagreement.[47] As Wellington talked to Jeannette and recruited friends to do so, he also argued that she would be harming the political careers of other women, as though her vote would indicate that no woman could face the challenges of protecting the nation. He asked her to go with him to New York to meet with suffragists that supported the war effort. Wellington also brought dedicated activist Harriet Laidlaw to Washington to plead with her concerning the damage that would be done to the suffrage cause by the first woman in office voting no to war.[48] On the day before the vote, after an argument lasting until midnight, Wellington once again tried to convince her. And then he finally said, "Well, you've heard it all. You go in there and vote your conscience."[49]

Because of her view that this war was not necessary, that it would put workers in jeopardy while enriching armament dealers and ambitious politicians, Jeannette made the difficult decision to go against her brother and many suffragists, and against what was a changing attitude in her state. As she indicated about the various viewpoints that she considered, "It was easy to stand against the propaganda of the militarists, but very difficult to go against friends and dear ones who felt that I was making a needless sacrifice by voting against the war since my vote would not be a decisive one. I decided to listen to those who wanted war and not to vote until the last opportunity. If I could see any reason for going to war I would try to change." She felt that her own political ambition should have no place in her decision: "Never for one second could I face the idea that I would send young men to be killed for no other reason than to save my seat in Congress."[50]

On April 6, 1917, only four days into her term, the House considered the resolution to enter World War I. Jeannette did not vote on the first roll call. On the second ballot, as was reported throughout the country, when she was called upon, she said that "I want to stand by my country, but I cannot vote for war" and added quietly, "I vote no." In speaking in this manner before voting, she had violated a House rule that forbade comment on a vote.[51]

Afterwards, Jeannette met Wellington in the hallway of the Capitol to walk home together, and Wellington told her, as he recalled to an interviewer years later, "You know you are not going to be re-elected. You know there will be a lot of feeling," and she replied, "I am not interested in that. All I am interested in [is] what they will say fifty years from now."[52] And then he said the more general "Think what you've done," a line he repeated when Belle Fligelman, in Washington to serve as Jeannette's secretary, let them into the house. The next week, in a letter to her brother, Jeannette wrote that "I am sorry to disappoint you. I still feel that this was the only way I could go." Many years later, given her strong convictions, he admitted concerning his protracted attempt at persuasion that "I've been a little ashamed of it since." He continued by recognizing that his sister "would consider it more dishonest not to vote your conviction than to rob a bank or steal something."[53]

The newspapers made much of her vote even though she was one among many opposing the war. While fifty members of Congress voted no, the *New York Times*, in the main article concerning the vote, led with the headline of "Seek to Explain Miss Rankin's 'No,'" a much smaller fifth headline mentioning the forty-nine other senators.[54] A subheading in the article called hers "purely a woman's vote." The article, like many others, described her as reacting emotionally right afterwards: she "threw her head back and sobbed ... her appearance was that of a woman on the verge of a breakdown." While the *New York Times* and newspapers across the country depicted her during the roll call as bordering on hysteria, witnesses said she was dry-eyed and controlled, as Jeannette also recalled: "I had wept so much that week that my tears were all gone by the time the vote came."[55]

While Wellington had supported Jeannette all through the campaign and felt that ultimately she had to vote her own convictions about war, he faced difficulties after her opposition vote, their careers continuing to be entwined. Right afterwards, he sought out interview opportunities to report that he opposed her decision.[56] He quickly joined the Tank Corps to further demonstrate his support for war. But many people in Montana never forgave Wellington for being her brother: even eleven years later, when he ran for governor, newspapers across the state reminded readers of her war vote, her work for peace that had continued in the 1920s, his inability to control her, and the family's seeming lack of patriotism.[57]

Though Jeannette hurt Wellington with her war vote, some of her other priorities as a legislator extended his power base in Montana, particularly as she opposed the Anaconda Mining Company. In his legal career, as he represented the interests of cattle ranchers, including himself, Anaconda had been his "long time nemesis"; the company and its newspapers "viciously attacked Rankin at every opportunity"—and he was glad to help his sister oppose this monolith.[58] In June 1917, a fire in a mine shaft turned into the worst disaster to ever occur in hard-rock mining, causing the death of 168 miners. Three days afterwards, a general strike erupted, with workers demanding better working conditions and wages.[59] In August, Jeannette introduced legislation asking Congress to authorize the president to nationalize the mines, as essential to the war effort, a direct attack on Anaconda. She told the *Washington Times* and other newspapers that she would be vilified in Montana as a result since the mine bosses "own the State. They own the government. They own the press."[60] Given the power of this mining company and the complications of a federal takeover, Congress failed to act.

In August, as the strike continued with no government response, Jeannette decided on a visit to Montana and to the mines, which would raise national attention, given the press' interest in her. Wellington first advised her not to take on this entrenched power, but then he met her train in Miles City, Montana, and escorted her west, to the mining center of Butte. There police would not allow her to speak to a group that gathered at the train station. The next day in town, however, accompanied by union leaders, Jeannette addressed a large crowd, which Wellington estimated at 15,000. He said afterwards that the response was the most enthusiastic anyone had received there: "And it wasn't the miners alone. It was all the people."[61]

In Congress, in the newspapers, and in the speech that she made in Butte, Jeannette had stood up to Anaconda as her brother did in courtrooms, thus extending the reach of his power. She tried to forge a compromise, which would at least include better working conditions if not higher wages, but the miners finally went back on the job without achieving much of anything. Like her war vote, this attempted intervention damaged Jeannette's career, given the power of this company in the state. But this opposition proved helpful to Wellington. Though, as his widely publicized narrative claimed, he had not controlled his sister's war vote, he had since then brought her to the state to stand up to his enemies, a construction of events that Jeannette never countered. Through the rest of her term in the House, Wellington and Jeannette continued to collaborate in small ways as well as big. When Teddy Roosevelt died in January 1919, she gave a eulogy for him in the House, extolling him as a model for youth. Roosevelt had praised the military above almost all else, enflamed the Spanish-American War, and expanded the navy while taking Panama, decisions with which Jeannette did not agree, but he was Wellington's friend and mentor.

The loyalty and connection of these siblings would be tested again in 1918 when Jeannette sought to run for re-election, another instance when her choices bolstered his power. That year they judged that she could not be re-elected to the House. Since 1916, Montana had been split into two districts, each with one representative. The new western district, including their hometown of Missoula, was heavily Democratic and would not support any Republican; the eastern district was more Republican but further from their home base. Given this new situation, Jeannette decided to run in the Republican primary for the U.S. Senate. Hampered by her anti-war vote and her support of miners, she lost to Dr. Oscar M. Lanstrum, a former state representative and publisher of the *Montana Record-Herald*, by the close vote of 18,805 to 17,091. To oppose him, the Democrats nominated incumbent Thomas J. Walsh, who had entered the Senate in 1912, a supporter of Wilson's reform program and a skillful and popular politician, the lawyer who had hired Wellington when he first returned to Montana from Harvard.[62]

After Jeannette lost the Republican primary, Wellington began nego-tiating with the Democrats, threatening that she might run against Walsh and Lanstrum as a third-party candidate. Given her opposition to Ana-conda, party officials feared that if she ran she would take away some labor votes and thus hurt Walsh. In sexist terms that highlighted Wellington's supposed power over her, Colonel C.B. Nolan, Walsh's law partner, wrote to Walsh on August 30, 1918, urging that "every influence possible be brought to bear on Wellington not to have her run."[63] Nolan and Walsh proposed to Wellington that a position be created for Jeannette, perhaps overseas, so that she could retire from the field gracefully. Walsh's cam-paign manager, A.E. Spriggs, also suggested that the Democratic Party might offer cash.

This discussion, of a payment and an overseas appointment, soon hit the state's newspapers, publicity that Jeannette judged as disgraceful. These rumors, in fact, may have led her to stay in the race.[64] That fall, Jeannette became a candidate of the National Party, an organization founded by socialists.[65] Besides providing her with a means to run—albeit an unlikely one, as the experience of her brother in 1912 and of many women candidates would indicate—this choice enabled Wellington to engage in further negotiations.[66] He had been in competition with Lanstrum for power in the Republican Party, and so with this choice he was promoting his own power within the party and in the state: without his backing, he was asserting, a Republican couldn't win. Wellington was also indirectly helping his friend and partner Thomas Walsh and thus emphasizing his influence within the Democratic Party as well. On November 5, the vote totals were Walsh 46,160; Lanstrum 40,229; and Rankin 26,013.[67] Lanstrum did not run for office again.

For the next two decades, Jeannette continued her work as an activist while attempting to help Wellington secure political office. While serving as a field secretary for the National Consumers' League in the 1920s and 1930s, she campaigned for legislation to promote health care for pregnant women and for children and to regulate the hours and wages of women workers. She then became an officer of the Women's International League for Peace and Freedom, established in 1915 by Jane Addams. In 1924, Jeannette came to Montana from her home in Georgia to stump for Wellington for the Senate, but he didn't win against Thomas Walsh, who had solid backing. In 1928, she returned to Montana again to help Wellington, who was run-ning for governor, another election that he didn't win. His connections and experience then led to his appointment as associate justice of the state Supreme Court and later as U.S. attorney for the district of Montana.

In 1940, Jeannette saw an opportunity to reenter the U.S. House. For the Republican nomination, she beat Jacob Thorkelson, from Butte, who had entered the House in January of 1939. In July 1940, the *Christian Science Monitor* excoriated him as a Nazi sympathizer who had "built up a reputation of having filled the Congressional Record with anti–Semitic diatribes."[68] In the general election, she secured 54 percent of the vote against Democrat Jerry O'Connell, a divorced Catholic with Communist sympathies. Wellington's long-term collaboration with Democrats, many of whom were not O'Connell supporters, helped her to win this seat. As she spoke at schools around the state during this campaign, she made clear to voters that she remained an isolationist, determined to oppose war, this stance again acceptable for a short time as Americans sought to avoid a second world war.

After entering office for a second time, Jeannette opposed the Lend Lease policy, enacted in March 1941 to supply warships and warplanes, along with other weaponry, to the allies. Following the attack on Pearl Harbor, Wellington urged her not to repeat her earlier vote, that the reaction would be much worse, but she once again voted against war, this time as the only member of the House to do so. Then when the House declared war on Germany and Italy, she voted solely as "Present."[69] Reaction was swift and fierce, beginning with hissing on the floor of the House. On December 9, the *New York Times* reported that Montana's Republican leaders had denounced her and that she needed to publicly change her vote "to redeem Montana's honor and loyalty."[70] Like other small-town and big-city newspapers, the *Acantha* in Choteau, Montana, described her as an irrational recalcitrant child: she needed to be spanked on the floor of the House.[71] The *Washington Post* concentrated on the immediate response of rational male leaders: "After she voted, there was a small procession of solemn-faced colleagues back up the aisle to her seat. They spoke earnestly to her, in the benign manner of men who strive to change a woman's mind ... but at the end of each conversation, she always shook her head."[72]

After these war votes, Jeannette basically waited out her term. She decided not to run again in 1942 and instead supported her brother's candidacy for the U.S. Senate, throwing herself "into the campaign with ardor." As they campaigned, she repeatedly asserted that they disagreed about war but not about Montana, about the need to advocate for the state's residents and to oppose the dominance of companies like Anaconda: he lost that election by just 1100 votes.[73]

This sister and brother pair differed in their political principles, with

Wellington furthering the rights of ranchers while supporting two world wars and his sister seeking an eight-hour work day, child labor laws, and better health care for women as well as an end to war. They also differed in their political skills, as Jeannette's biographer Norma Smith described the two: "He was not the politician she was. He was aloof, even arrogant, though, in Jeannette's words, he could 'pour on the charm' when he chose. Jeannette understood people better, she knew the complex technicalities of politics as well as he, and she was trusted."[74] As Wellington recognized in an interview, "she was one of the best single-handed campaigners I ever saw," a key skill that he lacked.[75]

But though they often disagreed and they had different strengths, this twosome forged a political family for themselves, in a generation in which parents might be furthering their sons' careers, as the Rankins did in sending Wellington to Harvard, but not their daughters' future in politics. Wellington's biographer Volney Steele contended that he was "the man who twice propelled his controversial sister, Jeannette, into Congress."[76] This claim perhaps went too far because she propelled herself, but he certainly helped her with party connections, knowledge of issues across the state, campaign organization, control over media representations, and fundraising. And she also continued to help him. Her celebrity, both as a Republican and as a potential spoiler of party plans, helped to establish his reputation as a powerful deal-maker. They together went beyond two sisters as outsiders or a brother who could help a sister get an appointed post. Certainly they showed that siblings could have different strengths, with the man not necessarily the better politician, that they could aid each other, and that there could be power in a political family even though members might advocate for conflicting principles. Without always being in agreement, family members could create an authority and independence that went beyond parties and beyond organizations like suffrage groups, enabling women to assert their priorities and power.

THREE

"Over His Dead Body"

Widow's Succession
as Family Connection

Victoria Woodhull and Tennie Claflin's attempts to secure election and Rankin's victory in the House involved collaborations between siblings—members of the same generation, willing to help each other, both with something to gain in eras when older members of a family might not forward the careers of women.

Into the 1920s and 1930s, few women would enter office even from the most politically engaged families. While Eleanor Roosevelt had the same family connections and intelligence as Franklin, she would not be encouraged to go to college and certainly not to run for office. Franklin, however, would go to Harvard and move into the family electoral space inaugurated in the seventeenth century by New York City alderman Elsie Roosevelt and continued in the nineteenth century by Cadwallader D. Colden, mayor of New York City, Nicholas Roosevelt, member of the New York Assembly, and Cornelius C. Roosevelt, New York City alderman, as well as Theodore Roosevelt into the twentieth century.

With full suffrage in 1920, the major parties declared the need to recognize women as voters and activists but not as elected officials: securing their votes and party work mattered but encouraging them to run for office or supporting them in that choice generally did not. In the 1920s, only one woman would enter the U.S. Senate, Rebecca Felton, who served as an appointee for just one day. In that decade, only eleven women entered the U.S. House.

After passage of the federal suffrage amendment, with little change in the electoral landscape and with few political families forwarding the goals of women, the most common means of entering office would involve another form of family connection, one that still occurs: the woman replacing a husband as his widow.

Through the decades, party leaders have anointed widows to finish their husbands' terms in Congress for several reasons: to honor the deceased politician, to tap voters' sympathy, and to exploit name recognition. Party leaders generally did not desire to "open up the field to women," but instead to hold onto a seat while more conventional—male—candidates prepared for the next, "real" campaign.[1] Some historians have associated this tradition with an older system of coverture, allowing a widow to inherit a small percentage of her husband's property: in 1933, Sophonisba Breckinridge described appointed or elected widows as "women who have taken political office as a dower right in their husband's estates."[2] So well known was the practice of wives succeeding husbands that the terms "widow's mandate" and "widow's succession" have been coined to identify it. And this succession has involved widows and not widowers. No widower has taken his wife's place though Reuben Spellman of Maryland tried to do so in 1980; he lost in the Democratic primary for the U.S. House.

Before widows began to follow their husbands into office, women like Victoria Woodhull and Jeannette Rankin represented the scary few, rebels in a new space, their viewpoints outside of what was accepted. Widows of the next decades would also be disparaged—not for being radicals but milquetoasts, involved in a pointless trend as faithful wives, their participation labeled as "sentimental nepotism."[3] But the group of women that entered the U.S. Senate and House as widows has included many well-prepared long-term legislators, who with the backing of family moved well beyond their husbands, often advocating for outsiders, in contradiction of their husbands and their parties. Though stereotypical judgments have relegated these women to a secondary status in congressional history, the truth of their service is much more complex and significant, with both the criticisms and the reality worthy of serious consideration.

A Key Assumption: That Widows Came Right into Office and Went Right Back Out

One of the criticisms has been that large numbers of these unpoliticians, primarily of another era, slipped into office on an old-fashioned wave of sympathy and left without their service involving much effort or impact.

This criticism involves the assumption that in the past every widow who had any inclination easily won a seat. These widows did win at a higher rate than other women running for office: among first-time House candidates from 1916 to 1993, for example, 84 percent of the widows won while only 14 percent of other women were victorious.[4] But widows were not as frequently elected as has sometimes been assumed: wives of only 14 percent of the men who died in office have succeeded their spouses, generally those women who had been involved in campaigning and were well prepared for the job. Widows are certainly not the majority of women who have served: through the 115th Congress, they constitute 16 percent of women in the House and 16 percent of women in the Senate. Forty-seven women had been elected or appointed to fill congressional vacancies created by the deaths of their husbands, eight to the U.S. Senate and thirty-nine to the U.S. House, the names provided in this book's appendix.

While a low percentage of widows have come into office, they often did so in highly competitive elections. Some of them did have a smooth path to short-term service. Catherine Small Long of Louisiana, for example, easily defeated her opponent for a seat in the U.S. House after her husband Gillis Long died in 1985. As Carson Killen, an aide to her husband and her campaign manager, declared during the campaign, "Let's face it, she is going to get elected this first time out as Mrs. Gillis Long and not as Cathy Long."[5] She remained in office only until the conclusion of her husband's term. But not all of these women trod an easy path. When Lindy Boggs ran in a special election to replace her husband, she had strong opposition in the Democratic primary, the key at that time to winning the state. Several men opposed her, claiming publicly that one of them should, and would, win. One strong candidate, real estate agent Woody Koppel, focused on Boggs as an older woman: he argued that as a much younger man, he could build seniority and bring more help to Louisiana. His supporters, from his years on the city council, emphasized his business acumen and his greater knowledge as a current state resident, with Boggs thus cast as a Washington outsider, an older, devoted mother just keeping the seat warm until it could be occupied by her son Tommy.[6]

Initially, in 1951, Elizabeth Kee was the underdog in the race to replace her husband, not the preferred candidate, beginning the race behind such powerful politicians as Walter Vergil Ross, who had served several terms in the West Virginia legislature, and Sheriff Cecil Wilson of Bluefield. Party leaders proposed that she should be retained as a secretary for the eventual nominee, a suggestion that infuriated her. With her son James, she campaigned heavily with leaders of the United Mine Workers of America, convincing them that John Kee had initiated several projects for the district that only Elizabeth Kee could complete. That strategy worked, causing mine workers to throw their weight behind her.[7]

When her husband John Sullivan died in January 1951, Missouri Democratic leaders refused to nominate Leonor Sullivan to run in the special election to fill the vacancy. "We don't have anything against you," they told Sullivan. "We just want to win." Their chosen candidate, Harry Schendel, lost to Republican Claude I. Bakewell. Lacking the funds to mount her own congressional campaign without the backing of the Democratic Party, Sullivan took a year-long position as an administrative aide to Representative Theodore Irving. In 1952, Sullivan announced her candidacy for her husband's reapportioned district. After that successful campaign, Sullivan was never seriously challenged: she captured her next eleven elections with between 65 percent and 79 percent of the vote, attaining the party support in these contests that was denied to her in the first.

Beyond assumptions concerning their ease of election, another common belief is that these women served for a short term and long ago. Again the stereotype relates to just some widows. These legislators include, in the House, Veronica Grace Boland of Pennsylvania, who served from 1942 to 1943, but it also includes in the House Edith Nourse Rogers of Massachusetts, in office from 1925 to 1960; Frances P. Bolton of Ohio, 1940–1960; Leonor Sullivan of Missouri, 1953–1977; and Doris Matsui, of California, 2005 to the present, re-elected to the 116th Congress in November 2018. Though some of these legislators simply completed a term, many served for a lengthy period, relative to the average tenure, developing into trusted legislators.[8]

This means of entering office may seem old fashioned, but it has continued into this century. The group includes in the Senate Jean Carnahan from Missouri, serving from 2001 to 2002, and in the House Jo Ann Emerson from Missouri, 1996–2013; Lois Capps from California, 1998–2013; Mary Bono from California, 1998–2017; and Doris Matsui. Many of these women served for long periods, prevailing in difficult elections to do so, withstanding the ongoing discourse that claimed widows had no right to be there, that these matrons should remain at home with their children.

These Women Judged as Lesser: A Group Disparaged

While their ease of entrance and their numbers have been overestimated, these widows' qualifications and impact have been underestimated.

This widow's mandate has engendered many humorous phrases, including "over his dead body," "the best husband is a dead husband," and "for some women to rise their men must fall" as well as "sentimental nepotism."[9] Commonly expressed judgments have made it easy to satirize these women as a group—and have led to repeated assertions that the many who have made a significant contribution are surprising or unique outliers, somehow separate from the whole.

Some early analysts recognized that even well-qualified women had few other options for seeking office. In 1925, Emily N. Blair, a vice chair of the Democratic National Committee, used the comparison to a dower to illustrate how a "self-conscious feminist," speaking to a younger woman, would respond to this slight bit of opportunity: "My dear child, inheritance of a man's political assets by a woman is a great step forward. Why, in our day, a woman did not even inherit her own money, or her own child, let alone the opportunities and responsibilities that she and her husband had built up together."[10]

But, beginning in the first decades of suffrage, many journalists used this image of inheritance to react much more negatively. In 1932, upon the retirement of widow Effiegene Wingo, who had replaced her husband Otis Theodore Wingo in the U.S. House in 1930, the New York *Sun* wrote of the six widows who had served: "It can be said that they submitted with dignity and good taste to a false code of chivalry, served unostentatiously and departed the Capitol quietly, wondering what the men who invented the term-by-inheritance thought they were doing." And the *Washington Post* declared ominously that "it is too soon to say that politicians and voters have learned that it is a bad policy to deal with offices as with dower rights. There will be other examples of chivalry in the future," a base form of "sentimentality."[11] After the first women gained offices as widows, many feminists also found the results disappointing, decrying both these women's lack of qualifications and the voters' lack of trust in independent women as leaders. Journalist Mildred Adams contended in 1932 in the *New York Times Magazine* that these widows were just doing the minimum, not changing the world or affecting women positively. She described them dismissively as "discreet, hard-working, generally obedient, and quite unspectacular."[12] Grace Adams in the *North American Review* in 1939 claimed that these widows seemed "simple, conventional and on the whole, rather mediocre housewives, who happened in their youth to marry men who later became statesmen and still later died in office."[13] And these denunciations, from varied sources, have continued to occur. Concerning Mary Bono, elected to the U.S. House in 1998 to replace Sonny Bono,

Kevin Ryder, host of a morning radio show in Los Angeles, declared that "just because you're Sonny Bono's wife really doesn't mean that you can do what Sonny Bono was doing. I mean, Michael Jordan isn't going to die and his wife go play for the Bulls." As scholar Irwin N. Gertzog depicted this criticism spanning the decades: "Widows are not given the benefit of the doubt."[14] Regardless of how well prepared they were or how hard they worked, the prejudice remained that they didn't deserve election, that they were taking advantage of an extreme situation—just piteous widows without qualifications.

Through the decades, negative judgments found expression in discourse about appearance and family, involving body shape but also these widows' first duty as the sole parents of their children. Concerning Katharine Byron, who replaced her husband, William D. Byron, in the U.S. House in May 1941, the *Washington Post* noted that she wanted to support the president's plans for national defense, but she was having trouble concentrating because of her eight-year-old son's poison ivy. The article continued by confiding that she "looked more motherly than official."[15] The *Post* commented in 1944 that "plump, gracious Mrs. Hamilton P. Fulmer" was one of the new legislators, having replaced her husband.[16] Such widely publicized judgments did not cease in later decades. In 1998, newspapers across the nation reported that Sonny Bono's mother opposed her daughter-in-law's run for office because it would hurt Sonny's children. "Mary Bono Loses One Vote" one newspaper used as a headline, with the text implying that his mother's decision should determine a district's.[17]

Regional stereotypes also displayed these women's lack of worthiness. One article labeled Willa Lybrand Fulmer as "more of a Southern gentlewoman than a career type." Concerning Fulmer, the *Washington Post* further indicated that she might be smart but as a Southern woman she was too used to stifling her intelligence to become an effective legislator: "She may be like many smart Southern gals who read popular magazines in the drug stores when the boys are around, and devour Shakespeare, history and Greek in their boudoirs"; such foolish, engrained deception would not prepare her for governing.[18]

While these women as a group have been mocked as unprepared, ineffective mothers, critics would frequently praise individuals from the group as surprising individuals—to account for Hattie Caraway or Frances Bolton or Edith Nourse Rogers or Cardiss Collins or Margaret Chase Smith or Lindy Boggs or Mary Bono or Doris Matsui. Though so many widows have served with distinction, they have been repeatedly seen as unique, their political beginning as widows often overlooked or forgotten as they undertook praiseworthy actions. While in 1925, Emily N. Blair had commented that a woman could forward the "opportunities and responsibilities that she and her husband had built up together" and then successfully move on to her own choices, critics have kept repeating negative judgments while claiming that only a very few have achieved any significant goals, certainly a restricted version of the actual story.[19]

In the Family Business

While prejudices concerning these women mark them as wives serving as placeholders, their story, as a group and as individuals, is much more complex. Part of this complexity, and indeed their service, is rooted in family.

These widows did provide assistance to their husbands' extended political families, a significant step beyond raising children. George S. Long was an Oklahoma state representative and then U.S. representative from Louisiana. His younger brothers were Huey Long, governor of Louisiana and U.S. senator from Louisiana, and Earl Long, governor of Louisiana. Rose McConnell Long, Huey's widow, who had been a stenographer before her marriage, won a special election on April 21, 1936, to serve the remaining months of her husband's term; she declined to run for re-election in November 1936 when the seat was won by Allen J. Ellender, who had been an ally of Huey Long and who remained in office until 1972. Rose Long's son, Russell B. Long, served as a U.S. senator from Louisiana for the long period of 1948 to 1987. Her husband's cousin Gillis Long was a U.S. representative from Louisiana, 1963–1965 and 1973–1985; he was followed into office by another family widow, Catherine Small Long, who finished her husband's term, from 1985 to 1987. Both women raised children but also served in Congress to help their family, party, and state.

Although these legislators are known for their status as widows, many were members of powerful political families themselves. In Maryland, a prominent political family engaged widows in more than one generation, the family power coming from both wives and husbands. Katharine Byron, elected to the U.S. House in 1941 to replace her husband, William D. Byron, after his death in an airplane crash, belonged to a prominent political family from western Maryland: Katharine's maternal grandfather, Louis Emory McComas, had served in both the U.S. House and Senate. After she finished her husband's term in the House, she left office. Her son, Goodloe Byron, would also be elected to represent the same district. After he died, his widow Beverly Byron served for him.

Through their own political connections, many of these women had helped their husbands get elected. Frances Payne Bolton, who served in the House as a widow from 1940 to 1969, was from a political family that forwarded the career of both her husband and son. Her grandfather Henry Payne, a railroad magnate, represented Ohio in the U.S. House and Senate, leaving office in 1891. Payne's nephew Sereno, a member of Congress beginning in 1882, co-authored the Payne-Aldrich Tariff in 1909. Frances Payne Bolton's husband, Chester C. Bolton, was elected in 1929 to the seat that Henry Payne had occupied. After a career in the army, Bolton worked in the steel industry and then raised cattle. Her family helped him to enter the state Senate and then move to the U.S. House. Much later, beginning in 1953 and for three terms, Frances Bolton would be in office along with her son, Oliver P. Bolton, with her legislative record and the family's background essential to his first campaign.

Of great help to her husband and to her own preparation for leadership were the generations of Marie Corinne Morrison Claiborne (Lindy) Boggs' family that had been in politics across the nation and especially in the South, including Thomas Claiborne (1740–1812), a U.S. representative from Virginia; William C.C. Claiborne (1773–1817), a U.S. representative from Tennessee, governor of Louisiana, and U.S. senator from Louisiana; and Claiborne Pell (1918–2009), a U.S. senator from Rhode Island. After Hale Boggs, from Long Beach, Mississippi, one of six children in a family faced with a "precarious" financial situation in the Depression, received a law degree at Tulane University in 1937, he married Lindy in 1938: it was her family with the connections and political history that helped him to become, in 1941 at age twenty-six, the youngest member of Congress. In a highly political family, no political future had been considered for her, but the family's connections forwarded her husband's goals.[20]

In Louise Goff Reece's case, she met her husband, Carroll Reece, after he had just entered office, as a member of the U.S. House from Tennessee. Both her great-grandfather Nathan Goff and her grandfather Nathan Goff, Jr., served as a U.S. representative and senator from West Virginia. Her father Guy D. Goff was U.S. attorney general for the eastern district of Wisconsin and was then elected as a U.S. senator from West Virginia, in 1924, taking his father's old seat. Louise Goff grew up in Washington, D.C., and then attended boarding schools, including the prestigious Miss Spence's School in New York City. As she grew up, Louise Reece later recalled, running for office was "the last thing I ever thought of." Any such aspirations had been discouraged—she recalled her father's exclusionary practices as indicative of his view of who should be engaged in government: "No woman ever got inside his office door."[21] But Guy Goff viewed his son-in-law's ambitions differently. As Carroll Reece's biographer claimed, "Reece's marriage connected him to a Republican family firmly established in national politics."[22] Her family helped him through a long career, providing political connections, fund-raising clout, and legislative knowledge not available to most first-time House members. She was well prepared and well connected when she entered the House after her husband's death in 1961.

Another well-connected widow was Jo Ann Emerson, daughter of A.B. (Ab) Hermann, executive director of the Republican National Committee. Bob Dole described him in 1978 as a "man for all seasons" in the party, at various times encouraging candidates, running campaigns, staffing a speakers' bureau, and administering the national office.[23] Jo Ann Hermann married Bill Emerson in 1975 when he was working as an attorney and lobbyist, her family connections essential to him when he ran in 1980 for the U.S. House from Missouri. She followed him into office and served from 1996 to 2013.

Their Education

Even though these women might not have been encouraged to enter political careers, or indeed any career, many of them were well prepared to do so: indeed, widows with more education and more involvement in politics were more likely to run and to win. These members of Congress, at much larger percentages than other American women, had been to elite boarding schools, traveled abroad, and attended college. In 1940, only 3.8 percent of women age twenty-five and older had graduated from college; the percentage had been lower in earlier decades and went up slowly after 1940, to 5.8 percent in 1960, 13.6 percent in 1980, 23 percent in 2000, and 26 percent in 2010.[24] But, in the Senate, two out of three, or 66 percent, of those widows who served before 1950 and seven of eight, or 87.5 percent, of the entire group attended college. In the House, nine out of fifteen women, or 60 percent, of those who served before 1950 and thirty of thirty-nine, or 76.9 percent, of the entire group attended college.

Marguerite Stitt Church, for example, developed an interest in foreign countries at an early age, from going abroad each summer with her parents. She earned an A.B. in psychology with a minor in economics and sociology from Wellesley College in 1914. After graduation, she taught biblical history at Wellesley for a year before enrolling in a masters program in economics and sociology at Columbia University. Following years of assisting her husband, Ralph Church, and working for various charities, Marguerite Stitt Church won election to the U.S. House to succeed him after his death in 1950.

Though their husbands were more likely to have studied law, many other widows had educational backgrounds that helped to prepare them for leadership. Texan Lera Millard Thomas, wife of attorney and congressman Albert Thomas, who briefly succeeded her husband in the U.S. House, attended Brenau College in Gainesville, Georgia, and the University of Alabama. Marian Williams Clarke, born in Standing Stone, Pennsylvania, studied art at the University of Nebraska for a year and then graduated from Colorado College in 1902. She worked as a reporter for a Colorado Springs newspaper before moving with her husband, attorney John D. Clarke, to New York. She was elected to Congress in 1933 to fill the vacancy caused by his death in a car crash.

Beyond higher education, some widows had elective experience when they assumed their husbands' seats. Maurine Neuberger, from Cloverdale, Oregon, graduated from the University of Oregon's College of Education and then took graduate courses at UCLA to prepare for a career in Oregon public schools, from 1932 to 1944. She married Richard L. Neuberger in 1945 after he completed his service in World War II. He was elected to the Oregon State Senate in 1948. Maurine Neuberger entered politics herself in 1950 when she was elected to the state House of Representatives, where she served until 1955. In 1952, when she was re-elected to the Oregon House and her husband to the state Senate, she won by more votes than he did. Richard was elected to the U.S. Senate in 1954. In 1960, when he died from cancer, Maurine won a special election to complete his term. At the same time, she won the general election for a term from 1961 to 1967, her political experience forwarding her goal of assuming his seat.

Campaigning with Their Husbands

By employing their connections, educational training, and work experience, these women had often served as key members of their husbands' campaigns. They were well prepared to take such a key role, by which they gained knowledge that would further their own political careers.

This dual effort might begin before marriage. Margaret Chase Smith tried out at a variety of occupations while also becoming a campaigner for Clyde Smith. As a teenager, she worked on a switchboard in her rural hometown of Skowhegan, Maine. Calling her every night to pursue her was Clyde Smith, local politician and businessman, recently divorced and twenty-one years older, their relationship continuing as she took a position recording tax payments, taught at a local school, worked at the telephone company, and then found employment at a newspaper where Smith was the publisher. Margaret Chase Smith said of their long courtship, during the time that he ran for and held a seat in the Maine Senate, that "mostly we went campaigning."[25] They married when she was thirty-two and he was fifty-three, in 1930. When he ran for the U.S. House in 1937, she was by his side as a seasoned campaigner, writing his speeches and arranging his schedule while meeting with women's groups and other constituencies.[26]

In at least one instance, the wife did all of the campaigning for the husband in his first election, while he was overseas. During the 1930s, George W. Andrews served as a district attorney in the Alabama circuit court system. He held the position until 1943 when he became an officer in the U.S. Naval Reserve, stationed in Pearl Harbor. When longtime representative Henry B. Steagall died in November 1943, Andrews announced his candidacy for the vacant seat. With her husband in the Pacific, Elizabeth Andrews led his campaign team, making speeches around Alabama on his behalf. While still overseas, her husband won the March 1944 special election. When he died suddenly in late 1971, after many campaigns waged together, friends convinced her to seek election for the remainder of his term.[27]

Margaret Chase Smith and Clyde Smith on the campaign trail, ca. 1930s. From Margaret Chase Smith's early personal photograph albums (courtesy Margaret Chase Smith Library Collection).

In the more common situation of wife and husband campaigning together, the wives could provide assistance in the home district and out from that base. When Lera Millard Thomas' husband, Albert R. Thomas, first ran for Congress in 1936, he faced a popular mayor of Houston, Oscar F. Holcombe. Lera and Albert found themselves in a hard situation, with no money for advertising and little name recognition, as she framed the comparison of their situation with Holcombe's: "He had been Mayor for twelve years. But the strange thing about it was, Albert Thomas was not known and he had to do it the hard way. He had to resign from the office of Assistant Federal District Attorney, and no one thought he could win. We had no money and he had to do it on his own personal contact." As she summarized their plan, "he walked the streets from morning until night and I would go in a different direction." Coming from Nacogdoches as did her husband, she could rely on local knowledge and connections, as she noted in an interview: "I grew up in East Texas politics and there everyone knew me, everyone knew his family, they knew my family.... I could ask them if they were going to vote for us, and I knew—as I said East Texas people—you know whether they're going to vote for you. They'll tell you." And beyond their hometown, as she continued to be highly involved in his campaigning, they relied on methods established at home: "He'd go in one direction to picnics and barbecues and I would go in the other direction. Just to meet people. So I think that way people—people look to the wives of the members—the politicians—I think very much."[28]

After the first victory, with their husbands fully engaged in Washington, wives often took over more of the campaigning in subsequent elections. Lindy Boggs indicates in her autobiography that "I had campaigned for Hale for so many years that I knew the aspirations and problems of our constituency, and I was always open to their suggestions. Because of the Washington experience I had been privileged to enjoy, I was conversant with national and international affairs." During his last primary election, she served as his surrogate: "He had been so busy in Washington he had sent me to campaign for him."[29]

During the long service of her husband, Louise Goff Reece regularly campaigned with him, also serving as his chauffeur since he didn't drive. She became as well known in the district as he did during Carroll Reece's eighteen terms in the U.S. House. One congressional aide remarked that "most East Tennesseans thought of them as Mr. and Mrs. Republican." She recalled of campaigning that "he stayed in Washington and I came home and ran things. In those days he only had to show at just one county rally to clinch another term." Such campaign experience helped Louise Goff Reece when she ran in a special election to succeed her husband after his death in 1961. As she campaigned for herself, she said, "I thought of a lot of back roads my husband had forgotten." And she claimed further, "I feel thoroughly at home with campaigning, I've done it so much."[30]

This experience with campaigning, along with the knowledge of constituents and issues gained from it, could make the difference in whether a widow would be elected, with a stark example occurring in 1972. While Lindy Boggs, a stalwart campaigner, would be elected that year to replace House Speaker Hale Boggs and would serve until 1991, her fellow widow from the 1972 disappearance of a campaign plane, Peggy Begich, the wife of Representative Nick Begich of Alaska, who had spent her time at home raising six children, was discouraged from running by party leaders and lost at a party convention. Though Hale Boggs' prominence in office forwarded his wife's chances for election, so did her family background and extensive campaign experience, both of which Peggy Begich lacked.

Running His Office

Beyond campaigning, many of these women had taken an active role in daily legislative work once their husbands were elected. This long-term experience, in both the district and Washington, helped propel them to victory when they ran for office.

In 1926, when a car accident severely injured Otis Theodore Wingo, who had first won election to the U.S. House in 1912, his wife Effiegene Wingo took on a far more active role in Washington. For four years she worked as an unpaid assistant, becoming his surrogate during long absences as he sought to recuperate from his injuries. That direct experience—tending to constituent requests, overseeing staff, and researching key issues—gave her valuable exposure to voters and a keen understanding of the district's priorities. She won a special election to replace him when he died in office in October of 1930.

Like Effiegene Wingo, other wives did the work of speech writers, legislative aides, and office managers. As Marian Williams Clarke told the *Washington Post*, "You see I was always interested in my husband's work and followed his activities very closely. It was a rare day that didn't find me in the gallery all eyes and ears for what was going on."[31] She recalled that she also served as a "general factotum" in her husband's office. Marian Clarke won election to the U.S. House from New York less than two months after the death of her husband. Elizabeth Kee helped her husband to plan his speeches and practice his delivery. She sat in the audience to judge the response, giving him signals so that he could make changes in tone and volume. She also managed his office and insured that all letters were answered, working with her brother and sister. She learned about the rights of labor and the needs of veterans as well as office organization, all of which would be essential to her when she replaced him in 1951.[32] When Clyde Smith ran for Congress, he put his wife, Margaret Chase Smith, on the payroll as his secretary: she helped write his speeches, handled his mail, studied pending legislation, and went on research tours. In 1940, when Clyde had a severe heart attack, he announced his plan to ask his wife to run in his place, his press release noting her professional experience: "I know of no one else who has the full knowledge of my ideas and plans or is as well qualified as she is, to carry on these ideas and my unfinished work for my district."[33]

Seemingly in Office Just for His Reputation and His Issues

Having gained experience campaigning with their husbands and running their offices, many of these women relied on the aura of helpmate as they sought election, thus making themselves acceptable to voters who otherwise might not chose a woman candidate. Though these widows' motivations might be more complex, they declared themselves to be seeking office just to fulfill their husbands' promises to voters, thus employing a reassuring type of rhetoric that remained similar through the decades. In also speaking publicly about their grief and about their need to support their children, they further positioned themselves as dutiful wives following through on family commitments.

When John Nolan died in November 1922, just weeks after being elected unopposed for a sixth term in the U.S. House from California, the Union Labor Party quickly nominated Mae Ella Nolan to succeed him; she would be the first widow to enter the House of Representatives. While campaigning, she embraced a platform that echoed her husband's support of labor and education. "I owe it to the memory of my husband to carry on his work," she repeatedly declared while enumerating his plans that only she could enact: "His minimum-wage bill, child labor laws and national education bills all need to be in the hands of someone who knew him and his plans intimately. No one better knows than I do his legislative agenda."[34] In 1939, Clara Gooding McMillan, elected as U.S. representative from South Carolina after the death of her husband Thomas Macmillan, said to reporters that she was not surprised about winning because "I told the voters I would carry on his work."[35] In 1941, Katharine Byron described her election as a "very fitting tribute to my late husband and it is my only hope to do the utmost to carry on the work he had begun."[36] Many other women who entered the Senate and the House reiterated this sole priority, including Willa Eslick, Elizabeth Gasque, Florence Gibbs, Veronica Boland, Willa Fulmer, and Jean Ashbrook in the House and Vera Bushfield, Muriel Humphrey, and Jocelyn Burdick in the Senate.

These declarations concerning the husbands' platform have continued to the most recent widows who have entered Congress. When interviewed for an article given the cheesy headline of "The Beat Goes On," Mary Bono stressed her desire to continue her husband's work, "to bring his common-sense approach to serving the people of this great nation."[37] She claimed in another article that "Sonny would have encouraged me to continue his work" and then she listed his priorities, including reform of the education system and of social security, which she would pursue.[38]

Besides emphasizing their husbands' agendas, some widows spoke of their need of a purpose right after their husbands' deaths, a means of reentering the world and staving off grief. They thus created an appeal to sympathy as they sought political office. Marian Williams Clarke, for example, spoke of her great sadness at the loss of her husband, telling a *Washington Post* reporter, "I wanted dreadfully to come, of course. I felt the need of some absorbing work." She mentioned her "great loss" frequently as she campaigned as well as the voters' ability to help her heal.[39]

Other widows, with families to support, depicted themselves as desperately needing

Mary Bono and Sonny Bono (Kathy Hutchins/ZUMA Press © Kathy Hutchins/ Alamy Stock Photo.

the salary, discussion of which could provide another sympathetic appeal and tie to the husband. When Thaddeus Caraway died in office as a U.S. senator in 1931, Arkansas governor Harvey Parnell appointed his widow Hattie Caraway to the vacant seat. With the Democratic Party's backing, she easily won a special election in January 1932 for the remaining months of the term, becoming the first woman elected to the Senate, her term to end in March 1933. When she decided to run for a complete term, she described financial problems that would immediately occur without this income: "It saddens one to think of the years and years of dependence one may have to endure." One son was then studying at West Point and two were in the Army; her only other choice would be to take away from the military and from family stability by depending totally on them.[40]

As part of this construction of themselves as needy, grieving widows seeking to further their husbands' priorities, some of these women openly eschewed any concern for women's rights. In an article entitled "Mrs. Nolan No 'Crusader,'" the subhead of which is "California member seeks only to represent interests of constituents, rather than appearing as champion of sex," Mae Ella Nolan declared that she was representing her district and not women particularly.[41] She had supported women's suffrage, as her husband had not, but she didn't advocate for further extensions of women's rights, largely because his core labor constituency was unsupportive. As she served in Congress, she even argued that women should not be there: "Politics is entirely too masculine to have any attraction for feminine responsibilities ... politics is man's business."[42] Like Nolan, other widows from the early decades spoke against women in politics and against gendered legislative priorities. Pearl Peden Oldfield prevailed in a special election in Arkansas after the death of her husband, William Allan Oldfield, and served from 1929 to 1931. In 1929, she explained that male legislators could successfully represent the entire citizenry: "I shall advance no strange or exceptional feminine governmental ideas, as I entertain none. I believe that a government, if properly administered in behalf of our husbands, our sons, our fathers, and our brothers, is equally safe and sound for our women."[43]

Some Indeed Short-Term, but Making an Impact Afterwards

Many widows finished their husband's term and then returned to their own lives, either not running again or not succeeding at doing so, thus fulfilling the task designated to them by state leaders. Though these widows might be denigrated for their service in Congress, they did what was asked of them, and they showed that women were capable of moving beyond their homes and states onto a national stage. And many of these women, though they left Congress, went on to further important work for the nation.

In 1934, after leaving office, Effiegene Locke Wingo co-founded the National Institute of Public Affairs, which brought college graduates into the federal government as interns, offering on–the–job training at a quickly growing list of federal departments.[44] Clara Gooding McMillan had graduated from the Flora McDonald College in Red Springs, North Carolina, and served as an aide for her husband, but had not pursued a career before she entered the House. After she left office in 1941, she began working as an administrator of the National Youth Administration, a New Deal agency then funneling young workers into the defense industry. After the war, she began working at the U.S. Department of State, where she remained until 1957.[45]

For other women, the years spent in office were part of a long career, not just of helping him, but of paid public service. Tennessean Edith Irene Bailey Baker, widow of Howard Baker, Sr., and the stepmother of Howard Baker, Jr., finished her husband's term in the U.S. House, from 1964 to 1965. She had been Deputy County Court Clerk of Sevier County, worked for the Tennessee Valley Authority (TVA), and served as a Republican national committeewoman. When her husband died suddenly, she vowed to enter office only a caretaker who would not seek further election; and she fulfilled that promise. After leaving Congress in 1965, Baker became a Director of Public Welfare in Tennessee, monitoring federal assistance programs for the poor and elderly, a position she held until 1971.[46]

Women Determined to Continue and Take Their Own Path

While most widows publicly declared their desire to continue their husband's legislative agenda and support his children, they also had other, varied reasons for choosing to seek elective office. Especially in the House, as we have seen, many women stayed beyond the single term: indeed 46 percent of widows did so through the 115th Congress even though they may have begun their service to just "carry on" for a short time. Like those who served for a single term, these women generally came from an educated group and had been active in their husbands' careers, but they went on to issues that did not begin with the spouse. As these legislators moved to their own priorities, they would especially speak for the other, for the outsider, seemingly more liberal and independent than their spouses and the majority of their party, either Democratic or Republican, perhaps spurred by the confidence and base of a political family.

This independence in office, this drive to establish and act on personal priorities, to speak forcefully for the outsider while facing criticism as the lesser politician, began right at the beginning of widows' service in Congress, with Hattie Caraway. Though she publicly stressed her husband's priorities and her financial need as a widow, Caraway also indicated to reporters that her election would show what women could do: "There's no sound reason why women, if they have the time and ability, shouldn't sit with men on city councils, in state legislatures or in the House and Senate."[47] Though she faced gendered attacks on her methods of legislating, and even had to defend herself from the men who helped her, she ultimately succeeded at changing the status of her state's residents, acting on goals that were not her husband's.

By the time that Hattie Caraway announced her decision to move beyond the status of temporary replacement and run for a second term, right before the filing deadline of May 9, 1932, six well-known candidates had already been campaigning for more than a month; her formidable opponents included a former governor, army major, deputy sheriff, and prominent attorneys. Officials in Arkansas, supporting these men, expected that, as a widow and an outsider to state politics, she would not run. But, after interviewing her, *New York Times* reporter R.L. Duffus indicated that she had never promised not to do so.[48] And she told another reporter, "I am going to fight for my place in the sun.... I want to deny again rumors that I will withdraw from the race. I have never said a word that would indicate withdrawal." She further maintained that "the time has passed when a woman is placed in a position and kept there only while someone else is being groomed for the job."[49]

Although she had not been expected to run, Caraway put on quite a campaign, relying on her husband's reputation as well as her own, even as she sought a strong, new connection from which she would later have to extricate herself. For the first eight days in August 1932, Huey Long went with her to Arkansas. She had met him when she attended a cotton conference in New Orleans in August 1931 with her husband. Long's motivations to help her may have been several: as he sought to defend a fellow southerner and outsider, he may have also wanted to extend his influence into the home state of his rival, Arkansas senator Joseph Robinson, to line up Caraway's vote for his legislation, and to enhance his national reputation by securing a win for her against great odds.

These two southern senators made a concerted effort together. First Caraway began speaking on the radio throughout Arkansas, combining her husband's history with her own: "I want all Arkansas to know I am asking for re-election to the senate in my own right, because I have had many years training from having heard discussions of pending legislation, both on the floor and in private, for many senators have been our personal friends." In the *Arkansas Gazette* in August, she defended the fact that she was not a strong or frequent speaker like other candidates and her husband: "I firmly believe that an ounce of common sense brought to bear on the problems in congress is worth more than pages of speeches in the Congressional Record, and is not nearly so expensive."[50]

Next she and Long sent out 125,000 copies of a speech by Long that endorsed her and, on July 19, announced a joint speaking itinerary, which ultimately involved thirty-seven stops in eight days. And then in August the Huey Long machine came to the state. In New Orleans, he ordered 30,000 circulars, to be distributed daily from his trucks. He brought a "caravan of automobiles, sound trucks, and literature vans," and together Caraway and Long added towns to the initial schedule, secured local dignitaries to make introductions, and advertised their route so that people lined the rural roads from town to town. Reporters wrote that Caraway increased her speaking skills as she toured with Long, learning, as the *Arkansas Democrat* declared, to "make a darned good speech before it was all over." Without his help, historians believe, she might have done better in the election than many skeptics judged, but she would not have won—as indeed she did.[51]

During her years in office, Caraway faced various forms of criticism, emphasizing that she shouldn't have stayed beyond one widow's term. Criticisms continued about her public speaking: she was known as Silent Hattie or The Woman Who Holds Her Tongue since she made few speeches on the Senate floor, with these titles preceding the judgment that she couldn't possibly be acting as a leader. She instead viewed herself as a strong force in committees, wielding real power while men often just talked without effecting any change. "And they say women talk all the time," she wrote in her diary. "I haven't the heart to take a minute away from the men. The poor dears love it so."[52] Additionally she dealt with critics who assumed that Huey Long controlled her voting. She had told Long when he offered to campaign with her and seemed to expect her support that "I wouldn't give a dime for my seat in the Senate if I couldn't vote according to my convictions and my conscience" and she had to repeatedly emphasize her independence from him.[53] She also faced additional gender-driven commentary: she was criticized for resembling a vapid housewife as she knitted at the desk, read Zane Grey novels, and purportedly worried about drapes in the meeting rooms instead of legislation. Indeed, she "faced some really daunting obstacles," but proceeded to fulfill her own agenda, what she felt that her constituents most needed, especially better education as a route out of poverty."[54]

Concerning university education particularly, she showed that she would not be following her husband's lead. When Arkansas State's main building, which housed classrooms, science labs, the library, and administrative offices, burned down in January 1931, a disaster for an institution founded just twenty-two years earlier, Representative Thaddeus Caraway had written to university president V.C. Kays that he was "tremendously disturbed" by the news and hoped the school had insurance. "If so, you will be all right." In the next sentence, he moved from the possible shared responsibility of "we" back to the problems to be faced by "you": "If not, I am afraid we are in for a hard time, aren't you?"[55] Thaddeus Caraway took no steps to help the university. But when Hattie Caraway came into office, she provided help with rebuilding the burned structure and with securing federal funds for nine additional buildings on the small campus, a huge effort on which she worked closely with Kays.[56]

Her efforts extended to other Arkansas colleges. She arranged for ten new buildings at the Arkansas State Teachers College in Conway and for large grants of federal money to extend the school's operating budget: this university received an allotment of $60,000 in federal funds for several years when the state just provided $94,000 a year. She also secured interest-rate reductions on loans for building projects at Henderson State Teachers College in Arkadelphia, the Agricultural and Mechanical College in Monticello, and Arkansas Tech in Russelville. Additionally, for the University of Arkansas in Fayetteville, she secured federal funding for four buildings, including a library, science labs, and a gym.[57]

Besides enlarging the physical plant of these universities, Hattie Caraway also built their student body, severely lowered by the Depression. With the state's general assembly debating whether to close some state colleges, she lobbied the federal government to establish military training schools at these sites. Hundreds of soldiers from across the country came to Arkansas State, for example, helping the embattled school to remain open. Naval and air force cadets, along with marine and naval reserves, secured training at the Arkansas State Teachers College, this group including 1800 members of the Women's Army Auxiliary Corps.

Funding and larger enrollments for Arkansas colleges, serving primarily a rural population, were not all that Caraway sought. During her 1938 re-election campaign, newspaper articles noted that she had secured funding for road construction, a hospital annex, a new high school, and a new Faulkner County courthouse. And as a member of Congress she didn't just seek to improve her impoverished state. All through the war, she pressed for school funding around the nation, citing higher literacy rates in Japan and Germany. As she ran for office in 1940 and 1942, Caraway declared that 1500 school buildings had been built across the nation due to her efforts; she also cited her ongoing support for the nation at war and for American soldiers.[58]

Even though disparaged, even though labeled as silent and silly, Hattie Caraway made a difference for her constituents and for the nation, moving well beyond her husband's priorities, which had primarily concerned segregation: on May 15, 1921, he had introduced a bill to prohibit the enlistment of African Americans in the army and navy. In the same congressional session, he sponsored H.R. 8112, which proposed ongoing segregation of public transportation in Washington, D.C., and H.R. 8113, which directed the "Commissioners of the District of Columbia to set apart certain sections, streets, blocks, or parts of blocks of the District of Columbia in which shall reside members of the Negro race only, and other sections ... in which members of the Negro race shall not reside." Though she had begun by stating her allegiance to her husband's priorities, Hattie Caraway did not continue with this effort as she sought improvements in education. In *Good Housekeeping*, in January of 1940, Eleanor Roosevelt commented about whether Caraway's supposed silence was just acquiescence to others: "At first one heard that she was under this or that influence; that she was a rubber stamp; that she did little thinking for herself; but of late one hears a great deal more about her being a useful member of the Senate and having a mind of her own."[59]

Like Caraway, many other legislators who remained in Congress for long periods developed their own priorities, often employing their confidence and independence to speak for outsiders. Elizabeth Kee, who had worked as her husband's executive secretary, served in the House of Representatives from 1951 to 1965, long beyond her completion of his term. Her husband had been on the House Foreign Affairs Committee, highly engaged in the Cold War and with the spread of American influence through foreign aid, but she turned her attention instead to economic redevelopment plans for West Virginia. Having secured little assistance from the Eisenhower administration, Kee threw her support behind John F. Kennedy, helping him to win the critical West Virginia primary. During the first year of the Kennedy administration, Kee's economic development plans found realization in the Accelerated Public Works Act, which pumped millions of dollars into recession–prone regions: through industrial loans, job retraining programs, and grants for water systems. With her influence, the program instituted in southern West Virginia became a national model. Comparing her work to her husband's, she claimed that foreign aid bills were important, "but not more important than bread and milk for coal miners' children, good jobs for their fathers, new industries and increased business activities for economically depressed American towns and cities."[60]

Other long-term representatives moved, with changing times and their own priorities, well beyond what their husbands sought to achieve, speaking for groups that their husbands might not have chosen to help. Along with her mother, Edith Nourse Rogers had volunteered at her church and with many charities. In 1907, she married John Jacob Rogers, newly graduated from Harvard Law School, who in 1912 was elected as a Republican representative from Massachusetts. During World War I, while her husband served in an artillery training battalion, Edith Rogers volunteered as a "Gray Lady" with the American Red Cross in France and then at the Walter Reed Army Medical Center in Washington, D.C. In France, she witnessed a stark contrast between women in the British Army, loaned to the American Expeditionary Force (AEF), and American women who worked beside them. Unlike the English, the Americans were civilians with no benefits, thus lacking insurance, legal protection, medical care, pensions, and compensation for their families in case of death. When Rogers returned from France, she spoke at civic groups on the need for more women to be recruited into the military with better training and a more secure status. Then in 1922, President Warren G. Harding employed her as an inspector of veterans' facilities, an appointment renewed by both the Coolidge and Hoover administrations. Though she had military and administrative experience, she did not consider a career in politics until her husband died in March 1925, in the middle of his seventh term. She then ran in a special election, beating the former governor of Massachusetts with a landslide 72 percent of the vote.[61]

In the House, John Jacob Rogers had sponsored the Rogers Act of 1924, which merged the diplomatic and consular services into the United States Foreign Service. Though his wife would also be interested in Americans overseas, her concern during World War II would be with the rights of women and men in the military, not with diplomatic service. Drawing on her experience in Europe during World War I, Edith Nourse Rogers, in her thirty-five years in the House, sponsored more than 1,200 bills, over half on veteran or military issues. In early 1941, with the support of Margaret Chase Smith, she introduced a bill to establish a small Women's Army Auxiliary Corps (WAAC), to support the army at war and in bases at home, but the bill didn't pass. After the attack on Pearl Harbor, Rogers approached the Army Chief of Staff George Marshall and with his backing reintroduced the bill, with a much higher total of 150,000 recruits envisioned, along with an amendment giving women full military status. The amendment was resoundingly rejected but the unamended bill passed, and on May 14, 1942, President Roosevelt's signature turned "An Act to Establish the Women's Army Auxiliary Corps" into law. While "Auxiliaries," and thus not part of the regular army, the WAACs attained a more secure status than American women had in World War I.

Continuing to seek equal treatment, Rogers introduced a bill in October 1942 to re-form the WAACs as a regular unit of the United States Army Reserve, no longer auxiliary. On July 1, 1943, Roosevelt signed "An Act to Establish the Women's Army Corps in the Army of the United States," officially dropping the "auxiliary" portion of the name and status. The WACs received the same pay, allowances, and benefits as male soldiers while additional army regulations covered marriage, pregnancy, and maternity care. In December 1948, the director of the WACs, Colonel Mary A. Hallaren, became the first commissioned female officer in the U.S. Army.[62]

Then in 1944 Rogers joined with Senator Champ Clark of Missouri to write and co-sponsor the Servicemen's Readjustment Act of 1944, the G.I. Bill, providing for education and vocational training; low-interest loans for homes, farms, and businesses; and unemployment benefits for returning military. On June 22, 1944, when President Franklin D. Roosevelt signed the Act, he handed Rogers the first pen. As a result of the bill, roughly half of returning veterans went on to higher education, with women entitled to the benefits as well as men.[63]

Another legislator who impacted women's professional lives during World War II and afterwards was Frances Payne Bolton. As teenagers, Bolton and her friends had volunteered in tenements in Cleveland, making the rounds with public health nurses, going where her father thought a young girl shouldn't go.[64] In high school, she spoke at the Lakeside Nursing School concerning the difficulties faced by urban nurses. During World

War I, when she inherited a trust fund from her uncle, Oliver Hazard Payne, a founder of Standard Oil, Bolton established the Payne Fund, with which, among other projects, she distributed grants to Case Western Reserve University, the largest gift that had been given to a university school of nursing. In 1935 this school, which Bolton had required to be a regular undergraduate unit and not a separate annex, was renamed in her honor.[65]

After Bolton entered the House in 1940, as a widow replacing her husband, she was expected to leave Washington as soon as possible and return to her charitable giving and her opulent life in Ohio. As she indicated concerning her election, Republican leaders "thought it would be a graceful gesture which would do them no harm since they were sure I would get tired of politics in a few months and flit on to something else."[66] She knew that her ability to fund Republican campaigns had contributed to her receiving even short-term support.

But she would remain in office, in the fall of 1940 defeating her Democratic challenger with 57 percent of the vote. And then she would move beyond her husband's priorities to her own. He had been a delegate to the Republican National Convention, and he centered his legislative choices within his party's platform. But, in her support for Roosevelt's war decisions, she showed independence from her party right away: all the other members of her state's delegation voted against the Lend-Lease Act in March 1941, but she voted for it. She also broke with her party in her support for arming merchant ships.

Additionally, in the House, Bolton was able to advocate for American nurses as her husband would not have done. To meet the quickly expanding need for their service during the war, some legislators wanted to recruit minimally trained volunteers, a plan advocated by the Red Cross. But Bolton spoke for thorough professional training to be sponsored by the army, with professional organizations, such as the American Nurses Association, in concurrence with her. She repeatedly secured funding for the Army School of Nursing, as well as schools at universities across the nation; a Bolton amendment to a 1941 appropriations bill set aside $1,200,000 to provide the staff and equipment required to support larger enrollments, a figure that she worked to have increased in 1942. During the war she continued to insist on more and better training: in 1943 she introduced and won the enactment of what was called the Bolton Bill, which provided funding for nursing schools to establish a complete curriculum taught at a faster pace, thirty months instead of the regular thirty-six, with successful applicants eligible for a government subsidy that paid for tuition and books as well as a stipend. Of the 1,300 nursing schools in the country, 1,125 participated. By mandating equality of access in the Bolton Bill, Frances Bolton ensured that African American, Native American, and Japanese-American nurses would gain training and become part of newly commissioned units. The federal government spent over $160 million on this program.[67]

After the war, Bolton continued her advocacy of nurses and nursing. In August 1949, she introduced legislation to provide for the appointment of male nurses in the Army, Navy, and Air Force. In 1951, she helped the National Association of Colored Graduate Nurses to disband and join the main organization. In the 1950s, she also sought to recruit more women into nursing and improve their working conditions through a Commission on Nursing Services. Her biographer David Loth concluded that "she was so closely identified with progress in nursing that some competent observers say she has done more than any other layman of her generation to make it the high profession it has become."[68]

Like Caraway and Bolton, other widows who remained in office for many years spoke for the outsider, as Bolton did for nurses during years when soldiers had the nation's attention.

Margaret Chase Smith filled her husband's House seat when he died in 1940, moved to the Senate nine years later, and remained in office until 1972. She was far more liberal than her husband. She spoke to women's groups about equal rights, not one of her husband's favored issues. She also worked with Edith Nourse Rogers to improve the status of women in the armed services, joining her in arguing for WAACs to become a regular part of the army. Later called the Mother of the WAVES, Smith introduced legislation to extend equitable service conditions to the Navy, a bill signed into law by President Roosevelt in July 1942.[69] She supported expenditures for military preparedness before World War II that Clyde Smith, a "categorical isolationist," had opposed.[70] As she demonstrated her independence from her husband, she also opposed fellow Republicans. In support of Roosevelt's New Deal, she worked with Democrats in Congress and with Secretary of Labor Frances Perkins, voting, for example, against a bill to freeze the social security tax. Along with Democrats also, she spoke and voted for the United Nations and the European Recovery Act.[71]

Not just in World War II decisions, or in advocacy for women, but into the Cold War, Republican Margaret Chase Smith was willing to oppose the Republican Party's power base as she spoke for the outsider, the dispossessed. In 1945, she voted against making the House Un-American Activities Committee a permanent body. In the Senate, which she entered in 1949 having won her seat without help from the party machine and therefore without obligations to it, her stand against Joseph McCarthy earned her a national reputation for independent discourse, as the first in Congress to criticize the tactics of McCarthyism in her 1950 Senate speech, "Declaration of Conscience."[72]

On Lincoln Day, February 9, 1950, at the Republican Women's Club of Wheeling, West Virginia, McCarthy had made a shocking claim: "I have here in my hand a list of 205—a list of names that were made known to the Secretary of State as being members of the Communist Party and who nevertheless are still working and shaping policy in the State Department." This speech resulted in a flood of news articles. In June 1950, with McCarthy intimidating politicians and accusing Americans with impunity, Margaret Chase Smith publicly replied to him in her first major speech in the Senate, her text co-signed by six other Republican senators.

Though she did not speak of McCarthy by name, she argued that his tactics had debased the Senate's deliberative character "to the level of a forum of hate and character assassination sheltered by the shield of Congressional immunity." Senate debates, she continued by arguing, had devolved into a "publicity platform for irresponsible sensationalism. I am not proud of the reckless abandon in which unproved charges have been hurled from this side of the aisle." She spoke of the Truman administration as a burden to the country while claiming that a Republican regime, lacking political integrity, would prove equally disastrous to the nation. And she continued by asserting that "the American people are sick and tired of being afraid to speak their minds lest they be politically smeared as 'Communists' or 'Fascists' by their opponents." She then spoke of the impact on American rights of McCarthy's unsubstantiated but terrifying claims: "Freedom of speech is not what it used to be in America. It has been so abused by some that it is not exercised by others."[73]

Smith's statement led to an immediate response from McCarthy. Afterwards, he released a statement referring to her and to the supporting senators as Snow White and the Six Dwarfs. He had her removed as a member of the Permanent Subcommittee on Investigations, a powerful group that investigated syndicated crime, giving her seat to Senator Richard Nixon. But many newspaper editorials supported her position, and President Truman told her that "your Declaration of Conscience was one of the finest things that has happened here in Washington in all my years in the Senate and the White House." McCarthy helped finance an unsuccessful primary challenger during Smith's re-election campaign in 1954; that year she voted for his censure.[74]

Many other widows, with the backing of political families, had the strength and independence to advocate for outsiders, for the less than powerful. Leonor Sullivan, a widow in Congress from Missouri, fought for consumer rights. After attending Washington University in St. Louis, she worked as an instructor of business and accounting during the 1930s, and then as director of the St. Louis Business School. She next worked as her husband's administrative aide while John B. Sullivan served four terms in Congress. Following her husband's death in 1951 and a short period of working for Congressman Leonard Irving, she was elected to Congress twelve times.

As one of America's early consumer advocates, Leonor K. Sullivan authored many of the protective laws that Americans have come to take for granted, initially a lonely undertaking as she recalled: "Those of us interested in consumer legislation could have caucused in an elevator." Sullivan urged her House colleagues to pass stricter consumer protection legislation by employing strong rhetoric: "You are faced with an arena of supreme importance to the lives and health and safety and well being of the American people—all of the foods we eat, all of the drugs and devices we use for health purposes, all of the cosmetics used not only by women but in increasing numbers by men, as well." In 1957 she wrote and successfully guided into law the first Federal Poultry Products Inspection Act. She also sponsored legislation to protect consumers from harmful food additives.[75]

One of Sullivan's great legislative triumphs came when she served as the House floor manager for the 1968 Consumer Credit Protection Act. The bill established "truth in lending" provisions, requiring lenders to provide consumers with information about the cost of credit. When President Johnson signed the legislation, he praised "that able Congresswoman from Missouri," noting that Sullivan "fought for a strong effective bill when others would have settled for less." Two years later, Sullivan continued her efforts to protect American consumers when she authored the Fair Credit Reporting Act, a bill prohibiting credit companies from distributing false credit information.[76] To extend the effectiveness of the Consumer Credit Protection Act and the Truth in Lending Act, passed in 1968 to extend credit protection, she sponsored legislation in the 1970s to end discrimination in the enforcement of these acts on the basis of race, color, religion, national origin, and age.

In 1959, as Sullivan strove to protect Americans and extend their rights, she worked with Senator Hubert Humphrey to author the Food Stamp Act. Under the new legislation, low-income Americans would no longer have to rely upon disbursements of surplus food. Though the legislation passed under Eisenhower, the Agriculture Department refused to allocate funding. Influenced by Sullivan's arguments, the Kennedy administration instigated an experimental food stamp program in 1961. In 1964, Sullivan authored legislation to increase this initiative, making food stamps available nationally. On the House floor, she maintained, "The States and localities, which now bear a heavy financial burden under the direct distribution system, would save added millions under the food stamp plan. Who loses, then, under the plan? Hunger. Only hunger loses." President Lyndon Johnson spoke of this newly passed legislation as a key element of his War on Poverty.[77]

Like many other widows, Lindy Boggs came into office seeking to finish her husband's agenda, but she soon moved beyond his goals to advocate for outsiders and especially for women. As she later wrote, "I never expected that I would develop my own agenda or that I would become a voice and a vote for many women during two tumultuous decades." As she attempted to succeed with her own issues, she recognized the power of accessing what her husband had built: "Congress was heavily male dominated; not much focus or attention was given to the role of women—within the Capitol or outside it. I set about trying to change that. As a freshman I had no seniority, so I had to use what leverage I had as the wife and helpmate of the former majority leader."[78]

Boggs fought to secure credit protection for married and unmarried women, her advocacy spurred by inequities she experienced after her husband was missing and declared dead. She was influential in composing the Equal Credit Opportunity Act of 1974, which made it illegal for creditors to discriminate based on sex, marital status, race, age, national origin, or reception of public assistance. When the Banking Committee considered this legislation, Boggs added the provision banning discrimination due to sex or marital status without informing other members of the committee, inserting the language on her own and photocopying new versions of the bill. She then told the committee, "Knowing the members composing this committee as well as I do, I'm sure it was just an oversight that we didn't have 'sex' or 'marital status' included. I've taken care of that, and I trust it meets with the committee's approval." The committee unanimously approved the bill. Boggs used her membership on the Appropriations Committee to advocate for other economic concerns of women, such as equal pay in government jobs and equal access to government contracts.[79]

While Boggs fought for economic equality for women, Cardiss

Collins, throughout her political career, was a champion of women's health. She was elected to Congress in a 1973 special election to replace her husband, George, who had died in the December 1972 United Airlines plane crash. While her husband was in office for two years, she would serve for twenty-five. In 1975, she was instrumental in prompting the Social Security Administration to revise Medicare regulations so that they would cover the cost of post-mastectomy breast prosthesis, which before then had been considered cosmetic. Her other legislative focuses included gender equity in college sports and improved federal child-care facilities.

Mary Bono also found her own voice for the outsider while she was in Congress, not always speaking for what Sonny Bono might have advocated. In a phone conversation with me, she said that when she ran for office, the name had been an asset, an identification, ceding her goodwill. As she made plans to assert her own priorities, some advisors said that she should take back her birth name, but she did not do so. As she indicated, regardless of names, women were often not taken seriously in government, especially when they tried to speak on traditionally male subjects like defense: every woman in Congress, in business, dealt with this ongoing prejudice, with the press as well as colleagues often hostile. But she said that her interactions had been 90 percent positive though governmental work did take a thick skin, with some reporters especially wielding an ax to grind that might be "sharpened on you," delivering a "thump on your head." But such viewpoints didn't affect her hard work.

In her fourteen years in Congress, Mary Bono served on important committees, such as the Committees on Energy and Commerce, on the Armed Services, on the Judiciary, and on Small Business. Though she voted primarily with the Republican Party, she could show her marked independence. She twice voted, for example, against the Federal Marriage Amendment, which would have defined marriage in the United States as a union of one man and one woman. In December 2010, she was one of just fifteen Republican House members to vote in favor of repealing the military's "Don't Ask, Don't Tell" ban on openly homosexual members of the service. In 2013, after losing re-election, Bono was a signatory to an *amicus curiae* brief submitted to the Supreme Court in support of same-sex marriage in the *Hollingsworth v. Perry* case.

The widows who have entered Congress have often been depicted as unworthy, with just a few singled out as surprisingly able legislators. But their story is more complex and more notable than has commonly been assumed. Most of these widows would not have considered a political career if they had not been asked to serve. But they generally had what it takes to succeed in politics: family ties, a superior education, a history of public service, and experience in campaigning, public speaking, and running a governmental office. When they entered Congress just to complete a term, widows generally did so to further the priorities of their husbands, a governor, or party chief, thus serving their family, state, and nation. After thus stepping onto a national stage for perhaps a short time, many of these women expanded their service to the nation by assuming other government positions. And other widows remained in office for significant periods, perhaps longer than their husbands, assuming their own political authority and forwarding their own issues. With the power of family behind them, they frequently took positions that separated them from their parties, speaking for outsiders, including rural citizenry during the Depression, nurses and other women in the armed forces, women who lacked economic equality and adequate health care, and American consumers. These women created a path for other legislators who might come into office by not just relying on a party, but on other means of support to fulfill their goals.

FOUR

Husbands and Wives

While women through the decades have entered Congress as widows, a larger group has come into state and federal office with other family connections. As we have seen, in the U.S. House through the 115th Congress, 44 percent of the women who served came from political families, with just 31 percent of this group, or less than a third, being widows directly appointed or elected, and thus 69 percent with other family ties, a rising percentage in the second half of the twentieth century and into the twenty-first. Since January 2001 through the 115th Congress, a period when only one widow, Doris Matsui, entered the House, 57 percent of the women elected came from political families, a marked increase over the general percentage of 44 percent. In the Senate through the decades, 64 percent of the women who had been elected came from these highly involved families, with only eight of this group (25 percent) being widows and twenty-four (75 percent) being other members of such families. Since January 2001 through the 115th Congress, there was a slight increase of women in the Senate with family connections—to 65 percent—with only one, Jean Carnahan, entering the Senate as a widow. Thus, of the fifteen women senators from political families serving from 2001 through January 2019, as the appendix with their names indicates, 94 percent have not been widows.

Beyond the older tradition of the widow taking the husband's seat, one common family connection has been that of husbands and wives who have supported each other and involved each other in politics, with the husband generally elected first until the most recent generations. Within this trend, scholars have noted the "double standard whereby women are punished for having a political partner while men do not incur a similar cost."[1] The wife might be judged as the lesser of the two, with the husband scripted as the mentor, the major player. And his choices, especially the poor ones, might be judged as also being hers. Considering specific instances of wives entering office at the state and federal level can reveal how political wives have come into politics and how they have been judged for doing so.

In Direct Competition

Certainly within a marriage the husband would be the assumed member of the political elite, the first one elected and the primary legislator; thus one controversial, and rare, possibility was for the wife to seek office in direct competition with him.

Women of other eras have been willing to run against their spouses. Martha Maria "Mattie" Hughes Cannon, in November 1896, in an election for the Utah Senate, defeated her own husband.[2] She was born in Wales and immigrated to New York City with her family at age three in 1860. In 1861, with the assistance of the Mormon church, the family went on to Utah. Cannon received a chemistry degree in 1875, at the University of Deseret, now the University of Utah, and then attended the University of Michigan medical school. After graduation, she returned to Salt Lake City and served as a physician at the newly founded Deseret Hospital.

In 1884, Hughes married Angus M. Cannon, superintendent of the new hospital and an official of the Mormon church, twenty-three years her senior. She became the fourth of his six plural wives. In April 1886, when federal officials attempted to convict polygamists, Mattie Cannon left Utah with her infant daughter to avoid providing federal marshals with proof of her marriage to Angus which, as she wrote, might lead to her "sending to jail a father upon whom a lot of little children are dependent."[3] She also feared being forced to provide testimony against others, based on information gathered through her obstetrical practice. Two years later, with the anti-polygamy crusade less active, Cannon resumed her Salt Lake medical practice. She then became involved with the Utah Equal Suffrage Association and the national women's suffrage movement.

In a much publicized election in 1896, after the state granted suffrage to women in 1895, Mattie Cannon was one of five Democrats running as "at large" candidates, in an open election involving both parties, for state senator from Salt Lake County. Suffrage activist Emmeline B. Wells and Cannon's husband Angus were among the Republicans seeking the seat.

Local newspapers, following their party affiliations, gave various forms of coverage to a well-known Mormon polygamist competing against his fourth wife. The *Salt Lake Herald,* a Democratic newspaper, argued that "Mrs. Mattie Hughes Cannon, his wife, is the better man of the two. Send Mrs. Cannon to the State Senate and let Mr. Cannon, as a Republican, remain at home to manage home industry."[4] The *Salt Lake Tribune,* proponent of the Republicans, countered that Angus M. Cannon deserved the readers' votes and that the *Herald* editorialist should be immediately disciplined along with Mattie Cannon: "We do not see anything for Angus M. to do but to either go home and break a bouquet over Mrs. Cannon's head to show his superiority, or to go up to the Herald office and break a chair over the head of the man who wrote that disturber of domestic peace."[5] The election also secured national interest, with the *New York Times* finding Mattie Cannon's "intense independence" ironic since she lived in a polygamist household controlled by the husband.[6]

On November 3, 1896, Martha Hughes Cannon became the first woman elected as a state senator, winning with 10,288 votes while her husband received 8,054 votes. She served two terms in the legislature, advocating for improvements in health and safety for state residents and especially the most vulnerable: she worked to secure funding for a board of health and a hospital at a school for hearing-impaired students; she sponsored the state's first pure-food law; and she fought to ensure that children received vaccinations before entering school.[7]

Unlike Mattie Cannon, some wives might decide not to run if it meant competing with their husbands. In the spring of 2017, Ann Ferlic Ashford of Nebraska was considering a run for the U.S. House seat that her husband, Brad Ashford, had previously held for one term: he had been elected in 2014 and then defeated in 2016, by Don Bacon. After graduating from Creighton University School of Law, she had specialized in health care law. As she spoke about running, she told reporters that she wanted to seek the seat on her own terms: "Simply because I am married to (Ashford) shouldn't disqualify me from pursuing something I want to. And simply because I am married to him shouldn't qualify me either.... I need to be looked at as my own individual person, because I am my own individual person." Ashford stated further that she had long wanted to run for Congress but would never have challenged her husband. By that June, he told reporters that he was also pondering a run for the seat. And then he quickly decided to run and she withdrew. He was unable to achieve a rematch with Bacon in the 2018 general election, however, because he lost in the Democratic primary.[8]

As Helpful Placeholders

While Mattie Cannon competed against her husband and Ann Ashford at least considered doing so, a more common route into politics was for the husband to have some level of success first and for his career to be in some way primary. At an extreme of women deemed as secondary were those who served as placeholders for a few months in the U.S. Senate or House, to aid in the careers of their still very alive husbands.

Dixie Bibb Graves entered the Senate after being appointed by her husband, Governor David Bibb Graves of Alabama, to fill the vacancy caused when Hugo L. Black resigned to become an associate justice of the U.S. Supreme Court. She served from August 1937 to January 1938. In August of 1972, Louisiana governor Edwin Edwards appointed his wife Elaine Edwards to the Senate after the death of Senator Allen Ellender. This decision allowed Governor Edwards to avoid immediately choosing his preferred candidate among several aspirants to the seat. Elaine Edwards agreed to resign after a new senator was elected, in November of 1972.

Extending His Power When He Can't Run: Term Limits and Jail

Besides being appointed by the husband to help fulfill his political goals, women have come into office because of term limits and criminal sentences, especially when the men wanted to keep a position, at least within the family. This choice might enable the wife to realize some of her own ambitions as well as her husband's.

When George Wallace failed in 1965 to get a constitutional ban lifted, which mandated that a governor of Alabama could not serve more than two consecutive terms, he asked his wife Lurleen Wallace to run for the office. To assure his supporters who might have been concerned about the transfer of power, she stated at her announcement that her husband would be her "No. 1 assistant," that she was running not as the former "Lurleen Burns," but as "Mrs. George C. Wallace," and she used the slogan "Two Governors, One Cause." At her general election campaign kickoff in Birmingham, Lurleen Wallace pledged that "George will continue to speak up and stand up for Alabama."[9] In order to facilitate their election plan, she hid the fact that she had begun radiation therapy in December

1965 for uterine cancer, the treatment having been followed by a hysterectomy in January 1966. Despite her ill health, she maintained a brutal campaign schedule all through 1966. Lurleen Wallace was elected and served from January 1967 until her death in May 1968.

Beyond the governorship, term limits and retirements in state legislatures have also led to women replacing their husbands. When Herman Ray Hill was term-limited in the Louisiana House of Representatives, having served from 1992 to 2008, Dorothy Sue Hill, his wife, succeeded him, winning her third term in 2015. Otto Beatty, Jr., was first elected in 1979 to the Ohio House of Representatives and served until 1999 when he retired and was succeeded by his wife, Joyce Beatty, previously a senior vice-president at Ohio State University. She remained in office through 2008; then in 2012, she ran in a newly redrawn U.S. House district and won a seat that she still holds. In 2015, Beatty's legislation to combat child sex trafficking unanimously passed the House and became the Justice for Victims of Trafficking Act. Beatty has also sponsored bills that designate tax deductions for elementary and secondary teachers, that require release of information about mortgages and credit reports, and that provide funds for small businesses. Inspired by her own experience as a stroke survivor, Joyce Beatty has also sponsored or co-sponsored acts intended to extend the care given by Medicare and other federal programs to stroke victims.

Another form of replacement could stem from the husband's conviction for crimes. As in the case of the term-limited husband, the election of the wife might indicate continuing support for him as well as for her. There could be complications, of course, stemming from a convicted spouse who might want the job back when he was released and who might not be all that popular with voters or the press.

James Ferguson, who served as governor of Texas from 1915 to 1917, was impeached, convicted, and removed from office at the beginning of his second term after he demanded that some faculty members at the University of Texas, his political foes, be fired. When the president refused to comply, he vetoed the state budget appropriation for the university. Other impeachment charges included misapplication of public funds for his own use and reception of a "secret" $156,000 loan. In 1917, the Texas Senate removed Ferguson as governor and declared him ineligible to hold office in the state.[10]

Refusing to accept this judgment, Ferguson ran for governor in the 1918 Democratic primary and for the U.S. Senate in 1922, and then announced his intention to run for governor in 1924. With even his supporters advising him that he needed to abide by the terms of his removal from office, he announced the candidacy of his wife, Miriam. From the beginning of this campaign, she spoke as his supportive wife, claiming that "he is conscious of no wrong." At many events, he indicated that her election would actually return him to office, that Texas thus would get "two governors for the price of one." A common campaign slogan, stressing voters' support for them both, was "Me for Ma, and I Ain't Got a Durned Thing against Pa." She was elected governor, serving until 1925 to 1927 and from 1933 to 1935, a busy legislator.[11] She opposed Prohibition and took a firm stand against the Ku Klux Klan; she pushed for a state sales tax and corporate income tax so that she could improve state highways and establish the University of Houston as a four-year institution.

In another situation, a wife took a seat in government after the husband was convicted and was given a sentence that included an agreement not to run again; in this case, of John and Katherine Langley, the husband would run against her in an attempt to return to politics, and she would seek to keep the seat by her own right and ambition.

Part of a political family herself, Katherine Langley taught speech at the Virginia Institute at Bristol, Virginia, after graduating from the Emerson College of Oratory in Boston. She then began to work as a secretary for her father, James M. Gudger, Jr., a member of the U.S. House from North Carolina. She met her husband, John Langley, in Washington where he was working for the Census Bureau. Like other women in political families, she used her family's contacts to forward his career. He represented Kentucky in the House from 1907 to 1926, while she served as his secretary and held influential party positions, including leadership roles in the Republican Party of Kentucky.

In 1924, John Langley was convicted of violating the Volstead Act, of selling alcohol illegally and attempting to bribe a federal officer. In 1926, after the U.S. Supreme Court denied his appeal, he resigned from Congress, and Andrew Jackson Kirk was elected to take his seat. Katherine Langley defeated Kirk in the next election, in November 1926. During the campaign, she relied on her own family connections: she told newspaper reporters that she had been drawn into politics as a child, working with her father, leading to an active role in the Republican Party. But although she "knew politics," like many widows, she indicated that she had never planned to run for office.[12] Like many widows also, she emphasized her financial need: their home had been mortgaged to cover his court costs, she declared repeatedly, and she needed the salary that a seat in Congress could provide. She also spoke, like many widows, about her husband's priorities for the state.[13]

Katherine Langley prevailed in a bitter election fight, in which much of the criticism heaped on her concerned her husband.[14] As she campaigned, in response to these accusations, she argued that her husband had been a victim of a government conspiracy, that he was not a criminal. As she gave speeches honed to the specific needs of each town and constituency, she relied on her speech training and knowledge of the issues: "John Langley wears the breeches," said one commentator, making a judgment widely repeated, "but the lady has the brains."[15]

In Washington, Katherine Langley needed all the political connections that she had since she was an outsider as a woman, as the wife of a felon, and as a seemingly "hick" southerner. She found herself marginalized and derided, as neither her father or her husband had been. "She offends the squeamish by her unstinted display of gypsy colors on the floor and the conspicuousness with which she dresses her bushy blue-black hair," one newspaper reported.[16] She was also criticized for her flowery oratory on the House floor, perhaps a result of her career as a speech teacher but portrayed as the exaggerations of a mountaineer. These attacks did not affect the voters she served, however: she was re-elected to Congress in 1928 by a larger vote than in her first election. In Congress, she advocated for flood relief for the eastern part of Kentucky, pensions for invalids and war widows, and a cabinet-level department of education.

While she was in office, Katherine Langley also continued to advocate for her husband, a choice that led to a competition between them. She lobbied President Coolidge to grant him clemency, which the president did with the understanding that John Langley would never seek office again, an informal proviso. Coolidge granted the pardon in December 1928, shortly after Katherine Langley won her second term. Almost immediately, John Langley declared his intention to seek a seat in the House again, denying that any condition had been set, causing his wife to assert that she would not step aside "for John or anyone else."[17] The result was a publicly aired disagreement that doomed the political futures of both husband and wife. She was ultimately the one that ran for the seat, but many Republicans stayed away from the polls, insuring victory for the Democratic opponent.[18]

While the popular felon could enable a career and could serve as lively competition, the tie to a political criminal could prove complicated when he became unpopular, with the wife's career inexorably tied to him. Jan Schakowsky moved from the Illinois State Council of Senior Citizens to the Illinois House and then to the U.S. House, where she serves in the 116th Congress. Her husband, whom she married in 1980 before running for office, is Robert Creamer, a political consultant and community organizer. In 2005, Creamer pled guilty to tax violations and bank fraud stemming from his direction of a public interest group in the 1990s. He had to repay the funds and was sentenced to five months in prison and afterwards to eleven months of house arrest.[19] Then, in October 2016, scandal again dogged Creamer. He resigned from a consulting position at a political organization after a video came out that showed him attempting to pay people to incite violence at Trump rallies.[20]

Illinois newspapers repeatedly evaluated Schakowsky's campaigns by Creamer's legal situation. She had the support of the *Chicago Tribune*, for example, during her elections for the state House and when she ran for the U.S. House in the fall of 1998, before either conviction occurred, the endorsement articles centering on her dedicated work for constituents. But in 2006, after her husband pled guilty and went to jail, the *Tribune* was no longer willing to endorse her and did not indicate why. The newspaper again endorsed her for her liberal voting record and strong support of her constituents in 2008, however, when Creamer was long out of jail, as they did again in 2010 and 2012.[21] But in 2016, with Creamer having been accused of inciting violence at a Trump rally, the *Tribune* declared the Republican to be the far better choice, with no liability named except her husband.[22] In her 2018 campaign, her husband again out of the news and thus her record being the one examined, Schakowsky won with newspaper support and 72.9 percent of the vote.

As a Political Partner, Taking Office in Tribute to a Dual Commitment to Activism

While some women came into office as a result of their husbands' term limits or criminal sentences, serving for various periods with various results, they also entered office, by appointment, as an accolade, in recognition of their own and their husband's service.

The first woman in the Senate served for a day in 1922, as a tribute to her decades of activism as well as the reputation of her husband. Rebecca Ann Latimer Felton, "a political power in Georgia for forty years," was a pro-lynching politician who spent a lifetime advocating for the rights of poor women and farmers as long as they were white.[23] Her husband, William Harrell Felton, had been elected to three terms in the

U.S. House, as a member of the Independent Democratic Party, a progressive who he had been a sharp critic of capitalism. Like many widows who followed their husbands directly into office, she had run her husband's campaigns and his office. He died in 1909 after which Rebecca Felton advocated with Georgia legislators and civic groups for prison reform, women's suffrage, and educational reform. In 1922, when Senator Thomas E. Watson died, Governor Thomas W. Hardwick became a candidate for his seat. In October 1922, seeking an appointee who would not be a competitor in the upcoming special election and who could rally white women voters alienated by his opposition to the Nineteenth Amendment, Hardwick chose Rebecca Felton. Congress was not expected to reconvene until after the election, so the chances were slim that Felton would be sworn in. However, not Hardwick but Walter F. George won the special election and, rather than take his seat immediately when the Senate reconvened, George allowed Felton to be sworn in, convinced by a supportive campaign launched by women from Georgia.[24]

Another tribute to a political family and especially to an activist woman occurred in the case of Eva Kelly Bowring, active in Republican politics in Nebraska, who was appointed to the U.S. Senate by Governor Robert B. Crosby to fill the vacancy caused by the death of Dwight Griswold. When Bowring's first husband died, she took over his business selling livestock feed, driving across the state to make sales. Her second husband, rancher Arthur Bowring, served as county commissioner and as a representative and senator in the state legislature. After Arthur's death in 1944, Eva Bowring operated their ranch, the Barr–99. To protect her cattle business, like Wellington Rankin in Montana, Bowring became involved with Republican politics, eventually serving as its director of women's activities. Bowring's transition to public office was sudden. Governor Robert B. Crosby appointed her in April 1954 to fill the vacancy caused by the death of Senator Dwight Palmer. Though she did not want to leave her ranch, the governor talked her into the appointment as a duty to her family, party, and state. She explained that after years of exhorting Republican women to engage in political activism, she could not decline, as she noted in the press by speaking directly to these citizens: "When a job is offered to you, take it. Men can refuse but women are increasingly important in political life." The Senate's only other woman member at that time, Margaret Chase Smith, wrote that Bowring's appointment "did the women of America as well as the women of Nebraska a great honor."[25] She served from April to November 1954.

As Political Partners, Forwarding the Wife's Career

It was not always or most frequently the case that the wife came into office amid special circumstances: as the competition, the quick replacement, the one chosen as a tribute. In other cases, the wife moved forward while husband and wife worked together as political partners.

In some of these situations, the political husband withdrew willingly and advanced the wife's career. This type of support had to be carefully handled—so that she could present herself as a legislator in her own right though not too aggressive, not intimidating to him.

As the husband reached the end of his career, he might be pleased to forward hers even if he would need to remain in the background. John D. Dingell, Jr., U.S. representative from Michigan from 1955 to 2015, came from a political family: in his election to this seat, he was succeeding his father, who held it from 1933 to 1955. His second wife, Deborah Dingell, has been serving in the same seat since he retired, re-elected in November of 2018, the first non-widowed woman to immediately succeed her husband in Congress.

Deborah Dingell had married John Dingell, twenty-eight years her senior, in 1981, but as reporters noted, she was "nearly as well connected as he is," her history combining philanthropy with politics.[26] Deborah Dingell is descended from one of the Fisher brothers, owners of Fisher Body Corporation. She served as president of the General Motors Foundation as well as a member of the Democratic National Committee. She chaired Al Gore's presidential campaign in Michigan in 2000 and helped to secure the Michigan Democratic primary and general election vote for John Kerry in 2004.

Dingell indicated that she planned to run for her husband's congressional seat after he announced his retirement, a choice that he publicly acclaimed. Reporters denigrated her as "lovely Deborah," running as a wife, the ultimate "heir to a political dynasty that dates to Franklin Roosevelt." Though she recognized her husband's name and popularity, and he was more than willing to help her, she refused to let him come to some events as she established her own political career: "I didn't want to be seen with him…. I needed to be Debbie Dingell and stand on my own two feet, period." As she indicated concerning the dual source of her reputation, "A lot of congressional wives feel lost in their husbands' shadows and have trouble finding their identity. I've never felt that way. I'm proud to be Mrs. John Dingell, but I very much have my own accomplishments."[27]

Instead of replacing the husband, the wife might go beyond him in politics. To thus move forward, she might need to carefully construct herself, as not too aggressive or scary. Martha Wright Griffiths graduated from the University of Michigan Law School in 1940, where she met and married Hicks George Griffiths, a lawyer and judge as well as chair of the Michigan Democratic Party. In the fall of 1948, Hicks was the law partner of a first-time candidate for governor, G. Mennen Williams, and very active in his campaign. That fall also, Martha Wright Griffiths was running for her first term in the Michigan House, where she would serve from 1949 to 1953. These three campaigned together, successful in electing both Williams and Martha Griffiths. In 1954, she entered the U.S. House where she remained until 1974.

When Martha Griffiths ran for state office, local newspapers described her as backed by the power of two party leaders. Then as she ran for federal office, she further constructed herself as not in competition with her husband, a soothing narrative. She told stories of his asking her to run: she did not have the ambition, she declared, but responded to his concern that his friends and family develop their capacities and serve their state.[28] A December 1954 Associated Press story repeated the construction of reality that they created on the campaign trail, involving her acceptable looks, his power, and their lack of children that would need a mother at home: "The stylish, 133-pound Mrs. Griffiths concedes Hicks 'wears the pants in this family.' He'll stay in Detroit except on weekends. They have no children." That fall Hicks frequently commented on her cooking: "'Among other things, she's a terrific cook,' says her proud husband. 'But to get her to make my favorite dish I have to invite guests. It's what we call waffle brownie, which she serves with ice cream.'"[29] As she presented herself as the good wife, doing what he asked of her, she seemed like an appropriate woman to elect.

In some of these families, the wife went further after the husband lost an election. A husband then withdrawing from politics occurred in the case of Pat Schroeder, who would spend twenty-four years in the U.S. House, prevailing in twelve elections during which both husband and wife campaigned together for her. Democrat Pat Schroeder and her husband Jim Schroeder graduated from Harvard Law and then moved to Colorado, where she did pro-bono work for Rocky Mountain Planned Parenthood and the Denver Fair Housing Group. She then became a hearing officer for the Colorado State Personnel Board and taught political science and constitutional law, at the University of Colorado and at Regis University. Jim Schroeder lost a 1970 state House election by forty-two votes.[30]

In 1972, he served on an ad hoc committee looking for someone to run against the Republican incumbent for the U.S. House. Clarence "Arch" Decker, a conservative Democrat with whom party officials sided, was considering a run, but ultimately he demurred: with George McGovern as the presidential candidate, running as a Democrat on the same ticket looked hopeless. In this situation, when the party might choose a woman, Jim Schroeder suggested his wife. As she later commented about this race, "In the old days, there were two ways for a woman to run for Congress: as the widow of an incumbent or as challenger in a hopeless race. Scenario number two was how I was chosen to run."[31] Party leaders thought that she might bring out liberal issues, about the war in Vietnam and about the environment, but that she could not prevail against the Republican incumbent, Mike McKevitt.

Pat Schroeder thus had party support but only for a limited purpose. And, as happened to Jeannette Rankin in 1916, many feminists thought that Pat Schroeder should not run at all or should run for a local office: the National Women's Political Caucus, which Schroeder had helped to found in 1970, didn't support her because they thought it was too early for a woman to run for Congress from that district and state. But, along with her husband, Pat Schroeder took the campaign seriously, making postcards and placards, sending out letters to friends, talking to people one-on-one, moving beyond the expectations of her own party and her fellow feminists. And she won, serving in Congress until 1996.

In Office Before and After Him

Instead of entering politics at the same time or afterwards, some women were already in political office when they met and married their husbands. These women's experience varied according to whether the spouse was from another state or not; she might no longer be judged as an appropriate representative of her home state after marriage to an out-of-state man, a pressure that husbands did not face.

Kay Bailey Hutchison, in a phone conversation with me, reported little effect on her career after she chose a husband from her own state who was also engaged in politics. As she noted to me, she had already launched her career when they met and married, and he was not perceived as intervening in her political choices although she had difficulty when she attempted to serve in the U.S. House from his district.

Following her graduation from law school, Kay Bailey Hutchison worked as a legal and political correspondent for a television station in Houston, as one of the first on-screen newswomen in Texas. In 1972, at age twenty-nine, she was elected to the Texas House from Houston. She remained in office until 1976 during the same years that Ray Hutchison served, representing Dallas County. As two Republicans elected in the same year, they found themselves working within a small group together, what she described to me as "a merry little band."

But Kay Bailey Hutchison would have problems, however, when after their marriage she attempted to run from his home district. In 1976, she became vice-chair of the National Transportation Safety Board (NTSB); Ray Hutchison also left the state House, to become chair of the state Republican Party and launch what would be an unsuccessful run for the governorship. She remained with the NTSB until 1978, the year that they married. She was a candidate for the U.S. House in 1982, from the Dallas-based Third District, in a part of the state to which she had relocated with him, but she was defeated in the primary by Steve Bartlett, who won the general election. Her husband did not run for office again.

While her husband left political office, Kay Bailey Hutchison went on to a long and successful electoral career. She became Texas state treasurer in 1990 and served until June 1993 when she ran against Senator Bob Krueger for the right to complete the last two years of Lloyd Bentsen's U.S. Senate term: he had resigned in January 1993 to become Secretary of the Treasury in the Clinton administration. She served until 2013 when she returned to her legal practice. In August of 2017, she became the United States' permanent representative to NATO.

Ileana Ros-Lehtinen of Miami, in the U.S. House from Florida from 1989 to 2018, the second woman to represent a Florida district, after Ruth Bryan Owen, also established her own career before her marriage. She was born in Cuba and came to the United States at age seven. A teacher and school administrator, Ros-Lehtinen had been elected to the Florida House in 1982, where she met state representative Dexter Lehtinen, whom she married in 1984. He became U.S. attorney for south Florida in 1988. As she went on to the U.S. House, her husband's political history and new job did not become major factors in her career, established in Florida before their marriage.

Other women, with husbands who came from other states and who remained in office for longer periods, found the situation more complicated, involving the ties of state and party as well as marriage.

When married politicians came from different states, voter reaction could be severe, especially for the wife. Indianan Andrew Jacobs, Jr., and

Kansan Martha Keys, both in the U.S. House, met and married after she came to Washington in 1975. Jacobs was a representative from Indiana from 1965 to 1973 and from 1975 to 1997, and so they were both in a sense freshman legislators in 1975. Both came from political families: Keys' younger sister had married Gary Hart; Jacobs' father had been a U.S. representative from Indiana. After they married in 1976, "we had quite a family caucus for a while," as Jacobs commented.[32]

When both Keys and Jacobs ran for re-election in the fall of 1976, she especially faced a strong challenge, her marriage providing "political ammunition" to her opponent, Ross Freeman. In the Kansas campaign, she was denigrated as the "congresswoman from Indiana," with Freeman's supporters calling for a congressman actually from Kansas. When Jacobs came to Kansas to campaign for his wife, Freeman declared that her husband was either coaching her or whispering sweet nothings in her ear. At Kansas events, she was repeatedly asked if she should be representing one state when she had a husband in another. On the other hand, as Jacobs reminded reporters, he was not referred to as a congressman from Kansas while he was campaigning in Indiana. And he spoke of the sharp difference and the difficulties that his wife was facing: "No one has said to me that because my wife lives in Kansas, I can't represent my district.... But there is an energetic campaign against Martha on this basis. If it is a double standard, which is what I suspect, I think it is rough." This attack meant that she could not come to Indiana to campaign with him without seeming like a traitor to Kansas and Kansans.[33] Jacobs won in Indiana by 38,000 votes and Keys in Kansas by just 6,000, his campaign much less affected by accusations of inappropriate residency and allegiance. Kristie Hill, an Associate Press reporter, commented that Keys' marriage "nearly cost her a second term in Congress" while Jacobs' campaign was "unaffected," the difference labeled as sexual discrimination.[34]

In the case of Stephanie Herseth Sandlin, marriage to an out-of-state legislator may have ruined a bid for re-election. In a phone conversation with her, she told me about the difficulties that she encountered in South Dakota, as someone with strong family ties there, after she married Texas representative Max Sandlin in 2007. During her unsuccessful re-election bid in 2010, for the U.S. House seat that she had first secured in 2004, much of the advertising and criticism concerned this marriage. Although her husband had sold his property in Texas and had moved to South Dakota after he lost a re-election bid in 2005, she was attacked for not marrying a native, for thus abandoning her home state and its priorities. Even though her grandparents and father served in state office and she had been a resident all of her life, she would not be viewed as quite so much of a South Dakotan after she married a Texan.

In our interview, Sandlin said that her opponent in the 2010 campaign focused state attention on bad Washington elites versus good local residents, with her marriage a key to this powerful construction. Sandlin's campaign slogan was Stephanie for South Dakota and her opponent Kristi Noem's was Kristi Is South Dakota, with Noem's supporters claiming that Sandlin had abandoned her identification with the state. Critical op-eds compared the candidates' lives, pointing out that Sandlin had gone to college at Georgetown, had waited to marry while she established her career, and then had chosen an outsider whereas Noem had gone to a state school, married a state resident, and raised a family in the state before entering politics, a more traditional and acceptable path in a conservative region, what editorialist Bob Mercer described as Noem's "strong personal story" that Sandlin could not match, the worst element of her story seemingly her out-of-state politician husband.[35]

Though Sandlin had to deal in 2010 with animosity toward Washington and toward a Texas husband, she said that she had the added reaction in South Dakota of Native Americans, displeased that she had married out of state, outside of a tight-knit group, ending the possibility that she might marry one of them or at least a state resident. She said that she has a Lakota name, which means "she who can bring the peoples together," that she has Sioux cousins and might naturally belong with them, her marriage certainly not bringing the peoples together as evidenced by their negative response.

In the newspapers, as she noted to me, reporters also zeroed in on how being a multi-state couple had affected their child care, an essential element of traditional family. In a small state, after Sandlin had her first child Zachary, in 2008, she felt that there was a sense of needing to know, of wanting to be involved, at a time when she was busy and not posting on social media, like Facebook. As Zachary got older, articles focused on the difficulties the couple encountered finding adequate child care as they moved between two states and Washington.[36] Sandlin commented to me that women in Congress face difficulties concerning where their children are: some critics believe that these legislators should leave their children in the home state, in some supposedly more settled and traditional situation there, thus demonstrating loyalty to their constituents and home, and some believe that the children should remain with their mother, even in far away Washington, and both factions feel they have the right to judge. When during the 2010 campaign, Sandlin was asked where her then two-year-old son would be going to school, she told reporters that he would stay with her, what she thought was best for her son and what should have seemed like an approved family value, but in fact did not. Sandlin lost the 2010 election. She then joined a Washington law firm and in 2017, she became the president of Augustana College in Sioux Falls.

As in the case of Stephanie Herseth Sandlin, many women with husbands also in the business of politics have experienced the good and bad of this situation. Women with a live political spouse have had another base, not just a party, from which to launch and continue a career. Very few women have entered into direct competition with their spouses, as did Mattie Cannon. Instead of competing, women have embarked on many forms of connection. Like Dixie Bibb Graves or Elaine Edwards, some have taken on the role of placeholder, enabling the husband to make political decisions about future candidates. Like Joyce Beatty or Katherine Langley, some have furthered their husbands' goals when term limits or jail sentences bring an end to a career, and from that beginning the wives might go on to their own issues and ambitions. As in the case of Debbie Dingell, there might also be support from a retiring husband. Alternatively, the husband might decide early in his career to withdraw from elective politics and aid his wife, as Jim Schroeder did with Pat Schroeder. A political husband might also provide support to an already developed career,

Stephanie Herseth Sandlin, her husband Max Sandlin and their son Zachary in 2017 (courtesy Stephanie Herseth Sandlin).

as occurred with Kay Bailey Hutchison and Ray Hutchison and with Ileana Ros-Lehtinen and Dexter Lehtinen.

Though this very live connection can help a wife to launch and continue a career, it can also have its difficulties. When a woman in a political marriage attempts to enter office, she has to make her own independence clear. As Martha Keys and Stephanie Herseth Sandlin experienced, the woman politician might be judged as a less appropriate legislator if her husband comes from another state or has priorities that differ from hers. She might be held responsible for his legislative agenda, as he would not be for hers. This marital power base can create opportunities as well as unexpected and even bizarre difficulties, as has certainly been true in two particular cases, those of Elizabeth Dole and Hillary Clinton.

FIVE

Elizabeth Dole
and Hillary Clinton
Two Wild Cases

When Debbie Dingell decided to run for her husband's congressional seat, her accession to power seemed to hold difficulty for him. One reporter, Sheryl Gay Stolberg, "feeling empathy," thus described the situation: "So you had that tug of her looking ahead and him looking behind, and the two of them trying to reconcile these feelings."[1] This situation, of the wife following the husband into office, whether he left because of term limits or jail or retirement, has proven to be a special gendered category, ceding opportunity as well as difficulty, the association with the husband extending to everything he had ever done.

In the case of two women who ran for the Senate and for the presidency, Elizabeth Dole and Hillary Clinton, this dynamic, this relationship and tension, has been especially telling. Concerning these two women, historian Betty Boyd Caroli noted "more similarities than differences": these comparisons include their childhoods in privileged circumstances; their allegiance to the Methodist church; their law degrees from Ivy League schools where they were presidents of their classes; their concern for women's rights; their activism in Washington; their successful runs for the Senate and unsuccessful for the presidency.[2] They also had both altered their career goals because of their marriages to ambitious men.

As these two women sought elective office late in their careers, their husbands were fully supportive during campaigns for the Senate, which one man had controlled for years and one had never sought to enter. But both men became more problematic concerning the presidency, which one could not attain in more than one try and one hated to leave, especially after having been impeached. Here is the apotheosis of both the opportunity and drawbacks, the good and bad, of marital allegiance to power.

Elizabeth Dole

While Elizabeth Dole's candidacy for the presidency was short-lived, it was the longest and most serious bid by a woman for a major party's presidential nomination in many election cycles. In the Republican Party, Margaret Chase Smith had sought the presidential nomination in 1964. After winning no state primaries, she placed fifth in the initial balloting at the convention and denied unanimous consent for Senator Barry Goldwater of Arizona by refusing to withdraw her name from the final ballot. In the Democratic Party, Congresswoman Shirley Chisholm became a candidate for the presidency in 1972. She received votes in primaries in fourteen states and secured twenty-eight delegates during the primary process. Pat Schroeder launched an exploratory campaign for the presidency in 1987, but withdrew quickly when adequate funding and party support were not forthcoming. And then the next serious candidate from a major party was Elizabeth Dole.

Throughout her training and career, Dole's choices seemed to place her both inside and outside of gendered expectations. She graduated from Duke University, with distinction in political science, in the fall of 1958, and took a job in the Harvard Law School library. Then she pursued postgraduate work at Oxford, after which she took a job at a Massachusetts high school. While teaching, she pursued her master's degree in education at Harvard University, which she earned in 1960, followed by a J.D. from Harvard Law School in 1965; of 550 members of the class, there were just two dozen women.[3] She had thus experimented with traditional careers for women, teaching and library work, before making the overwhelmingly male choice of Harvard law.

When Elizabeth Dole entered a government career, a primarily male space, she did so within divisions of the federal government deemed appropriate for women's care and concern, including departments dealing with education and consumer safety. As a Democrat, she campaigned for the Kennedy–Johnson ticket in 1960, and after graduation from law school she worked in the White House for the Johnson administration. At the Department of Health, Education and Welfare, she planned a large conference on education for the deaf, with emphasis on federal funding for research and schools. As she later declared about this time, "While Bob

Dole was voting against the Great Society, I was working for it." In April 1968, she took a job in the White House's Office of Consumer Affairs. When Nixon took over, Dole switched her party affiliation from Democrat to Independent, and became executive director of the President's Committee for Consumer Interests. Nixon maintained this position, Dole has written, because it was "the heyday of consumerism" and he was "aware of the political realities."[4] The consumer affairs division, run by Virginia Knauer, the highest-ranking woman in the administration, promoted recycling, nutritional labeling, and other consumer and family-friendly legislation. In 1973, Nixon appointed Dole to the Federal Trade Commission (FTC), her emphasis continuing to be consumer protection.

Though Elizabeth Dole established herself in government through appointed roles, her marriage would lead her into electoral politics. Her husband Bob Dole, whom she married in 1975, had been a U.S. representative from Kansas from 1961 to 1969 and then served as a U.S. senator from 1969 to 1996. He was the Republican nominee for vice president in 1976; a candidate in the primaries for the Republican nomination for president in 1980 and 1988; and the Republican nominee for president in 1996.

As Hillary Rodham Clinton would do also, Elizabeth Dole allowed her husband's career priorities to shape her own. In 1976, she took a leave from her post at the FTC for several months to campaign as Bob Dole ran for the vice presidency on the Republican ticket with Gerald Ford. She later resigned from the FTC, in 1979, to campaign during his 1980 presidential run. She had become a Republican in 1975.

After the 1980 campaign, under Reagan and Bush, Elizabeth Dole moved on to other positions in which just part of her work involved consumer protection. She served as director of the White House Office of Public Liaison, from 1981 to 1983, communicating with various interest groups. She then became a cabinet secretary for two federal departments. For the Department of Transportation from 1983 to 1987, she oversaw Reagan's deregulation efforts, of the airlines for example, but also worked to ensure automobile safety through seatbelt and airbag regulations. During her tenure, the National Highway Traffic Safety Administration mandated the installation of center-mounted stop lamps, sometimes called "Liddy Lights," on new cars. She worked with Mothers Against Drunk Driving to pass laws withholding federal highway funding from any state that had a drinking age below twenty-one. Then she served as Secretary of the Department of Labor under George Bush, from 1989 to 1990, arbitrating strikes in the coal industry along with advocating for a number of OSHA reforms to protect American workers from injury and illness.[5]

In 1991, Elizabeth Dole became president of the American Red Cross, serving in that position until 1999. In January of 1999, colleagues urged her to run for president, to thus help bring more women into the Republican Party and attract more moderate voters, and she quit the Red Cross to prepare for a campaign.

From March 1999, when she formally declared her candidacy, to October 1999, when she withdrew, opinion polls gave Elizabeth Dole high favorability ratings and showed her consistently running a strong second to George W. Bush. Support for Dole was so widespread that in August 1999, when the public was asked which of the seven Republican candidates should stay in the race for the nomination, 77 percent said that Dole should stay in, second only to Bush at 96 percent. Polls also showed her beating Al Gore if she ran against him in the general election. From a high of 24 percent of support among Republican voters in April 1999 to a low of 8 percent in June 1999 (which had rebounded to 13 percent by August), Dole was always ahead of every contender other than Bush.[6]

Elizabeth Dole brought to the campaign a superior education and experience in government. She had spoken well on prior national occasions, especially at the 1996 Republican National Convention, during which she walked out into the audience while talking conversationally about her husband's qualities. Reporters and voters also responded positively to the first speeches of her campaign.[7]

But negatives also surfaced, including the appearance discourse encountered by many women candidates. Based solely on her standing in the polls, Dole should have received less press coverage than George Bush, but more than the other contenders for the Republican nomination. As Caroline Heldman, Susan J. Carroll, and Stephanie Olson reported, George W. Bush was mentioned in 73 percent of the articles examined between March to October of 1999, but the strong second was John McCain, at 33 percent, with Dole at just 19.7 percent. And, in newspaper articles, reporters repeatedly paid attention to her personality traits and appearance, suggesting that she was a pretty novelty in the race. Part of what these stories did was to make her look overly contained, unable to speak frankly. On the positive side, she seemed "chipper," "poised," and "gracious." But in these depictions her control signaled the robotic: she was "canned," "rehearsed," "scripted," "choreographed," and "inauthentic."[8] Though Elizabeth Dole got credit for being intelligent and hard-working, she became a picture of the "overly cautious, overly rehearsed, robotic perfectionist who oozed charm but lacked substance": an opinion piece by Arianna Huffington in the *Los Angeles Times*, for example, compared Dole to "a

late night infomercial host" who "is plying us with well-rehearsed bro-
mides."[9] Some of this control criticism centered on her southern roots. In
January, Maureen Dowd commented in the *New York Times* that "her aides
ironed the Magnolia's skirts to perfection before she stepped in front of
the cameras."[10]

Elizabeth Dole had problems, with her gender and her controlled
presence—as well as with a seeming vagueness on some issues, a lack of
electoral experience, and a mixed record with the Red Cross. But she also
faced the issue of Bob Dole.

Certainly Elizabeth Dole was able to move from appointed positions
in government to a national campaign for the highest office in part through
her husband's influence and record, but there were also complications
stemming from his political history and ambition. Her husband was commonly referred to all through her campaign. As the Heldman article
reported, of the in-depth stories focusing on Elizabeth Dole, 61.9 percent
discussed his record. Moreover, 41.3 percent of the stories made multiple references to Bob Dole.[11] Some writers maintained that she owed her
entire career to her husband even though she had worked in the White
House long before they met: Michael Kramer of the *Daily News* referred
to the "lofty cabinet positions she held" as just "sops to her husband, the
Bobster, whose control of the Senate meant it was only smart for Ronald
Reagan and George Bush to throw her some crumbs."[12] Other writers
claimed that she was just recycling his positions on the issues and had no
independent ideas. One mentioned that they gave "his and her speeches,"
all based on his political and economic analyses. And repeatedly writers
evaluated her positions by how they squared with his record. She had no
right to speak against special interests, Arianna Huffington claimed, when
"her life has been intertwined for so long with Mr. Special Interest himself."[13]

Though negative coverage stemmed from her husband's power and
from his record, it also derived from his means of constructing himself as
a political spouse: indeed from many choices, made by a generally savvy
politician, that seemed likely to hurt her chances to prevail.

From the beginning of her campaign, his focus seemed to be on
himself, on the politician who had not achieved everything that he
wanted—and on her liabilities. During the week that she began discussing a candidacy, in January 1999, her husband called himself her
biggest supporter, but he also referred to his own past and needs in a
way that other political spouses would not do: "Well, I've still got one
chance to get to the White House, and that's if Elizabeth runs for

president."[14] In early February, in a widely circulated AP story, he reminded voters of his campaigns as he made fun of himself but also of her ability to give speeches responding to the priorities of various types of voters: "I'll do what she's done for me the past two times—stand there smiling while she makes the same speech over and over and over."[15]

And then Bob Dole signed on as a spokesman for Viagra. He had been diagnosed with prostate cancer in 1991 and had undergone surgery; in May 1998, he acknowledged that he afterwards had participated in trials for Viagra, which he called "a great drug." In 1999, he appeared in print and television ads for the drug in which he employed the word "courage." As the print ad quoted him, "It may take a little courage to ask your doctor about erectile dysfunction. But everything worthwhile usually does." He had also frequently used the powerful word "courage" in discussing all that soldiers endured for their country in World War II: "everything worthwhile" that men had achieved, in war and politics perhaps, is here tied to getting an erection. In the television ad, he further developed this comparison by associating Americans that "risk their lives" with those that have the courage to get Viagra.

As the ads came out, many influential commentators, and especially women, questioned whether Bob Dole was trying, on a conscious or subconscious level, to ruin his wife's chances of being elected president. In the *Chicago Tribune*, Geraldine Ferraro responded to the television ads by noting that sex had been discussed in Congress with the case of Bob Livingston, but then Bob Dole was "looking straight at me and my grandson in my living room and talking about erectile dysfunction." She then considered what these ads might do to Elizabeth Dole's campaign: "His wife should speak to him because she needs the support of the religious right, which might not care for the ad. It's her turn and she'll find it a lot easier if her husband isn't on television talking about their sex life." Ferraro created a hypothetical example of a candidate's wife suddenly doing birth control or feminine hygiene product ads to further argue that this spouse was acting inappropriately, in an unprecedented manner.[16] He had a disease to fight, a proper activity of a first spouse, as Ellen Goodman noted, but cataracts would have been a better choice.[17] Gail Collins commented in May 1999 that "people have been wondering why Bob Dole chose to appear in TV commercials about erectile dysfunction right at the time that Mrs. Dole was launching her bid for a prize he had always wanted for himself. The effort to educate fellow prostate cancer victims was commendable, but the timing seemed peculiar. Was it principle or a deeply sublimated desire to distract attention from his wife?"[18]

Bob Dole worsened this situation by making comments not just about sex but about their sex life. As *New York Post* reporter Deborah Orin commented, when she asked him what he planned to do if his wife was elected, "Bob Dole gave a big grin and replied: 'I just want to be able to go to bed with her,'" a line that the *Post* made into a headline.[19] Other articles focused on how such personal references, not just the ads, would alter her campaign. Joan Silverman wrote that at least on this issue no one could any longer "separate the public political figure from the private man," and his commentary would cause the questions about her, already gender based, to change from hairdos to sex: "'Does she, or doesn't she?' was once the domain of Clairol, referring to hair color. In a millennial flip, it will now have become something else altogether."[20] As Ellen Goodman quoted a woman at a beauty parlor, "She'll be giving a speech late one night and somebody will wonder if he is back at the hotel wasting a $10 pill."[21]

During the spring, Bob Dole also continued with awkward joking about his own diminished role in governing if she won. As he told a reporter, "she'd make history—and I'd be history." And then he continued, humorously but also piteously, about being left behind: "'All I want is a driver and a car, something to toodle around town in,' he said. 'But I also want a beeper in case I get left behind after some state ceremony.'" When asked about the campaign's decision that he not appear with his wife during the primary campaigning in Iowa and New Hampshire, as she attempted to establish her independence, he commented testily that he would obey: "'I have to be in the background.... I've been doing this—taking orders—for 25 years,' he said. 'The only difference is that I'd be doing this in the White House.'" He also discussed the difficulty he would have in the role of first spouse, dealing, as he said, with "dinners, lunches, meetings of the Cabinet wives." To cope with this sort of nonsense, he said, 'I'd have to take up knitting." But he also indicated that this role would not just be humiliating but almost impossible: "I'd feel a lot of temptation" to interfere.[22]

While the spring went on, Bob Dole further hurt his wife's campaign by voicing his lack of faith in it, his responses surprising reporters and leading to many reprinted articles, his comments unlike those of any other political spouse. In a May 1999 interview with Richard L. Berke of the *New York Times*, he declared that his wife's campaign had "growing pains, was slow to raise early money, and was only beginning to hit its stride." As he continued, he already seemed to be easing her out of the race: "If there's no response out there or if it looks impossible, this is not her whole life." And going further, Dole added, "If she can't raise the money, obviously it's pretty hard to be a candidate."

In this interview, Bob Dole continued by voicing his preferences among the other candidates. Since his wife might not stay in the race, he claimed, he "wanted to give money to a rival candidate who was fighting for much of her support." That rival was John McCain. "'I've thought about it,' Dole continued. 'McCain's my friend. And he's not raising the money that George Bush is. I think we need to keep good people in the race. So I've thought about ways to help McCain in particular.'" He also commented, as Richard L. Berke quoted him, about the notable skills of George W. Bush: "Mr. Dole said Governor Bush—whom he called 'the absentee candidate' because he has been holed up in Austin—would probably be 'very impressive' on the stump. 'He's in a strong position, no question about it.'" Dole also refused to confirm the positive news about his wife's ability to compete against Vice President Al Gore in a general election: "'It's too early to tell.'"[23] The title of this interview piece was "As Political Spouse, Bob Dole Strays from Campaign Script," and he certainly seemed to have done so.

Bob Dole's remarks quoted in this interview received considerable publicity, and even weeks later stories about Elizabeth Dole's campaign referenced them. In the *New York Times* on the following day, Gail Collins commented that Elizabeth Dole needed to lock up her husband: "With spouses like this, who needs opponents?" And then Collins reviewed the couple's political past: he had "benefited mightily" from her "abnegation of self and perpetual cheerleading" when he ran for office; she had never criticized his fund raising ability or stated her support for another candidate. And Collins considered the motivation behind his comments. There was, she concluded, "a drop—well, perhaps a whole gallon—of bile in the former Presidential candidate's remarks," which may have been determined by his history: "Perhaps a person with the psyche of a candidate is simply incapable of spending months directing all conversations towards the merits of somebody else."[24]

The candidate herself felt the need to turn from key issues to this fracas. Elizabeth Dole responded to Berke's article by declaring that her husband had apologized and that "I joked with him about it. I told him I loved him. I told him he was in the woodshed." The folksy "woodshed" quotation made great copy, so headlines like the *New York Times'* "Elizabeth Dole Exiles Mate to Woodshed" continued to appear for weeks.[25] In a column entitled "Bile in Bloom," Maureen Dowd succinctly summarized the results of the interview for the main actors affected by it, including, most importantly, the candidate:

The Doles, who have spent decades promoting themselves as close partners, are, for the moment, beyond the inspiration of Viagra.
   Sugar Lips is mad at Bob for his loose lips. As Dick Armey puts it, "He is going to be singing 'Strangers in the Night' for a long time."
   Liddy's strategists are mad at Bob for knocking the campaign off track just as it was getting on track and launching a big fund-raising drive.[26]

While Bob Dole hawked for Viagra, complained about his changing role, and spoke to reporters about his wife's liabilities, McCain's strong record, and Bush's chances of winning, he also questioned whether his wife had the background to make the right decisions on the issues. *U.S. News & World Report* reported that he said that "his wife might need help sorting out the issues and he would be willing to 'direct her' if asked." That article, dealing with their disagreements about the appropriate preparation for high office, had a troubling headline: "Psst, Bob Dole Beats His Wife."[27]

As Dole questioned his wife's preparation for leadership, he also quite publicly advocated for different positions on issues. As the *New York Post* commented, when she was in Iowa criticizing Clinton's recent foreign policy decisions, her husband was in Washington defending "the very same Bill Clinton's policy on Kosovo as a way to save lives and fulfill America's role on the world stage—he's just back from the Balkans as Clinton's special envoy."[28] Richard Berke also noted Bob Dole's quite public espousal of policies that contradicted hers: "As Elizabeth Dole has been walking the streets of New Hampshire, building a base for her campaign there, Bob Dole has been glowing on the Sunday morning talk shows, giving his opinions—not necessarily hers—in cozy chats with Tim Russert and candidates like McCain and Lamar Alexander. 'Where's the Dole who's running?' I've wondered."[29] Concerning his independent positions on the issues, another reporter claimed further, "That's fine leadership talk coming from the man who remains titular head of the Republican Party. But it's disastrous talk coming from the spouse of an opposing GOP presidential candidate. It exposes Elizabeth Dole to that deadliest of campaign viruses—ridicule."[30] When Bob Dole spent two days in Iowa campaigning, as Maureen Dowd commented, he didn't stay with her script or even seem to care about it: he seemed "fuzzy" about his wife's ten-point agricultural policy, but spoke "wistfully" about his thirty years of leadership on the congressional Agricultural Committee.[31]

After months of hawking for Viagra and boasting about his superior knowledge of the issues, by the early fall Bob Dole was forecasting the probable end of his wife's campaign. On September 16, for example, he told the *Democrat and Chronicle* in Rochester that Bush's lead might be insurmountable: the article's title was "Bob Dole Still Plays Politics." Employing highly judgmental statements for a political spouse, he said that his wife was having trouble raising funds and he wasn't sure how much further she could go. Elizabeth was finding, he continued, that she couldn't run a car without gas.[32]

On October 20, 1999, Elizabeth Dole dropped out of the race, before the first primary. After this announcement, critics continued to focus on her husband's role in what happened. Mary McGrory commented in the *Washington Post* that "Arizona Sen. John McCain had been his first choice, even when his wife was still a contender."[33] Bonnie Erbe wrote that "while she played the loyal campaign spouse for years, it wasn't a mantle he willingly embraced when it came her time to shine."[34] As Richard L. Berke concluded, "The Dole-Dole dynamic is fraught with personal and political land mines, a sense of missed opportunities—and perhaps even competition. On the one hand, Mr. Dole wants Mrs. Dole to be President. On the other hand, he spent much of his career trying to be President himself."[35] Into 2000, as George W. Bush considered Elizabeth Dole as a vice presidential choice, her husband still focused on his own political power: reporter Kenneth R. Bazinet noted that when Bob Dole was asked about his wife's future, he segued to himself and his own unfulfilled ambitions: he "piped up, 'I would accept it if it's offered.'"[36]

Although Bob Dole certainly hindered his wife as she sought the presidency, he would be much less problematic when she ran for the U.S. Senate, a site in which he had already long prevailed. In late December 2001, Elizabeth Dole began considering a campaign for a seat made available by the retirement of Republican Jesse Helms. She shifted her official residency from the Doles' condominium in Washington to her mother's home in Salisbury, North Carolina. Although Elizabeth Dole had not lived in North Carolina since 1959, the state and national Republican establishment quickly cleared the field for her. She won the Republican primary on September 10, with 80 percent of the vote over a lesser-known candidate, Dr. Ada Fisher.

As was true at the beginning of the presidential campaign, in this state election, the connection to her husband created political capital. By July, President Bush and Vice President Cheney had appeared in the state with her five times; Bush repeatedly declared that if she called the White House after she was elected, her call would be answered; and he raised two million dollars for her campaign. Press coverage on help from Washington mentioned her husband as the reason for it: "And so why not help Bob Dole's missus? The people running against her aren't the sons-of,

daughters-of or wives-of anyone to worry about. What made these nobod-
ies think they could get elected?"[37]

In the senatorial campaign, Bob Dole continued to provide powerful
connections but also to cause difficulties. As in the previous campaign,
he reflected on his own career and needs. Speaking at Mercer University
in April 2002, he quipped that if she were elected, he would be in the Senate spouse club with Bill Clinton and could beat him for head of it, his
ultimate chance to finally beat his rival, his own elections still his prime
subject matter.[38]

In the period since the presidential election, Bob Dole also had continued his Viagra promotion and had extended its popularity and earning
potential. At the 2001 Super Bowl, Pepsi debuted an ad that parodied the
commercials he had made for Viagra. In this one, he walks on the beach
with his dog and sees two young women scantily dressed. Then the viewer
realizes that this time his "faithful little blue friend," which causes him to
turn a flip and then receive an admonishment to use only as directed, is
actually not Viagra but Pepsi. Then, in March 2001 during the Academy
Awards, another ad featured the extreme effect that a dancing Brittany
Spears, seen on television, had on a sequence of men. In this ad, Dole sits
alone in a darkened room watching Spears, holding up his Pepsi can, and
making the penis joke of "easy, boy," with his dog by his side. By 2002,
when his wife was busy campaigning, Dole was no longer trumpeting
Pepsi and Viagra, but the ads still existed and he was still associated with
them.

But during the Senate race, even though Bob Dole still had the ethos
of Viagra man and he still seemed to seek power for himself, he did not
prove as problematic to his wife as he had in the presidential campaign.
As Elizabeth Dole ran for an office that he had held for twenty-seven years
and did not seek to regain, Bob Dole did not seem as intimidated or judgmental. And this time she may have known better how to contain him.

On the campaign trail in North Carolina with her, he went to veterans
hospitals, just discussing the bravery and the needs of the military; he
appeared with her at parades and other events without speaking. Then in
September, Bob was off with Bill Clinton raising funds for scholarships
for children of victims of 9/11, busy and important, but staying out of the
North Carolina and his wife's campaign. In late September, he began campaigning for Republican candidates in other states while also speaking
about the effect of rap music and violent movies as well as the importance
of family. In these excursions well outside of North Carolina, he was setting himself up as bigger than one state election, as the party leader and

a public moral authority. Eyeing a possible run at the presidency in 2004, his aides discussed these speeches as crucial for "fleshing out the senator's whole range of concerns"—and he was not interfering in his wife's Senate election as he had with the presidential campaign.[39]

In the November general election, Elizabeth Dole defeated her Democratic opponent Erskine Bowles, a former chief of staff to Bill Clinton, by an eight-point margin. In the senatorial and presidential contests, she had seen the good and bad of the political family: the connections, the fund raising ability, and the campaign help, but also the husband's frequent need to be in the game, not to become the supporter, especially if he sought power for himself. Elizabeth Dole's electoral history reveals the complexity of first being helped by a family member and then attempting to move beyond him, with his issues but also his sexual and business choices becoming his wife's.

Hillary Clinton

Like Elizabeth Dole, Hillary Clinton ultimately failed at running for president while being "helped" by a popular but uncontrollable husband, with the opposition and the press emphasizing her husband and sex. In this case, similarly, the husband did a good job of supporting the wife as she ran for the Senate, a job that he didn't want, but became amazingly negative when she sought a job that he valued so much more, one that he had held, had difficulties keeping, and didn't want to leave. The Clintons handled Bill's sexual proclivities well when she ran for the Senate in New York, just as Bob Dole's Viagra escapades had subsided by the time that Elizabeth Dole ran for the Senate in North Carolina. But his history became quite problematic in presidential races, his sexual choices symbolically becoming hers and impacting her quest for a presidential ethos. Like Bob Dole, Bill Clinton continued to want to be the leader, not the leader's spouse. Indeed, both husbands were good at helping their wives to achieve only what they didn't want.

When four-term New York Senator Daniel Patrick Moynihan announced his retirement in November 1998, his seat came open for the 2000 election. New York City Mayor Rudy Giuliani, who was prevented by term limits from again seeking the mayoral office in 2001, immediately indicated his interest. Due to his high profile and visibility, Giuliani was supported by the state's Republican Party. Late in 1998, prominent Democratic politicians, including New York Representative Charles Rangel, urged Hillary Clinton to run. Patrick Halley, her advance man, later wrote that she had been considering a run for a Senate seat in Illinois and "I thought she'd have a better shot as a native daughter than as a transplant to New York." But Halley recognized that against Rudy Guiliani in New York, "Democrats were desperate to come up with a marquee name."[40]

As she undertook a New York campaign, given the impeachment and the "hostility of people fatigued with the Clintons' soap opera," Hillary Clinton worked to separate herself from her husband. She chose to use just her first name in a campaign video, on her posters, and on buttons: "her husband's name has been deep-sixed."[41] And he did not speak when she went to New York City to campaign along with Chuck Schumer, but instead he sat on the stage and clapped like a proper political spouse: her aides feared that if Bill Clinton spoke he would be the one making the news.[42] Concerning their demeanor at her announcement and many campaign events, reporters like Sandy Grady noted that "gagging Bill was smart politics."[43]

But even though Hillary Clinton sought to avoid exposing voters to too much of her husband, she was attempting to employ his political strategies. As Halley indicated, in the battle for the vote upstate, an area all too likely to choose a Republican, she immediately launched a listening tour, visiting with people from town to town, "borrowing a page from her husband's playbook" to seem more personable and connected than she often did.[44] And she also relied on his fundraising connections. In reviewing this gift of support, Dick Morris commented that "Hillary Clinton's Senate campaign is Bill Clinton's 'I'm sorry' gift."[45]

As Hillary Clinton worked to establish herself, she also attempted to manage her husband's sexual history. She announced her candidacy four days after his impeachment proceedings concluded, taking advantage of her higher public approval, "something of a cultural apotheosis," created by this situation.[46] With the public expressing sympathy, she could portray herself as the victim, as a loving and understanding wife dealing with family hardship in a noble manner. In Tina Brown's *Talk* magazine, in an article entitled "The Intimate Hillary," the candidate charitably described her husband's cheating as rooted in his childhood: in his boyhood lack of a father, years in which he was "scarred by abuse" because of the ongoing conflict between his mother and grandmother. These experiences, Hillary Clinton argued, led him to need to please more than one woman at a time. Additionally, she maintained that he lied about Monica Lewinsky to shield her from bad news. And he cheated on her after the deaths of his father and mother and Vince Foster, she continued, because of his grief.[47]

This construction of events received mixed reviews. As Hillary Clinton defended her husband and his adultery, she was keeping her marriage before the press, a decision that conflicted with her vaunted independence. One reporter, Bill Press, in an editorial entitled "Hillary, Please Shut Up Now," portrayed himself as speaking to her about her desire to appear as separate: "So stop talking about your marriage," he told her, stop appearing as the "oft-cheated-upon spouse needing sympathy." And Press continued by claiming that "she not only stands by her man, she cooks up dumb excuses for him."[48]

The construction of events that Hillary Clinton debuted in *Talk* magazine, however, brought her more sympathy than derision. As one reporter commented, the "adoring media" had fallen for it: she had successfully made herself into a "suffering but strong victim, a role that this super feminist ironically plays better than Tammy Wynette," a reference to her January 1992 claims about not standing by her man like the iconic star.[49]

While Hillary Clinton experienced both press derision and sympathy for her husband's infidelities, she also had to face the voters' complex reactions to the choices she so publicly made concerning her marriage, a further entanglement of Bill Clinton in her campaign. An erosion of support throughout 1999 may have reflected mixed feelings about her staying with him and excusing him, about the power she had derived from him—and about her choice of leaving during the waning days of his presidency. On *ABC World News Tonight*, for example, Peter Jennings asked her if women resented her for her fidelity—and then asked how Bill Clinton would handle his exit from power alone, without his wife there to aid him.

Although Hillary Clinton worked to manage the effect of the Lewinsky scandal and her husband's impeachment, his sex life would continue to plague her. At the end of October 2000, Juanita Broaddrick, from Arkansas, sent a publicly released letter to Hillary Clinton claiming that Mrs. Clinton knew about her rape by Bill Clinton twenty-two years earlier and had sought to cover it up. Broaddrick had made, and denied, the rape claim before, but here, without evidence given, was her first claim of collusion, a charge that Hillary Clinton publicly ignored though it again brought out her husband's infidelities and lack of trustworthiness.[50]

While Hillary Clinton coped with the fallout of her husband's adultery and impeachment, she also dealt with the complications of still being first lady. In November 1999, she went on an official two-day visit to Israel that offered the possibility to further her own campaign: the trip would be a prime opportunity to woo the crucial Jewish vote, typically about 12 percent of the New York electorate. On November 11, however, the plan backfired: at the dedication of a U.S.-funded health program on the West Bank, she exchanged kisses with Suha Arafat, wife of Palestinian President Yasser Arafat, after Mrs. Arafat delivered a speech claiming that Israel had deliberately attacked Palestinians with poisonous gas. The following day, Hillary Clinton denounced Suha Arafat's allegations, and said that she had been told that Arafat had been referring to "tear gas" and not "poison gas." As Clinton claimed, "Had I been aware of her hateful words, I would have denounced them on the spot."[51] And she noted further that the difficulty had arisen from her being first lady: she could not just walk away or refuse the kiss without sparking a diplomatic incident and harming the peace process.[52]

But this explanation, combining a bad translation and official duties, did not calm the furor. Cal Thomas labeled her "belatedly issued" objections as "too little, too late." He likened these two "smooching each other" to the kiss of death from Judas or a mafioso boss.[53] And Rudy Guiliani repeatedly mentioned this "embracing and kissing," which he conflated with Bill Clinton's willingness to pander to Palestinians.[54] A series of ads came out quickly from Republicans replaying the kiss and hug with the tag line "Arafat spreads hatred and lies and Hillary embraces her." As the *Chicago Tribune* asserted, Hillary was not able to "juggle the Clinton administration's desired neutrality in the region with her own need to cozy up to the Jewish state known as New York City's 'sixth borough.'"[55]

These difficulties, along with her husband's sexual life, helped Giuliani: an early January 1999 poll showed him trailing Clinton by 10 points, but by January 2000 he was up by 9 points.

But then so much happened to Rudy. On April 26, television channel NY1 reported that Giuliani had undergone tests for prostate cancer. Two days later, he held a news conference to announce that he did in fact have cancer, in an early stage. He was unsure which of several types of treatment he might undergo, he told reporters, and that decision would impact whether he could stay in the Senate race.

Giuliani's own marital situation also created problems for him. His relationship with his wife, broadcast journalist and actress Donna Hanover, had grown distant, and the two were rarely seen together in public. Beginning in October 1999, another woman appeared with him at mayoral functions and at restaurants. On May 3, 2000, the *New York Post* published photographs of Giuliani with this woman, identified as Judith Nathan. With vague rumors of affairs and then cancer and romantic outings, he had gone "from run-of-the-mill philanderer to emotional basket case and swashbuckling bon vivant."[56]

As Guiliani's sexual choices as well as his health began to hinder his career, Hillary Clinton would find herself with an easier candidate to beat. On May 10, Giuliani held what the *New York Times* described as an "extraordinary, emotional news conference" to announce that he was seeking a separation from Hanover. Then, on May 19, he dropped out of the Senate race. After Giuliani withdrew, lesser-known Long Island congressman Rick Lazio took his place. He had been persuaded by Republican leaders not to enter the campaign against Guiliani since he was "unseasoned and nowhere near as skilled": Lazio had not given a major speech or delineated specific policy goals.[57] While he was attempting to establish himself, he made a big mistake during a debate: in violation of the rules, he crossed the stage, brandishing an agreement to forgo soft money in the campaign, demanding that Hillary Clinton sign it. This aggressive choice of looming in on another candidate, and especially a woman, appeared to many critics as "belligerent and bullying."[58] She won the election with 55 percent of the vote to Lazio's 43 percent, scoring surprising victories in upstate counties, areas in which she campaigned heavily.

In this Senate race, Hillary Clinton utilized many of her husband's connections, enabling her to run unopposed in the primary, in a state where she had not resided, just as Robert Kennedy's family connections helped him to win a Senate seat there in 1965. As Hillary Clinton tried to appeal especially to upstate voters, she relied on her husband's methods of meeting with small groups as well as large. She overcame the burden of his sexual proclivities, and the impeachment, by recasting this history to emphasize her own courage and steadfastness. Since Bill Clinton was still in office in Washington, he was generally not with her as she campaigned. He thus stayed within the script, as Bob Dole did during his wife's Senate race. But everything would be different in 2008 and in 2016 when she sought the job that he had left. As in Elizabeth Dole's run for the presidency, she would face the complications of a man who still wanted the job, and his sexual choices would be presented as her own.

Running for President, 2007–08

Hillary Clinton would find Rick Lazio a manageable candidate in the 2000 Senate race, but she would not do so well against Barack Obama in the 2008 Democratic primary campaign for the presidency. At the beginning of the campaign in 2007, she seemed to own the nomination. At the time, political analyst and pollster Matt Towery declared "Hang It Up, Obama—It's Hillary's Nomination." He offered the explanation that "the old Bill and Hillary Clinton machine awaits, well-oiled and ready to rumble."[59] But this judgment would of course prove incorrect, in part because of Bill Clinton's involvement in the campaign.

Though she began as the party's favorite, Hillary Clinton had her own liabilities coming into the primaries for the 2008 election, as Elizabeth Dole had in 1999. These negatives, with Democratic primary voters, included Clinton's 2002 Senate vote to authorize the use of force in Iraq, her centrist and inconsistent issue positions, and her continuing difficulty with creating a rapport with voters.[60] All through that campaign she also faced the negative body commentary that can assail women candidates. In May 2007, the *Economist* commented on her "pearls and perfectly coiffed blonde hair" and further that that she was "sharp elbowed" and "strong but brittle," echoing body and personality criticisms of Elizabeth Dole.[61] Then in July 2007, in the *Washington Post*, Robin Givhan discussed Clinton's cleavage, as displayed on the Senate floor, labeled in the article as "a teasing display," "provocative," and even "unnerving." She was also criticized for her squeaky bird-like laugh. As Howard Kurtz noted, also in the *Washington Post*, "Forget the cleavage. It's now about the cackle."[62] Along with her hair, chest, and voice, commentary also concerned the body of the older woman. After a photo of a tired-looking Clinton appeared in *The Drudge Report*, Rush Limbaugh opined that "as you age—and ... you know women are hardest hit on this.... America loses interest in you." He summarized what he viewed as a key voting criterion: "Will this country want to actually watch a woman get older before their eyes on a daily basis?" Limbaugh talked about Bill Clinton having dyed his hair, and then commented, seemingly praising Bill as he drew the contrast, "But men aging makes them look more authoritative, accomplished, distinguished. Sadly, it's not that way for women."[63] Hillary Clinton also faced the problems of running for this most authoritative of jobs as a woman of any age. Her advisor Mark Penn having determined that she needed to look tough, she "sidestepped mention of her gender" and emphasized her aggression and drive. As political commentator Rebecca Traister noted, Penn sought "to hide Hillary's femininity under a bushel of boxing metaphors," a choice that may have confused and alienated voters.[64]

For many analysts and voters, Hillary Clinton also lacked a coherent reform message, as she attempted to construct herself both as the candidate with the most government experience and as an outsider who would bring change to Washington. Many Democratic voters "saw just another ambitious politician who didn't represent change of any kind, a no-holds-barred campaigner who possessed all the feminine charm of Lady Macbeth."[65] Ann Lewis, one of her advisors, said that "what we missed, and what's painful, is that at a time when what the American people really wanted was change we had a candidate who had spent her life making change and we missed it."[66]

But in this election there were also the complications of Bill Clinton, by that time out of office. As Jonathan Allen and Amie Parnes commented about 2008, "She'd let her husband run wild on the trail."[67]

This political spouse certainly brought some positives. For this campaign, Bill Clinton played a large role in fundraising strategy and policy formation. As *New York* magazine commented in October of 2007, "he's been furiously active behind the scenes—fund-raising, reading over important speeches, speaking to her several times a day—and Hillary, being a quick study and disciplined in the extreme, has clearly absorbed a great deal of his advice." This writer went on to comment that he served as "her wartime consigliere—he's a brilliant strategizer and tactician."[68] But, especially in this race, her connection to Bill Clinton's presidency would also harm her.[69] Lori Cox Han, in *In It to Win: Electing Madam President*, claims that Hillary Clinton's lack of a victory in 2008 reflects more "Clinton bias" or "Clinton fatigue" than gender bias or any other issue: Hillary Clinton faced the "near guarantee that all the baggage of Bill Clinton's presidency would be relitigated ad nauseum in the press and by Clinton's opponents."[70]

As Bill Clinton introduced his wife at events and even headlined a few rallies, some observers felt that he was overshadowing her, with Obama claiming that he sometimes "did not know which Clinton I was running against."[71] At these events, Bill often brought up his own presidency and seemed unable to segue to her plans and future, a problem that Bob Dole also had. As Rebecca Traister recalled, "Bill was locked in on two subjects, his legacy and his wife, and I wondered whether he would be able to let go of the former in order that the latter might go it on her own."[72]

As he appeared regularly, both politicians and reporters created an ongoing joke about his inappropriate body for a "first lady," a riff on the appearance discourse that assails women. Mitt Romney and Fred Thompson, Republican primary candidates, joked on the campaign trail about their wives making prettier, sexier first ladies than would Bill. Then in Playboy.com's "Battle of the Sexiest," a contest for first ladies, he beat out Ann Romney. A *New York* magazine cover story, in October 2007, featured Bill Clinton in drag, with conservative hair, pearls, and red dress, a much less pretty version of Jackie Kennedy.

Just as humorous seemingly as his appearance was how he might be named. A *New York* magazine article queried: "How are the two Clintons introduced? As the Former and Mrs. President Clinton? Mr. and Mrs. Presidents Clinton? President Clinton and Mr. Clinton?" And Bill Clinton himself added to this amusement. On *The Oprah Winfrey Show*, for example, he joked that his Scottish friends said he should be called "First Laddie." A popular button issued by the Hillary Clinton campaign in the Iowa primary, in pink, read "Bill Clinton for First Dude."

Cover of *New York* magazine, Bill Clinton as First Lady, October 8, 2007 (*New York* magazine).

Then there was all the seeming silliness, and the complications, of what Bill Clinton's duties might be when he became first lady. In a televised interview, Barbara Walters asked him if he would oversee the Easter egg hunt and Christmas decorations—thus if he could accept the embarrassing moments of a much reduced role.[73] But if he would not be picking out decorations, there remained the more complicated issue of what he would actually do. During the second primary debate, Hillary declared with surprising directness concerning foreign policy: "When I become president, Bill Clinton, my dear husband, will be one of the people who will be sent around the world as a roving ambassador to make it very clear to the rest of the world that we're back to a policy of reaching out and working and trying to make friends and allies and stopping the alienation of the rest of the world." Such a declaration opened a door to continuing Republican attack: at a MSNBC debate among the Republican candidates, Mitt Romney reiterated one of his common themes as he warned voters that Bill Clinton would be a co-president and that he would "try and help manage the economy and help manage world affairs."[74] And then though Hillary Clinton had spoken of a key role for her husband, she grew increasingly vague about the best duties for him. As Dick Morris described her changing approach, "I think Hillary will go to great pains to make clear that She, not he, is president, just as Bush has done with his father.... She'll have to disempower Bill to empower herself."[75]

Though the situation was inherently complex, Bill Clinton's many problematic moments on the campaign trail made it much worse. He lashed out at reporters, and his lack of control became a repeated story, certainly not his wife's preferred message. He seemed angry that journalists questioned many of their policy choices, including her vote for the war in Iraq and their support of DOMA and NAFTA. On January 8, 2008, while campaigning in New Hampshire, Bill Clinton also claimed that reporters who criticized their every move had been giving Obama a pass, concerning his lack of experience and his supposed anti-war record, and that this junior member of the Senate would never survive the campaign: "Give me a break. This whole thing is the biggest fairy tale I've ever seen." Concerning press coverage, on January 9, Obama countered that "the real fairy tale is, I think, Bill Clinton suggesting somehow that we've been just taking a cake walk here." He commented further about Bill Clinton that "I understand he's feeling a little frustrated by now." Kathleen Parker of the *Baltimore Sun* referred to the Clintons' attacks on Obama that month as a "four-fisted pummeling against one skinny guy, but Bill Clinton seemed especially angry about their opponent's growing popularity and ability to parry their attacks."[76]

Then in South Carolina in January 2008, Bill Clinton appeared perhaps like a racist and indeed like a "hyperdefensive former president." In his speeches, he challenged black voters to remember how good the Clinton years had been for them and argued that Obama couldn't win at the national level. Then, when asked about Obama's victory in the state, where he beat Hillary Clinton by 48 percent to 37 percent, Clinton commented that "Jesse Jackson won in South Carolina twice, in eighty-four and eighty-eight, and he ran a good campaign. And Senator Obama's run a good campaign." Jackson was a native son who had basically run unopposed in the state, not a strong national contender; this comment derided Obama's possibilities of going forward. This error in judgment, as Rebecca Traister claimed, might have indicated "that he was losing his never-fail buddha charm, either due to old age or because it had been usurped by another compelling politician."[77] In response to Clinton's remarks, Obama claimed that his South Carolina win indeed showed that he could secure both black and white votes, which would enable him to succeed in subsequent states. Though Obama was countering successfully, the Clinton denigration of him continued. In August 2008, when reporters asked Bill Clinton if he thought Obama was qualified to be president, he replied curtly that the Constitution sets qualifications. When asked whether Obama was "ready," Clinton replied, "You could argue that no one is ready to be president."[78]

Bill Clinton awkwardly continued in his attempts not just to attack Obama but to defend his wife and himself, as though their construction of the past should not be questioned. At more than one event, in February and March 2008, Hillary Clinton had claimed that she landed under sniper fire in Bosnia as first lady in 1996. A video, and even her account in her autobiography *Living History*, demonstrated that this recollection wasn't factual. She later said that she had misspoken. But then on April 10 at more than one campaign stop in Indiana, when no one else was still talking about this error, Bill Clinton criticized the media's coverage of it. And, in making this unhelpful defense, he called attention to his wife's age and resulting forgetfulness as he compared her to younger reporters: "When they turn sixty, they'll forget things too." By the last stop of that day, Bill Clinton was no longer mentioning Bosnia; he told reporters that his wife had asked him to stop doing so and that he had said, "Yes, ma'am," as though she was older, his own mother, attempting to reform his manners. Of his various attempts to defend her that day, Cynthia Tucker of the *Atlanta Constitution* commented that "outbursts like that made me wonder whether, subconsciously, he was trying to sabotage her," a point that could be made about Bob Dole as Elizabeth Dole campaigned for the presidency in 2000.[79]

While Bill Clinton made mistakes in his opposition to Obama and in his support of his wife and himself, he also commented in a non-spousal manner about his wife's chances in the race, as Bob Dole had done also. Before the primaries in Ohio and Texas, Bill said that Hillary had to win both states to stay in the race, and he thus speculated about the possible end of her candidacy.[80] Though she ultimately did win both of these primaries, his widely reported declaration made her route to the nomination seem less sure, as though one state in the wrong column could spell the end, certainly not what political spouses would generally claim.

In 2008, the coverage ceded to Bill Clinton seemed to be less about his sex life than it had been in her Senate race, but instead it concentrated on his need to portray himself as the thoroughly popular president, able to control the vote of African Americans as well as the depiction of past events. As a former president, he seemed subsumed by his record, his popularity, and his need to be right—and he seemed to subsume her. Like Bob Dole when his wife ran for the presidency, Bill Clinton appeared to be working against Hillary, as many commentators at the time noted. "Every time she seems to get some traction," Cokie Roberts asserted, "Bill Clinton comes along and says something that throws her off again.... He secretly feels more comfortable when the power is in his hands."[81] Blythe Stanfel described Bill Clinton in the *Des Moines Register* as "good ole wanna-be-a-candidate-again hubby." Michael Tackett in a widely reprinted article concluded, "Though his name is not on the ballot, the race for the Democratic presidential nomination seems in many ways to be about Bill Clinton."[82] After Hillary Clinton conceded on June 7, 2008, many commentators, such as Rekha Basu, commented on his role in the campaign's demise: "Some of us had cheered on Hillary for emerging from the humiliations her husband had dealt her in the White House and building her own political career. But then, there he was trying to control the race, playing entitled, petulant bully and raising concern that all the things that made people queasy when he was president could resurface when she was. Could keeping him at bay in her race have solved that for Hillary? I don't know, but it could have helped."[83] As Rebecca Traister commented in 2010, "Maybe if she hadn't been married to Bill, the outcome of the election might have been different."[84]

Running for President, 2016

When Hillary Clinton ran for the presidency again in 2016, against a very different man in the general election than Barack Obama in the 2008 Democratic primary, her marriage would again create a difficult narrative, with the stress on sex as in 2000 but with her own construction of herself as victim no longer applicable—instead Donald Trump would construct her as her husband's enabler of sexual harassment, adultery, and rape.

A complex situation as well as campaign errors would be part of the loss in 2016. In an interview published in April 2017, Hillary Clinton said of her defeat that "certainly misogyny played a role.... That just has to be admitted," with voters having reservations about a woman in power.[85] In her book *What Happened*, she claimed further that with so much tumult in people's lives, with uncertainty in the Middle East and in the economy, a woman president seemed like a particular risk. She also noted her e-mail predicament and FBI announcements on that subject in the last week of the campaign as well as Trump's appeal to disenfranchised voters. But her book also lists her own mistakes, like her "basket of deplorables" remark concerning half of Trump's supporters and her decision to lie about having pneumonia, choices that made her seem less empathetic and trustworthy, extending long-term doubts about her. She also admitted that her heavily nuanced policy arguments caused her to lack one consistent, appealing message.[86] But as she considered what happened during the

2016 election, Hillary Clinton did not attribute any blame to her husband. Though her staff worried about Bill Clinton's excesses from 2008, in 2016 they sought to take advantage of his still formidable speaking skills and popularity. "There's debate about how publicly to use him," Julian Epstein, a Democratic strategist, had declared in October 2015. "The point of view that's winning, and that I agree with, is that you don't want to make the Al Gore mistake and keep your most gifted surrogate and campaign mind on the sidelines during the most formative months."[87]

Making Bill Clinton central to the effort created an association with his policies, a liability with Bernie Sanders attracting voters on the left. Some of his accomplishments—welfare reform, telecommunications and financial deregulation, NAFTA, DOMA—had become targets as had his "don't ask, don't tell" policy on gays in the military. As a *USA Today* columnist judged the situation, "Hillary Clinton is running against her husband's legacy almost as much as she is running against her GOP opponents."[88]

Besides having his legislative choices to explain and even run against, Hillary Clinton also dealt with the actuality of her husband loosed on the campaign trail, as had occurred in 2008. As this campaign commenced, he began making self-deprecating comments, like Bob Dole, about his reduced role and influence. In 2014, Bill Clinton told *The Denver Post* that in his wife's political stratagems he was "a bit player, and whatever she wants to do is fine by me." In October of 2015, he said of his reduced role that "I'm kind of like an old horse that they keep in the stable." Critics of both political parties concluded that this bit part to which he kept referring would actually be impossible for him.[89]

As Bill Clinton campaigned, he continued with other unfortunate habits from 2008. He publicly denigrated his wife's chances for success, by demarcating her road to failure, as he had in 2008 and Bob Dole did in 2000. In 2015, when asked about his wife's chances, Bill Clinton commented that there was no sure path, indeed that "a thousand things could happen" during the race. Besides alluding to the "long road" ahead for her, he called attention to the difficulties of attempting to replace a fellow Democrat: "It's hard for any party to hang on to the White House for 12 years."[90] Oddly, he also continued his criticisms of Obama, as though he still needed to assert his superiority as well as his wife's. At a campaign event in Spokane on March 21, 2016, in a construction of recent history that his aides later said was unintended, he declared that "If you believe we can rise together, if you believe we've finally come to the point where we can put the awful legacy of the last eight years behind us and the seven years before that where we were practicing trickle-down economics, then you should vote for her."[91]

As Bill Clinton campaigned, he still seemed to need to be the unquestioned, foremost leader. As Jonathan Allen and Amie Parnes commented, "Bill's temper, never far from the surface, would emerge time and again in the 2016 campaign."[92] In February 2016, his temper flared at a rally in Bluffton, South Carolina, when a former Marine interrupted his speech. The veteran asked him to address what his wife was going to do about problems within Veteran's Affairs. Instead, Clinton turned the question back on him: "What do you think should be done with the VA?" The Marine replied that "the thing is, we lost four lives in Benghazi, killed, and your wife tried to cover it up." Clinton then became visibly angry as though the man had no right to make such an assertion. "You listen to me now," Clinton shouted. "I'm not your commander in chief anymore but if I were, I'd tell you to be more polite and sit down."[93]

In April 2016, Bill Clinton got into a more protracted altercation, with two Black Lives Matter protestors who interrupted him at a recreation center in Philadelphia. One held a sign with "superpredator," echoing a remark that Hillary Clinton made in a 1996 speech about violent crimes committed by the worst felons: a speech and descriptor that she had apologized for in February 2016. As he had in 2008 about Bosnia, Bill reopened a difficult issue when he stepped up to defend this depiction, employing racial stereotypes: "I don't know how you would characterize the gang leaders who got 13-year-old kids hopped up on crack, and sent them out in the streets to murder other African American children. Maybe you thought they were good citizens—she didn't." By fanning this previously died-down flame, Bill Clinton portrayed his wife as stereotypically judgmental on the subject of race and crime, and thus as alienated from many voters and from the progressive wing of the Democratic Party.[94]

Along with making Hillary Clinton seem judgmental and conservative, Bill Clinton wielded his power as a past president in a heavy-handed manner, certainly well beyond what any other candidate's spouse could or would do. On June 27, 2016, just weeks prior to the Democratic National Convention, he talked to Attorney General Loretta Lynch on a tarmac in Phoenix, Arizona, for approximately thirty minutes—when she had power over whether his wife would be charged in the e-mail case. The meeting raised questions concerning the Department of Justice's impartiality in the investigation and Bill Clinton's dual roles of political spouse and powerful ex-president.

Though Bill Clinton created challenges for the 2016 campaign through his anger and his assertion of authority, he caused a greater problem, with Trump as Hillary's opponent, with his sex life.

Trump's own pronouncements on women marked his campaign from the beginning. When Megyn Kelly hosted the first Republican debate, on August 7, 2015, she questioned Trump on accusations of sexism against him. After the debate, Trump responded on Twitter by just slightly demurring from calling her a bimbo: "I refuse to call Megyn Kelly a bimbo, because that would not be politically correct. Instead I will only call her a lightweight reporter!" Later, in a CNN interview, he suggested that her style of questioning resulted from her menstrual bleeding: "You could see there was blood coming out of her eyes. Blood coming out of her wherever." On September 9, 2015, in another debate, he employed body rhetoric to insult Carly Fiorina and other women politicians: "Look at that face. Would anyone vote for that? and "Can you imagine that, the face of our next President? I mean, she's a woman, and I'm not supposed to say bad things, but really, folks, come on. Are we serious?"[95]

Trump's outrageous remarks, combined with his sexual past, seemed to make a space for Hillary Clinton to gain the high ground, as the moral leader, with a natural appeal to women. But then there was her husband—as Trump skillfully brought Bill's proclivities back to the forefront to overshadow his own. In December of 2015, Hillary Clinton responded to Trump's use of the word "schlonged" to describe her loss to Obama in 2008: "It's not the first time he's demonstrated a penchant for sexism." That same month, Trump tweeted that "Hillary Clinton has announced that she is letting her husband out to campaign but HE'S DEMONSTRATED A PENCHANT FOR SEXISM, so inappropriate!" He followed up the next day, on *Fox and Friends Weekend*, by accusing Hillary Clinton of playing the "woman's card" and by declaring that her husband was "fair game because his presidency was really considered to be very troubled, to put it mildly, because of all the things that she's talking to me about." He continued on *Face the Nation* on January 3, 2016, claiming that "it hasn't been a very pretty picture for her or for Bill. Because I'm the only one that's willing to talk about his problems. I mean, what he did and what he has gone through I think is frankly terrible, especially if she wants to play the woman card."

As Trump made claims about Bill Clinton's sexual past and involvement in the current campaign, many reporters noted the logic in his remarks. In December 2015, *Washington Post* columnist Ruth Marcus asserted that Bill Clinton's sexual history, and especially his predatory behavior, did merit reexamination since he was campaigning as his wife's surrogate. Trump had denigrated particular women because of their looks, the article continued, but Bill Clinton had preyed upon women, and in a workplace setting where he was by far the superior. The comparison of the two men was uncomfortable for Hillary Clinton supporters, Marcus noted, but accurate.[96]

Into the spring of 2016, through her advertisements, Hillary Clinton attempted to fire back on the subject of Trump's sexual history, thus countering claims that her husband was worse. One of her super PAC's ads, called "Speak," showed voters lip-syncing some of Trump's caustic remarks about women—about blood and Megyn Kelly, for example—with the tag line question of "Does Donald Trump really speak for you?"

And then Trump decided to reciprocate, again concentrating on Bill Clinton, but extending the accusations by claiming that his actual opponent was also involved in sexual offenses as his wife. On May 8, he tweeted that "Amazing that Crooked Hillary can do a hit ad on me concerning women when her husband was the WORST abuser of woman in US political history." And then on May 17, at a rally in Eugene, Oregon, he made an additional connection and claim: "Bill Clinton was the worst in history and I have to listen to her talking about it? Just remember this: She was an unbelievably nasty, mean enabler. And what she did to a lot of those women is disgraceful. So put that in her bonnet and let's see what happens."

On September 27, after the first debate, Trump quite publicly congratulated himself on not bringing up Bill Clinton's specific "sexual indiscretions" and hinted that he was considering "rough attacks" on Hillary and her family: he was thus praising his own tact and preparing for so much more. "I was going to hit her with her husband's women and I decided I shouldn't do it because her daughter was in the room," he told Fox News. His comments were widely interpreted as a threat to name these women in future debates, tying Bill's infidelities to Hillary's willingness to protect and enable him. Asked if such accusations would expose him to attacks about his own marital and sexual history, Trump replied, "No not at all, I have a very good history."

Other moments seemed to give Hillary Clinton the upper hand with women voters. During that first presidential debate, she accused Trump of having called Alicia Machado "fat," as well as "Miss Piggy" and "Miss Housekeeping," after she won the Miss Universe pageant in 1996, which he then owned. At the debate, Trump declared that Machado had increased in weight from 118 pounds to more than 160 pounds during her reign: "She was the winner and she gained a massive amount of weight, and it was real problem for us." In a series of tweets, he claimed further that Machado had starred in a sex tape, an accusation for which there was no evidence. As a next step Clinton released ads in which Machado discussed the cruel treatment that she endured throughout the year of her reign.

And then, Trump had a worse problem with his own sexual proclivities. On October 7, 2016, in a video obtained by the *Washington Post* that immediately became infamous, he discussed "grabbing (women) by the pussy" and that "when you're a star, they let you do it." Speaking with Billy Bush, then a host for the TV entertainment show *Access Hollywood*, Trump also talked about an unnamed woman: "I moved on her and I failed. I'll admit it. I did try and f–– her. She was married. And I moved on her very heavily.... I moved on her like a b––, but I couldn't get there."

Here was a low, a possible election changer. But Trump employed the same defense that he had before: that both of the Clintons were worse. He was just engaging in "locker room talk," he argued, but she was enabling a rapist, as a colluder in crimes.

And then Trump went on the attack again, quite publicly and dramatically, concerning Bill Clinton's sexual history and Hillary's long-term involvement with it. Right before the debate on October 9, he staged an event, purportedly a news conference, with three women who had accused Bill Clinton of sexual harassment and of rape along with a fourth woman who was raped by a man that Hillary Clinton defended in 1975. To introduce this session, Trump again apologized for his "locker room talk" of years earlier and then asserted that Bill Clinton had been abusive to and violent with women—and that three of them were there. Then, during the debate, this foursome sat together in the hall. Though Hillary Clinton prevailed in most of the night's questions, Trump's manipulation of the media overshadowed her performance, blunting the effect of the *Access Hollywood* video and taking away the argument that she was fully on the side of women.

In the campaign leading up to the 2016 election, Hillary Clinton had been seeking the support of women, and certainly she would have expected to inhabit the higher ground of respect and advocacy as she opposed Donald Trump. But she was not to have it, with her husband's sexual history being effectively made into her own. While Bill Clinton's need to be the unquestioned leader caused problems throughout the campaign, so certainly did decades of his sexual choices.

For both Elizabeth Dole and Hillary Clinton, political husbands ceded opportunities to move from careers in law and public service to national campaigns—to start their elective histories at the high level of the U.S. Senate and the presidency, not with a local or state office. Both husbands ceded access to fundraising sources, to endorsements from influential politicians, and to experienced campaign staffers. But, as happened with widows, this support made both women seem less than serious, as though they had glommed onto powerful men, trading on who and what these men knew. And very much alive husbands could create difficulties for their wives that widows did not encounter. These men might be intimidated by their wives' success, and thus do as much to hurt their careers as to help them, by commenting on their wives' chances for victory, for example, or even advocating for other candidates. Additionally, there was the complication of the husbands' insecurities, their continued assumption of authority, their unpopular policy decisions, and their sex lives. Both Elizabeth Dole and Hillary Clinton, certainly with different specifics involved, saw a husband's entire history, both the good and the bad, become their own.

Six

Family Members in Generations

Women coming into office as widows and as wives enter a complex space, in which they may have connections and fund raising help, but they may also be held responsible for everything that the spouse has done, in the legislature and in the bedroom. Both widows and wives have faced judgments, as lesser, as undeserving, even as they have proven themselves in office.

Along with widows and wives, entering politics through connections with their spouses and in-laws, another big group has come into the American power structure through their own families, as the appendix indicates. As Kenneth Prewitt describes in *The Recruitment of Political Leaders,* even democracies involve an elite, and one of the most direct means of obtaining elite status has been through family membership."[1] And Judith Horstman has said of the generations of Americans entering politics from the same families that "they tend to think of it as going into the family business—only the business happens to be running the country and they have to be elected to get into it. Congress is loaded with kin, including sons and daughters who grew up in the trade, licking stamps and stumping the campaign trail with their parents."[2]

Though in 1984 Horstman did mention daughters, most of the research on this phenomenon has concerned sons. When Stephen Hess wrote about American political dynasties in 1966, he considered seven hundred families and concentrated on men in office. Indeed his definition of a dynasty seemed to preclude women if they had a married name: "A dynasty is any family that has had at least four members, in the same name, elected to political office." In this book, he spoke of the job of elite women as producing sons: "The dynastic daughters were used as pawns in this chess game of political eugenics."[3] In the 2016 edition, he continues to use the phrase "the same name" to define the political family although he does note the "mix and match" that can occur through families joined by marriage.[4]

While much more research has concerned men, ever since women could run for office, they have been launched from political families, involving grandparents, parents, aunts and uncles, cousins, brothers, and sisters in office. Through the decades women have entered politics with the backing of their own families, not just those of their husbands and in-laws, and some of these political dynasties have been formed by women. These supportive groups have ceded power both in many generations and in one.

Three Generations and More

Some families with many generations of political involvement have only recently fostered careers for women. Beginning with P. J. Kennedy, a member of the Massachusetts House of Representatives from 1884 to 1889 and of the Massachusetts Senate from 1889 to 1895, fifteen members of the Kennedy family have been elected to office or appointed as ambassadors. At least one Kennedy family member held elective office in every year between 1947 and 2011, and from 2013 onwards, thus for more than a quarter of the nation's existence, now including Ted Kennedy, Jr., a member of the Connecticut Senate from 2015 to 2019; and Joe Kennedy, III, a member of the U.S. House from Massachusetts since 2013, re-elected in fall 2018. In earlier generations of the Kennedys, men had been encouraged into politics and women into helping their husbands, raising families, and engaging in philanthropy. As Barbara Perry, Director of Presidential Studies at the University of Virginia's Miller Center, remarked concerning Rose Kennedy, she was a highly ambitious family leader and campaigner, daughter of the mayor of Boston, who "trained her sons to be leaders, her daughters to raise lots off Catholic children."[5] Not until 1995 was the first female Kennedy elected to office: Robert Kennedy's daughter, Kathleen Kennedy Townsend, served as lieutenant governor of Maryland from 1995 to 2003. As she said in a phone conversation with me, in her first elections in Maryland, the state's Democrats needed a Kennedy and wanted a woman; she loved campaigning and getting things done; and her connections helped make her a leading fundraiser even as she dealt with criticism for exploiting the family name.

Like the Kennedys, many other multi-generational families that began with men have included women in office in their latest generations. Gwen Graham's grandfather, Ernest R. (Cap) Graham, was a Florida state senator; her father, Bob Graham, a Florida state representative, Florida state senator, governor of Florida, and U.S. senator from Florida. Gwen served as a U.S. representative from 2015 to 2017 and ran for governor of Florida in 2018, losing in the Democratic primary to Tallahassee mayor Andrew Gillum. Susan Molinari's grandfather, Italian-born Republican politician S. Robert Molinari, was a state assemblyman. Her father, Gaetano Victor "Guy" Molinari, served as a U.S. representative and then as borough president of Staten Island. Susan Molinari secured election to the New York City Council in 1986 and then to the U.S. House in 1990 to replace her father, when he sought the position of borough president. She served in the House for three terms before becoming vice president for public policy at Google, a job that she held until November 2018.

Some candidates have had three generations of politicians in both their own and in their husband's families. Christine Todd Whitman, governor of New Jersey from 1994 to 2001, had a grandfather, John R. Todd, who was a delegate to three Republican national conventions, beginning in 1928. Her father, Webster B. Todd, chaired the New Jersey Republican Party for many years and her mother, Eleanor Schley Todd, was a Republican national committeewoman. Her husband's grandfather, Charles S. Whitman, served as governor of New York, and her brother-in-law, Charles S. Whitman, Jr., as a New York judge.

Some families with a long history in American politics have involved women in office not just recently but from the first decade of suffrage. Ruth Bryan Owen, in 1929, was elected as Florida's (and the South's) first woman in the U.S. House. Her father was William Jennings Bryan, U.S. representative from Nebraska; U.S. secretary of state; and a Democratic nominee for president. Her grandfather Silas Bryan had been an Illinois state senator and judge, and her uncle Charles W. Bryan served as governor of Nebraska. After Owen entered the House, the family in politics continued with her daughter Rudd Brown serving as a delegate to the Democratic National Convention in 1956 and 1960 and as a candidate for U.S. representative from California in 1958 and 1960.

These multi-generational political families provided opportunities for unconventional paths to office, otherwise difficult to access. Choosing to enter national office late in life, as few could have done, Millicent Vernon Hammond Fenwick came from a long line of American political elites, reaching back to John Stevens, a member of the Continental Congress from New Jersey. She was the daughter of New Jersey Assemblyman Ogden H. Hammond, later ambassador to Spain, and sister of U.S. Vice Consul Ogden H. Hammond, Jr. During the 1950s, Fenwick became involved in politics through the civil rights movement. As a member of the U.S. Commission for Civil Rights, she sponsored meetings of low-income housing residents in Newark and worked to secure job training, mentoring programs, and college scholarships for them.[6] She was elected to the New Jersey General Assembly in 1969 and the U.S. House in 1974, at age sixty-four, where she served for four terms, advocating for control over lobbyists and interest groups, labeled by Walter Cronkite as "the conscience of Congress."[7]

While some of these multi-generational families formed by men helped women to enter politics in recent generations, others involved women in initiating family power. Thelma Engstrom served as an Alaska Territory representative, in the state House, from 1947 to 1949. Her son, Elton Engstrom, Jr., became an Alaska state representative and state senator. And a granddaughter in this family, Catherine Nora (Engstrom) Muñoz, became an Alaska state representative in 2009, remaining in the state House until 2017, where among other legislation she supported the inclusion of sexual orientation in Alaska's and the nation's anti-discrimination laws.

In some families, women in the earliest generations served in state offices with their descendants headed to national office. Ralph Herseth was born in Houghton, South Dakota, his father a Norwegian immigrant. He served as governor from 1959 to 1961; and his wife, Lorna Herseth, as South Dakota's secretary of state, from 1974 to 1980. Their son Ralph Lars Herseth was a member of the South Dakota House and Senate. And his daughter Stephanie served in the U.S. House from 2005 until 2011, advocating on the Agriculture Committee and the Natural Resources Committee for the farms, ranches, and national forests of her state. In 2007, she extended the political family connections when she married Max Allen Sandlin, Jr., a U.S. congressman from Texas.

Though some of these families didn't involve women in their first generation, these politicians could be key to creation of an ongoing power base. In Tennessee, Robert Clement served as mayor of Dickson, Tennessee, and then as city attorney for forty years. His son Frank became governor of the state while his daughter, Anna Belle Clement O'Brien, first served as Frank's chief of staff and then as a member of the Tennessee House, in office from 1975 to 1977, and the Tennessee Senate, from 1997 to 1991. Her marriages further involved her in state politics: first to A. W.

Lucas, mayor of New Johnsonville, Tennessee, and then to Charles H. O'Brien, a Tennessee state senator who later became chief justice of the Tennessee Supreme Court. In a third generation of this political family, she was the aunt of Tennessee Regulatory Authority chair Sara Kyle, of U.S. Congressman Bob Clement, of Court of Appeals Judge Frank Clement, Jr., and of state senator Jim Kyle. In the Nashville *Tennessean*, in an article entitled "In a 'Man's World,' O'Brien Was Political Pioneer," reporter Chas Sisk stated that "Mrs. O'Brien helped found a Tennessee political dynasty."[8] As the Nashville *Post* commented, she was known as "the first lady of Tennessee politics, coming from a family that was arguably the state's version of the Kennedys in terms of political influence."[9]

In families with a long history of political involvement, women have been key members, not just in the latest generations but from the beginning of women's suffrage. This power base was not just delivered to them or made available to them, but in many instances formed and extended by them as they worked for their states and the nation.

Two Generations

While political families of three or more generations have engaged women ever since they attained the vote, women have also flourished in political families of just two generations, with particular combinations ceding especially powerful opportunities.

The Clout of Grandparents, Long Ago in Office

Some of these two-generation connections involve a grandparent and granddaughter, with the aura of an earlier political figure ceding power—and enabling the candidate to avoid the possible complications of following a more recent relative into office.

These connections could involve grandmother and granddaughter. Kirsten Gillibrand's maternal grandmother was Dorothea "Polly" Noonan, a founder of the Albany Democratic Women's Club who became a leader of the powerful political machine of Erastus Corning, 2nd, a member of the New York Senate and then mayor of Albany for more than forty years. Besides becoming Corning's "closest confidante," Noonan served as a secretary to three senators and as a member of the National Democratic Committee. In the fall of 2018, Edie Falco played this influential political operative in an off-Broadway play, *The True.* Gillibrand has said that she learned about campaigning from Noonan: her grandmother, her "greatest political hero," taught Gillibrand how to be "a grassroots activist," lessons she used to secure support as she fought against sexual assault in the military and sexual harassment.[10] Beginning in her first year in office, Gillibrand established "Congress on your corner" events, what she described as "open substantive forums" held "at local grocery stores, book stores, farmers markets, coffee shops and community centers," these ongoing discussions of key issues reflecting her grandmother's style.[11]

Not only grandmothers but also grandfathers lent their experience and commitment to their granddaughters. Katherine Harris, Florida state senator from 1995 to 1999, Florida secretary of state from 1999 to 2003, and U.S. representative from Florida, from 2003 to 2007, is the granddaughter of Ben Hill Griffin, Jr., Florida state senator and representative, a prominent citrus grower and patron of college sports and higher education in the state. "With her name, political and family history in Florida," as the *South Florida Sun Sentinel* claimed, she was able to "leapfrog" other Republicans in the primary race for the U.S. House in 2002 though Democrats certainly had problems with her role, as Florida secretary of state, with hanging chads and the 2000 presidential election.[12]

Some of these women had the connection with a powerful grandfather as well as a large political family influential in both parties. Michelle Lujan Grisham, a Democrat who served as a U.S. representative from New Mexico from 2013 to 2019, is the granddaughter of Eugene Luján, judge of the Supreme Court of New Mexico and the first Latino to serve as chief justice. Her additional relatives, elected as Republicans in New Mexico, include great-uncle Manuel Luján, Sr., mayor of Santa Fe, and uncle Manuel Luján, Jr., who served as Secretary of the Interior under George Walker Bush after spending twenty years in the U.S. House. This powerful lineage now also extends to other Democrats from the state: to Ben Luján, New Mexico state representative, 1975–2012; and Ben Ray Luján, a U.S. representative from New Mexico since 2009. In 1989, at a Senate confirmation hearing for Manuel Luján, Jr., as Secretary of the Interior, Senator Pete Domenici jested that his state could claim three major political parties: the Democrats, the Republicans, and the Lujáns.[13]

This family power enabled Michelle Lujan Grisham to come back from a corruption charge as few politicians could do. After earning bachelor's and law degrees from the University of New Mexico, she became director of a program designed to provide legal services to seniors. She later became secretary of the New Mexico Department of Health, which had 3,800 employees and a $440 million budget. In 2007, the Justice Department filed a lawsuit against New Mexico in response to substandard conditions at the state-run Fort Bayard Medical Center. A settlement was reached four days later, but Lujan Grisham resigned within a month. She went on to secure a seat on a county commission, and then ran successfully for the U.S. House in 2012, with many newspapers criticizing her work at the Department of Health but praising her service on the county commission—and her family. Indeed, support for her claim that she could foster cooperation with members of both parties started with her own relatives in politics. And buttressing her reputation was the aura of her grandfather and his role on the Supreme Court. Lujan Grisham, an early supporter of the Hate Crimes Act in 2012 and co-sponsor of the Paycheck Fairness Act in 2017, was elected governor of New Mexico in November 2018.[14]

Mothers Starting Dynasties in Two Generations

While legendary grandparents could enable the transfer of a revered political past, another effective combination could involve parents, with the parental politician sometimes being the mother.

Some political families starting with the mother have stretched to a son. Carolyn Cheeks Kilpatrick, Michigan state representative from 1979 to 1996 and U.S. representative from Michigan from 1997 to 2011, is the mother of Kwame Kilpatrick, who served as the mayor of Detroit. Carrie P. Meek, U.S. representative from Florida, 1993 to 2003, is the mother of Kendrick Meek, who also served in the U.S. House from Florida. Patsy A. Danner, Missouri state senator, 1983 to 1993, and U.S. representative from Missouri, 1993 to 2001, is the mother of Steve Danner, who served as a Missouri state senator.

These connections in two generations have also led from mother to daughter. Chellie Pingree, the Maine Senate majority leader from 1996 to 2000 and a U.S. representative from Maine since 2009, is the mother of Hannah Pingree, a member of the Maine House from 2002 to 2011, where she served as majority leader and speaker, the youngest female speaker in the country. Chellie Pingree was re-elected in November 2018 to serve in the 116th Congress.

These connections could even involve a daughter's appointment to a seat that her mother had held. Barbara Snelling served as lieutenant governor of Vermont and then as a Vermont state senator. When she retired, her daughter Diane B. Snelling took over the Senate seat, appointed by

Governor Howard Dean to the remainder of the term. She remained in office from 2002 to 2016 and then became head of the Vermont National Resources Board.

Mothers and Fathers Starting Dynasties in Two Generations

Some of these family connections involved not just the mother but both the mother and father influencing the daughter, with the political family often dominant in a particular state. This dual influence can create a sense of assurance and purpose for both women and men of the second generation.

These families of mothers and fathers in politics can include stepmothers and stepdaughters, as in the case of the Roberts family in Oregon. State senator Frank L. Roberts remained in office from 1974 until his death in 1993. His second wife was Supreme Court justice Betty Roberts. His third wife, Barbara Kay Roberts, also launched a political career. When she married him, she was a stay-at-home mother advocating for educational programs for her autistic son; Frank Roberts listened and introduced a disability services bill in the legislature. His total involvement with his constituents impressed her—and provided something to emulate. A Democrat, Barbara Roberts served as majority leader in the Oregon House and won two terms as Oregon secretary of state before becoming governor. And Frank's daughter from his first marriage would also serve the state. Mary Wendy Roberts became the youngest woman, at twenty-eight, ever elected to the Oregon Legislative Assembly, serving first in the state House and then in the state Senate. In 1978, she became state labor commissioner, as position that she held for sixteen years. "The Roberts' surname has dominated Oregon's Democratic politics since the 1960s," a Salem, Oregon, paper declared, and it certainly had done so.[15]

In situations in which the mother might not remain in politics, the daughter could still profit from the example of both parents. Sheila Simon served as a city council member in Carbondale, Illinois, from 2003 to 2007, and then as lieutenant governor of Illinois, from 2011 to 2015, an office her father had held. Her mother was Jeanne Hurley Simon, an Illinois state representative from 1957 to 1961, and her father was Paul Simon, who also served as an Illinois state representative as well as lieutenant governor, state senator, U.S. representative, U.S. senator, and a candidate for the presidency in 1988. Jeanne Simon did not seek re-election after two terms, but instead chose to support her husband in his career. In a

phone conversation, Sheila Simon told me that her father's career had
helped her gain a reputation for "honesty and straightforwardness," traits
she tries to embody. As she also said, people might not agree with her
father, but they had a positive association with him, as honest and dedicated, and the memories people had of him helped her to start conversations with them. Since her mother remained as an active party member
and campaigner until her death in 2000, older women especially remem-
bered her, as a woman of loyalty and integrity. Friends said that Jeanne
Simon would have been "ecstatic" about her daughter's successes.[16]

These connections could enable a daughter to go further in politics
than the parents had. Mary Jo Copeland and Joseph Newton Copeland,
husband and wife, each served terms as mayor of Tecumseh, Oklahoma,
where they raised their daughter, Mary Fallin, who became governor of
the state. After beginning her career by working in several state agencies,
Fallin entered the private sector as a regional hotel manager and real estate
broker before launching a career in politics, which included serving as a
member of the Oklahoma House, as lieutenant governor of Oklahoma, as

Left to right: Paul Simon, Sheila Simon, Jeanne Hurley Simon, Martin Simon
and an unidentified bystander in 1968 (courtesy Jeanne Simon).

a member of the U.S. House, and then as governor from 2011 to 2019, when term limits kept her from running again. Especially in her first campaigns, she frequently mentioned the concern for families and the value of public service—and the political confidence—that she had gotten from her parents.[17]

Father to Daughter, Taking His Seat in Office

This connection in political families of two generations included not just mother or both parents with a daughter but father to daughter. "I find it off that female writers and women's magazines have spent years obsessed exclusively with mothers and daughters," Susan Molinari wrote in her autobiography, since many women have also come into politics and other careers through the influence of their fathers.[18]

The decision to follow the father directly into office can cede opportunity—but can also create a situation similar to what many political widows have experienced. The daughter might seem like a lesser politician, not fit to hold office beyond a short period of replacement.

Two years after the granting of suffrage, Republican Winnifred Huck, who had worked for her father, William Mason, as so many widows had with their husbands, was elected to fill the vacancy in the U.S. House created by his death. Propelled by sympathy and the desire to hold the seat, Illinois Republicans supported her in a special election to finish out his term. Huck defeated Democrat Allen D. Albert, with 53 percent of the vote.[19]

When Huck decided to run for a full term in 1923, voters did not judge her as an appropriate choice for an ongoing career. Her father had been re-elected after being one of fifty representatives who, including Jeannette Rankin, had voted against declaring war on Germany in April 1917. In her re-election campaign, Huck's own pacifism was deemed inacceptable, a sign of the softness of women: opponents constructed her as a dedicated wife and mother of four children but not a proper legislator. In the Republican primary for the full term, she lost the nomination to Henry R. Rathbone, a graduate of Yale, an attorney in Chicago, who had been a delegate to the Republican National Convention in 1916. As he ran for office, he touted his own family's past: the service of his grandfather, U.S. senator Ira Harris, and especially the valor of his own father, a military officer who, sitting in Lincoln's box at Ford's Theatre, had been seriously wounded when he attempted to stop John Wilkes Booth from getting away—Rathbone's family would act to protect the nation as Winnifred Huck would not. After defeating her, Rathbone held the seat until his death in 1928.[20]

Another controversial means by which a daughter could enter office was through appointment by her father. Frank Murkowski, U.S. senator from Alaska from 1981 to 2002, appointed his daughter to replace himself when he resigned the seat after being elected as governor, the first time that a daughter or son was appointed to the U.S. Senate. His daughter, Lisa Murkowski, had served as Alaska state representative, beginning in 1999, and had been elected majority leader of the state House. As a child, she was involved in campaigning and then began working for the state Republican Party, gaining a level of exposure that would stand her in good stead. Through those years, as she told me in a phone conversation, she viewed herself not as a possible candidate but as an "on the side." But her family experience did help her to realize that politicians were "all human beings," all with failings, people that she could decide to join. Her father's political style taught her to make a human connection, especially with the senator, ambassador, or president who might seem especially scary. As an example, she told me that when as a new senator she found herself in an elevator with Ted Kennedy, she connected with him through their shared love of dogs.

When her father appointed her to the U.S. Senate, he said that he wanted someone who would further his goals for the state, who shared his beliefs and basic philosophy. In interviews, Lisa Murkowski agreed with this assessment of their shared stances, as had so many widows: "We have a great deal in common besides sharing a name.... We share the same vision for the state. We share the same values."[21] Without the sympathy ceded to widows, much of the public response was negative. In a phone conversation with Kay Bailey Hutchison, she spoke to me of Murkowski's appointment as a two-edged sword, as an opportunity but also as a source of widespread complaint. As the *Los Angeles Times* reported similarly, "a big hoot and holler" occurred as a result of Frank Murkowski's decision. Tammy Troyer, head of the state's Democratic Party, declared in response that "this is supposed to be a democracy, not a nepotistic monarchy," and she sarcastically labeled the appointment as "a very nice gift from a father to a daughter."[22] During Murkowski's first term in office and afterwards, as she said in a phone conversation with me, "I put a high bar for myself," her plan to do "the best job for Alaskans." She told me that she tried to remind state's residents that she had served them well in the state House and that she was prepared to go forward: "watch as I work," she told them.

In 2004, when Lisa Murkowski ran for a full term, she still faced strong judgments about the initial appointment. One article claimed in a subheading that she "runs from nepotism charges," and it repeated the "nepotistic monarchy" descriptor. That year, Murkowski's opponents distributed bumper stickers that read "Yo, Lisa! Who's yer daddy?"; her Republican primary opponent repeatedly labeled her appointment, two years earlier, as a "scandal"; and Democrats put a highly publicized initiative on the ballot to stop Alaskan governors from making such inappropriate appointments in the future.

Additionally, negative reporting in 2004 dramatized a rift between father and daughter that had supposedly resulted from the "gift." Articles claimed that Frank Murkowski had lost popularity and that Lisa Murkowski was seeking to "distinguish and distance herself" from him. In response, she labeled the conflict as an invention of the press and her opponents, seeking to "fan the flame." But though she sought to deemphasize this conflict, it did seem to affect how she constructed her campaign in 2004: she circulated signs featuring her first name and not her last, and she repeatedly asked voters to move beyond their feelings about the initial appointment: "I haven't asked anybody to like it. What I'm asking is for people to judge me on my performance."[23] When her father was not re-elected in 2006, as she told me, there was negative fallout for her, and so she had to continue seeking a balance, of stating her respect for him while separating her career from his.

When Murkowski ran for a second full term, in 2010, she lost the Republican Party nomination to Tea Party candidate Joe Miller but, as a write-in candidate in the general election, she defeated both Miller and Democrat Scott McAdams, becoming the first senator elected by a write-in vote since Strom Thurmond in 1954. In my phone conversation with Kay Bailey Hutchison, she said that it was amazing that when losing the primary Murkowski ran as an independent: an act she described as "gutsy." The confidence that Murkowski demonstrated in accepting the initial appointment, in winning re-election as a Republican, and then in running successfully as a write-in candidate reflected her impressive record of service as well as power stemming ultimately not from party but from family.

Another path to office, instead of seeking the father's seat immediately or being appointed to it, was to run for it at a later date. Liz Cheney, for example, is the elder daughter of Vice President Dick Cheney and Lynne Cheney. She held several positions in the U.S. State Department during the George W. Bush administration. In 2013, she was briefly a candidate

Lisa Murkowski is greeted by her father Frank Murkowski as the results of the 2010 election show her in the lead (ZUMA Press, Inc./Alamy Stock Photo).

for the U.S. Senate in Wyoming, challenging a three-term incumbent, but dropped out of the race. In 2016, she won the U.S. House seat held by her father from 1979 to 1989, and she was re-elected in November of 2018. As her mother Lynne Cheney said of her own youth, "I think it's worth observing that women in my generation generally didn't have mentors. We didn't even know they were a good idea. And so we often didn't have anyone familiar with the challenges we were facing who could give us advice and guidance as we tried to deal with the obstacles we came up against."[24] Her daughter Liz Cheney would have more opportunities for mentoring, but also the powerful influence of family.

Father to Daughter,
an Influence on a Career

More common that being elected to a father's office or being selected by him to fill a seat is moving into politics with his backing and his connections, even if his first choice would not be for a daughter to run.

These connections might involve movement from state to state, with political confidence moving along with the candidate. In Iowa, Ralph Stark served as a Burlington city council member. After his daughter Kay Orr

Liz Cheney and her father Dick Cheney, 2011 (courtesy Dr. Robert M. Humphries).

moved with her own family to Lincoln, Nebraska, in 1963, she worked her way up through the Republican Party and was appointed in 1981 to fill a midterm vacancy as Nebraska state treasurer, a post to which she was elected in 1982. In 1986, she secured the Republican nomination for the Nebraska governorship by winning an eight-way primary and was elected, as the first Republican woman governor. As she indicated, her father had "talked about the joys of giving, and the rewards of your effort," about the need of politics to be grounded in local interests, his example influencing her as she made her own way in Nebraska.[25]

In some situations, a family established a political base and furthered a daughter's career, not through a father but a stepfather. Clare Boothe Luce first established a theatrical and writing but not a political career. She understudied for Mary Pickford on Broadway in *A Good Little Devil* and had a small part in Thomas Edison's 1915 movie *The Heart of a Waif.* As an adult, she reentered the theatrical world as a dramatist. After the failure of her initial playwriting effort, the melodrama *Abide with Me* (1935), she followed up with the popular satirical comedy *The Women.* In the 1930s, she wrote two more successful plays, *Kiss the Boys Goodbye* and *Margin for Error*, while also becoming a caption writer at *Vogue* and then associate and managing editor of *Vanity Fair.* In 1935, she married Henry Robinson Luce, the publisher of *Time* and *Fortune.* As a correspondent for *Life* magazine, a new publication that she suggested to her husband, she became a war journalist: her profile of General Douglas MacArthur appeared in the December 8, 1941, issue of *Life*, on the day after the Japanese bombed Pearl Harbor. After the United States entered the war, Luce toured military installations in Africa, India, China, and Burma, compiling a series of reports for *Life*.[26]

While Clare Booth Luce created a substantial career in drama and journalism, her stepfather, whom her mother married when Luce was sixteen, helped her to launch a political career. Albert E. Austin served as a health officer in Greenwich, Connecticut, a state representative, and then as a U.S. representative, from 1939 to 1941. In 1943, Luce won the same U.S. House seat than Austin had held, running against Leroy Downs who had defeated her stepfather two years earlier, and she served until 1947.[27] In her first election, she was criticized as the wife of the wealthy, reactionary, highly-anti–Rooseveltian Henry Luce, but her relationship to Austin was widely noted as a positive connection for a new politician, a sign of her independence from her husband.[28]

Help from Fathers, in Minority Families

While white fathers and stepfathers have enabled their daughters to enter politics, such help can also be crucial for women from African American and Latina families. Although Michelle Lujan Grisham represents a third generation in politics, in many families the involvement is of more recent origin. This power base, whether it engages one or several generations, can help women to cope with the realities of being "doubly disadvantaged" in politics, by gender and by minority status.[29]

Infrequently these power networks, which might extend to a son or daughter, begin with offices held by mothers as well as fathers. Arthur Anthony Morrell, for example, a member of the Louisiana House from 1984 to 2006, is married to Cynthia Hedge-Morrell, on the New Orleans City Council from 2005 to 2014. Their son Jean-Paul Morrell was a member of the Louisiana House from 2006 to 2009, succeeding his father, and has been a member of the Louisiana Senate since 2009. In my phone conversation with Hedge-Morrell, she discussed her experience as a school principal in New Orleans and as a lobbyist for education, leading to her election to the New Orleans city council. She also credited her work on her husband's campaigns as essential to her political career. When her son considered emulating them both as he followed his father into office, she encouraged him to do so if he had that "fire in his belly."

In minority families, as with white, the more common occurrence has been for initial acceptance to be of the man in office, which for minority candidates may have occurred fairly recently, and then for women to enter state and national offices in a second generation.

In African American families, a father or brothers have often preceded a daughter or sister in politics. Newton Jackson Ford, for example, was unsuccessful in his attempt to enter the Tennessee House in 1966, a difficult time for an African American to be elected in the state. But his sons would go into office: John, a member of the Tennessee state senate; Harold, a member of the U.S. House; and Edmund, a city councilman in Memphis. And their younger sister Ophelia would serve in the Tennessee Senate from 2005 to 2014. In Georgia, Cynthia McKinney, a state representative from 1989 to 1993, was in office along with her father, Billy McKinney, who had entered the state House in 1973. She then became a U.S. representative from Georgia, from 1993 to 2003 and 2005 to 2007, and a candidate for president with the Green Party in 2008.[30]

In recent generations, Latina families also have witnessed a path to power that engages father and daughter, leading to the first Latina women to assume federal office. Catherine Cortez Masto's father, Manny Masto, immigrated to the United States from Chihuahua, Mexico. After serving four terms as a Clark County commissioner and working as an attorney for the county, he became head of the Las Vegas Convention and Visitors Authority, where he wrote the slogan "what happens here, stays here" for his city. A major power in Nevada politics, he developed a longstanding friendship with Harry Reid, whose seat his daughter ultimately won.

After graduating from Gonzaga University's law school in 1990, Catherine Cortez Masto worked as chief of staff for Nevada governor Bob Miller, as a criminal prosecutor for the U.S. attorney's office in Washington, D.C., as an assistant county manager in Clark County, and as the attorney general of Nevada. She then was elected as the first Latina in the U.S. Senate. She ties her success to her father's lessons in politics: "He taught me that you need to be honest with people, and they'll respect you. They may not like what you say, but they'll respect you."[31] When she ran for office, his contacts across the state, as well as her own background, helped propel her to victory.

In the Roybal family, similarly, the father has helped to create opportunity for the daughter. Democrat Lucille Roybal-Allard is the daughter of Edward R. Roybal, a Los Angeles councilman and a U.S. representative from California. In 1990, the *Los Angeles Times* described him as "the leading Latino politician in Los Angeles": he was the first Latino on the city council, in the state assembly, and in the U.S. House from California.[32] In 1992, Lucille Roybal-Allard ran successfully for her father's U.S. House seat when he retired, becoming the first Mexican-American woman to serve in Congress, and has held it since then; she was re-elected in November of 2018. As a public relations officer and fund-raising executive without political experience, she recognized that her father's contacts and reputation helped her to campaign and win. Edward R. Roybal also helped to launch the political careers of other women, including Gloria Molina, who served on the Los Angeles County Board of Supervisors.[33]

Other Latinas have come into office from families engaged in politics before they immigrated to the United States. In 2012, Nydia Velazquez of New York City became the first woman of Puerto Rican descent to be elected to Congress. Her father, Don Benito Velazquez, was a sugarcane worker who became a labor organizer and founded a political party in Puerto Rico.[34]

Brothers and Sisters, on from the Rankins

While many families have established political power through parents and grandparents, politicians who are siblings, like Woodhull and Claflin and the Rankins, have also supported each other. As occurred in those two families, siblings often enable each other to overcome the challenges encountered by outsiders and move into the status of political elite.

Madeleine Kunin and Edgar May were born in Zurich, as outsiders, their mother a widow with two children, a Jew leaving Europe for her family's safety in 1940, when Edgar was eleven and Madeleine was seven. When the children came to Queens, they did not speak English. To support her family, their mother did sewing and babysitting, and she urged both of her children to take advantage of every opportunity in the United States.

As these siblings attempted to establish careers, May encountered more opportunities in their chosen field of journalism than his sister did. Kunin went to the University of Massachusetts in Amherst and the Columbia University School of Journalism, but found few opportunities for professional employment beyond part-time society-news assignments. Her brother, however, secured a job as a clerk at the *New York Times* while studying at Columbia, continued his journalism education at Northwestern University, and then worked as a reporter for small-town newspapers in Vermont and Massachusetts and for the *Buffalo Evening News*. In Buffalo in 1960, May investigated the New York state welfare system, publishing a fourteen-part series entitled "Our Costly Dilemma," for which he won a Pulitzer Prize. The series resulted in a book, *The Wasted Americans*, in 1964, which brought him to the attention of Lyndon Johnson, who hired him as inspector general of the Office of Economic Opportunity, helping to establish Head Start programs throughout the country. He also became deputy director of VISTA, a domestic version of the Peace Corps.

While May went further in journalism and in appointed service than his sister, her political career would first parallel and then exceed his. In 1972, Kunin was defeated in her bid to join the Burlington, Vermont, Board of Aldermen. Later that year, she became a Vermont state representative. Following her re-election in 1974, she served as minority whip of the state House. Her brother joined her in the Vermont House that year. After Kunin was elected to a third term in 1976, she became chair of the Appropriations Committee, the first woman to assume this position, which her brother later held. While May remained in the Vermont House until 1983, in 1978 Kunin was elected to the first of two terms as lieutenant governor. She did not run for re-election to this post in 1982, when her brother entered the state Senate, but instead ran for governor. Kunin was unsuccessful that year but in 1984 she won the first of her three terms as governor while her brother remained in the state Senate until 1991. No longer outsiders, both sister and brother took on extensive public service, investigating social and economic wrongs and attempting to right them. Ultimately, like Jeannette Rankin with her brother Wellington, Madeleine Kunin would rise further in elected office than Edgar May as both had long-term successful careers.

As siblings supported each other, through the generations, some of these outsider connections involved sisters who were more successful at securing office than Victoria Woodhull and Tennie Claflin. Raised by parents who immigrated from Mexico to Anaheim and secured jobs at a local manufacturing plant, the Sánchez sisters entered the U.S. House by repeatedly helping each other. In 1996, after working as a financial manager for the Orange County Transportation Authority and running her own consulting business, Loretta Sánchez defeated long-serving incumbent Republican congressman Bob Dornan by fewer than 1,000 votes even though he had a much stronger record of fund raising and establishment support. Her sister, attorney Linda Sánchez, worked on this campaign and again when Loretta ran in 1998. Linda then lectured around the country on how to mount a grassroots effort to seek office. In 2003, Linda also entered the U.S. House from California. In that campaign, the sisters appeared together at many events and in advertisements, asserting a joint power generally wielded by brothers, as an Associated Press reporter commented: "Brother acts come along fairly often in Congress, but never sisters—so far." During the campaign Linda's opponent Tim Escobar denigrated her through a comparison to Loretta: "If it wasn't for her sister, she would have no political qualifications." But these sisters helped each other to get elected and served in Congress together until 2016 when Loretta chose not to seek re-election, instead opting to run for the U.S. Senate, an election in which she was defeated by California Attorney General Kamala Harris.[35] Linda was re-elected in the fall of 2018, for the 116th Congress.

Women have come into local, state, and federal office with many connections to power, in families in which there might be three generations or more involved; two generations, either grandparents and grandchild or more commonly parents and child, and sometimes mother and daughter; and the one generation of siblings. This opening into the electoral elite began for women as soon as state and federal suffrage became law and they have participated, not just as wives and mothers but as elected officials, in building and extending political families. These relationships, from childhood onward, can cede the confidence and insider status crucial to independent political success.

Loretta Sánchez (left) and Linda Sánchez at the 2016 Democratic National Convention (Ron Sachs/CNP, dpa picture alliance/Alamy Stock Photo).

SEVEN

The Development
of the Connected Politician

Since the granting of suffrage, women have entered legislative office from political families, with assistance from the distant and revered grandparent, the fully involved parent, and the supportive sibling. These powerful connections in minority families have especially ceded opportunities in recent generations. Not just with the connection of widows and wives, not just through the power of in-laws, but with the backing of their own families, many women have launched careers that have opened up the possibility of elected office to others.

And what does a life and a career rooted in family involvement look like? Beyond the many types of families, beyond stereotypes or assumptions, are stories of the women themselves: of childhood involvements, of the assistance offered, of problems caused by this background and solved by it. These individual experiences have established codes and traditions for women, with various iterations ceding opportunity and independence.

From Childhood: Understanding
Political Realities

Beginning in childhood, members of political families can gain an awareness of political realities—including prejudice against women in office. Though bias voiced by fathers and grandfathers might be tough to hear, it could prepare potential candidates as they sought to enter the public arena.

William Jennings Bryan involved his daughter, Ruth Bryan Owen, in his own career, providing lessons that she would later use even though he would not have chosen such a path for her. When she was "just a girl," she often stayed with him in Washington as he served in the U.S. House from Nebraska. As a young woman, when he was the secretary of state, she wrote some of his speeches, kept unwanted visitors away from him, dealt with his correspondence, and studied legal and foreign policy issues on which he would need to voice an opinion. Then at age twenty-three, she served as secretary of her father's 1908 presidential campaign, receiving further "inside lessons on politics." But he was emphatically opposed to her going further instead of concentrating on being a mother and wife. He felt there were limits to what women could and should do: campaigning and working for others, yes; but running for office, no. Oddly enough, he had no negative view about his daughter making other risky or daring choices. During World War I, Ruth Bryan Owen served as a nurse in the Sinai and Palestine campaigns, from 1915 to 1918. She then became a pioneer in the film industry: writing and directing a feature film, *Once Upon a Time/Scheherazade* (1922), a tale involving infidelity, eastern harems, and scanty costumes. She also became a professor and member of the Board of Regents at the University of Miami in Florida and lectured across the country on the Chatauqua circuit, her topics including opposition to war, the power of the fine arts, and the history of profanity. She associated her public speaking skills with her father and with the family business, making the further connection that he would not: "Just as a soldier's daughter would have a certain familiarity with the usages of the Army, and a doctor's daughter with medical terms, I—the daughter of William Jennings Bryan—knew speaking and it led me into politics."[1]

To make a move into electoral politics, Ruth Bryan Owen waited until 1926, a year after her father's death. She lost that year in a race for a U.S. House seat by fewer than eight hundred votes. Then in 1927, as an administrator at the University of Miami, she played a significant role in the city when a hurricane hit; with an enhanced public reputation, she was elected, in November 1928, as Florida's (and the South's) first woman in the House.

Even though Owen's father would not have approved of her running for office, in this second race she used his methods and his commitment to independent judgment to win. She was, a reporter commented in 1928, "gifted with her father's eloquence, statesmanship and insistence on sticking to her side of a question." Employing his skill at emphasizing what was essential to the electorate, in this case hurricane protection, she won by bypassing the party and campaigning directly to the people, as her father had also done.[2] Her opponent William C. Lawson claimed that she had no right to run because she had married a British citizen, but she spoke at length about her family's long history and her allegiance to her country as well as her rights under the Cable Act of 1922, guaranteeing independent female citizenship. Employing the family speaking skill, as reporter Ruby Black noted, she made her case "most movingly."[3] Without any additional commentary on her citizenship, Owen ran for re-election in 1930, defeating Daytona Beach attorney Dewitt T. Deen by a wide margin in the Democratic primary and retaining the seat in the general election in the fall. In 1933, President Roosevelt appointed her as ambassador to Denmark.

In a later decade, elected to the U.S. Senate from Kansas in 1978, Nancy Landon Kassebaum also ran for office with political skills gained from her family and with a father who thought she shouldn't run. Her father was former Kansas governor Alf Landon. As she told a reporter, when she began considering a campaign, he frequently declared his opposition: "Dad had a lot of reservations about me running for the Senate in 1978 and being a woman.... He said so publicly, but I got him to stop that after I decided to run."[4] In March of 1978, she let reporters know that she hoped to win his endorsement, which she subsequently did; he then claimed that she had "a pretty good grasp of the political realities," certainly faint praise.[5] After she made her own way, however, he began to help her prepare for speeches and for press conferences, for assuming a position of power in the state.

Many other political families and fathers in later decades engaged daughters in campaigning, in the political life, but did not expect them to run for office. Mary Landrieu, a U.S. senator from Louisiana from 1997 to 2015, was encouraged by her father, Moon, a mayor of New Orleans as his son would become, to marry a politician, not to become one. Her brother Mitch was intended to carry on the family's political traditions.[6] Mary was expected not to run for office but to engage in politics as a supportive family member: at fifteen, when her father first ran for a seat in the state legislature, she helped him canvass local neighborhoods. At age twenty-five, in 1980, after working as a real estate agent, Mary Landrieu beat a three-term incumbent to become the youngest woman to serve in the state House, securing the seat that her father had occupied fourteen years earlier. She said that her father did not think she was serious about running until he saw five hundred signs in the neighborhood and knew that it was time to add his support.[7]

Some of this familial discouragement may have stemmed not from an assessment of a daughter's proper sphere but of the difficulties that

Mary Landrieu with her brother Mitch Landrieu in 2016 (Richard Ellis/Alamy Stock Photo).

this profession presented for women. In earlier generations particularly, a father might judge that there was no space for even the most well-qualified daughter in this world of male privilege, as in the case of Olin DeWitt Talmadge Johnston, who served first as governor of South Carolina and then as a member of the U.S. Senate from 1945 until his death in 1965. Beginning a career in the 1970s, ten years after his death, his daughter Elizabeth J. Patterson would become a councilwoman in Spartanburg, South Carolina, 1975–1976; a South Carolina state senator, 1979–1986; and a U.S. representative from South Carolina, 1987–1993. From childhood, Elizabeth Patterson's father quite publicly took her to work. While growing up outside Washington, D.C., she frequently came to her father's Senate office. In 1949, when she was ten, a *Life* magazine reporter wrote about her roller-skating around the Capitol building. Colleagues would find Olin Johnston temporarily absent, this feature article claimed, with Lizzie "in his place, her feet up on the desk."[8] Patterson became active in politics by managing her father's last campaign for the Senate in 1962 as well as working on Lyndon Johnson's 1964 campaign. In 1978, a reporter noted that she had "cut her teeth on politics" with her father and speculated that she would go further in electoral politics than just serving on a campaign staff, as indeed she did.[9] When Liz Johnston Patterson decided in 1986 to run for the U.S. House, she spoke about what her family had ceded to her. "My family taught me that our world is only as good as you make it, and one of the ways to make it better is to participate in the political process." Reflecting on her career in 2015, Patterson noted, "Our father used to say that he believed one of his daughters would marry a man who would become governor someday." But she felt that he held this opinion only because of the situation that he observed, with only one woman serving in the U.S. Senate, widow Maurine Brown Neuberger, in the 1960s. "Opportunities for women opened up in politics after he died," she said, "and I think he would have been pleased with my political career."[10]

And even though some fathers offered assistance, they might still prefer a son or grandson to enter politics. Susan Molinari thought of her father, Guy Molinari, as a role model and her supporter, as she wrote in her autobiography: "My father raised me to be tough in a world where people believe that women can't handle power. He taught me to take risks and be prepared to fail." Though father and daughter worked together closely, as she also noted, he would have preferred to focus his efforts on the political career of a grandson: "Despite his protestations to the contrary, he had always pointed me in that direction," she wrote, "although I suspect that he wouldn't have done so if I'd had a male heir to his mantle."[11]

Role Models

Though women in political families were not always encouraged to run for office, they were learning about government realities at home. Beyond providing realistic discouragement, family members could serve as role models, especially explaining what might be needed for a woman to enter a complex and often hostile space.

When Stephanie Herseth Sandlin considered running for office, as she said in my phone conversation with her, her father, Lars Herseth, who served for twenty years in the South Dakota House and Senate, had reservations about this choice. As the son of a politician, a member of the elite, he recognized the difficulties involved in appearing entitled, and he knew the challenge of raising money as a Democrat in a conservative state. Though he pointed out pitfalls, Sandlin's father also served as a mentor, offering specific advice, especially about the need to meet with state officials as she entered politics and make it clear that his battles were not automatically becoming hers.

Sandlin also had the guidance and support of an earlier generation, and especially of her grandmother, Lorna Herseth, who had been South Dakota's secretary of state and knew about how women and men might be treated in politics. In my phone conversation with her, Sandlin said her grandmother made her well aware of what had been achieved by her grandfather, Ralph Herseth, a governor of South Dakota, who died two years before Stephanie was born. Sandlin grew up spending summers with her grandmother, who told her stories about him and took her to see his portrait at the capitol.

But it was the grandmother who became a unique role model for her; they were commonly compared for their looks and for what she described to me as their "gumption." Lorna Herseth told Sandlin stories of her career achievements in the Depression, before her marriage: of attending Northern State Teachers College in Aberdeen, South Dakota, where she earned a two-year teaching certificate, of teaching in rural schools, and of serving as the Brown County superintendent of schools.

With her granddaughter, Lorna Herseth also emphasized what had been expected of women in her generation. After dating her husband for nine years, she married him and became a supportive political wife and first lady of the state, dutiful and unemployed. Ralph Herseth could be dictatorial, the grandmother made sure that Sandlin understood, with a big ego and the confidence needed for politics, not someone who would have been comfortable with a wife in this male game. In our phone conversation, Sandlin told me that state activists Sylvia and Goldie Wells approached her grandmother about the secretary of state job, four years after her husband's death. Sandlin was not sure whether they would have done so if her grandfather had still been alive or whether her grandmother would have declined. Lorna Herseth served as South Dakota's secretary of state from 1974 to 1980. She schooled her granddaughter in the realities of political careers and the entitlements of men while also encouraging the ambition that would be appropriate for women of a younger generation. In the year before she died, she was proud of her granddaughter's enrollment in law school, Sandlin declared in her phone conversation with me, and would have been proud of her political career.

Along with so many family connections, Sandlin had access to a wider group of political elites, from her own generation. She came to politics with more knowledge than many other women, but she recognized the difficulties even in her situation. She needed a group and knew how to reach out to one—to a friend from New York who was in politics; to both Tom Daschle's ex-wife and current wife, Laurie Fulton and Linda Hall; to Judy Olson, the South Dakota state party chair; to colleagues that she met at a leadership retreat—as she sought the confidence and organization that her grandmother and father had discussed as necessary in running for office.

The Dining-Room Immersion

Family mentors could teach lessons based on their own experience, but they could also provide daily immersion in a political conversation. Especially in the early decades of suffrage but afterwards as well, this absorption into the business could make a huge difference, to bring women into an elite circle. They might be criticized as too privileged, too dependent on family, but they did have the opportunity to enter a daily discourse of leadership.

According to one critic, Ruth Hanna McCormick's engagement in politics as a child merited a modern diagnosis—"father fixation"—but it also taught her all things Washington. When her father, Mark Hanna, came to the capital in January of 1897 as a senator from Ohio, having campaigned along with the new president William McKinley, he became one of the strongest forces in town. During the campaign, when Ruth Hanna McCormick was sixteen, her father lost his voice from so much public speaking, and she delivered his talk to hundreds of people from the back of a campaign train; she had heard the speech many times before. In Washington, McCormick served as host for the influential group meeting at the family home, the Little White House, thus heightening her own political awareness as she shared in the famous cooking of the family chef, Maggie Maloney, as a reporter noted about McCormick years later: "She now realizes that her future was largely wrought over Maggie's appetizing hash as she listened to the nation's 'best minds' discuss and decide this or that political issue."[12] Instead of going to college, Ruth became her father's assistant, analyzing upcoming legislation and sitting in the congressional gallery to take notes when committee meetings kept him from attending. An article about the campaigning that she did at the 1928 Republican convention when she was running for office commented that "she is no novice at a national convention. She had begun attending these gatherings in 1896, accompanying her father."[13]

Ruth Hanna McCormick learned politics through her husband's family as well as her own. She married Joseph M. McCormick, grandson of Chicago mayor Joseph Medill and son of U.S. Ambassador Robert Sanderson McCormick. Joseph McCormick became an Illinois state representative, U.S. representative from Illinois, and then U.S. senator from Illinois, from 1919 to 1925, the year that he died. Four years later, Ruth Hanna McCormick won the U.S. House seat that her husband had occupied before entering the Senate. About her approach to running for office that fall, she commented that "I didn't run for office as a woman. I ran as a daughter of Mark Hanna and the wife of Medill McCormick, and therefore equipped for office by heredity and training."[14] And as she campaigned, to extend the public memory and reach of her political heritage, she claimed that she had helped President McKinley to deal with the death of his daughters, both of whom had died in childhood in the 1870s. Thus, as she argued further, a lifetime of political conversations, with McKinley as well as her father and husband, had prepared her for her own career.[15]

Although McCormick stressed her positive family connections, some critics made her choices seem like just a neurotic need to enter the world of Dad. After she announced her intention to run for Congress in 1928, one widely reprinted article noted the intense bond that develops between fathers and daughters, the manic desire to please him, here pegged as her sole motivation for attempting to enter his profession. The article continued by asserting that modern psychology would label her ailment as a "father fixation." She was thus not establishing her own career, with family help, but trying desperately to be the good daughter.[16]

The importance of this immersion, however critics might deride it, has extended to women entering politics in recent decades. One result of these daily lessons, indeed, can be a reticence toward entering the career, as in the case of Jeanne Zeidler.

As members of the Socialist Party, both Carl Zeidler and his brother Frank served as mayor of Milwaukee, Carl from 1940 to 1942 and Frank from 1948 to 1960. In 1976, Frank ran for president as a candidate of the Socialist Party. His daughter Jeanne, a Democrat, served as mayor of Williamsburg, Virginia, from 1998 to 2010, her political life delayed by an engrained wariness about politics.

Having spent twelve years growing up with her father as mayor of Milwaukee, Jeanne Zeidler knew the difficulties of living under public scrutiny, the strain it can cause in a family. In a phone conversation with me, Zeidler said that with her father in the mayor's office, she had busy parents when she was in elementary and middle school and she sometimes felt that she was judged by their activities. In 1956 when she was nine, for example, she went to her father's inauguration but was criticized for skipping school, as though she had left for a Milwaukee Braves game—as though she was asserting an unfair sort of privilege. Her family also lived with the tension caused by Senator Joe McCarthy's opposition to much of what her father stood for: she was picked on at school and heard nasty comments when she answered the phone at home.

When Jeanne Zeidler moved from Wisconsin to Williamsburg in 1971 to study history at the College of William and Mary, she had non-political plans: "I always said I'd never do politics because I knew leading a public life can be difficult on families.... I wanted to study history and I started working in museums. I was lucky." She spent nine years at a small museum in Hampton, Virginia, before launching a twenty-one-year career as director of the Hampton University Museum.

Finally drawn into politics because of local issues affecting her own family, in 1994 Zeidler ran successfully for a city council seat and two years later was elected vice-mayor. In 1998, she became the city's first female mayor.[17] In a phone conversation with me, Zeidler said that even though she had felt negative about a political life, when she decided on it, her background was an asset. She understood the career since she had seen her father succeed at it. She also found her own priorities—a concern for schools, libraries, and a safety net for the poor—close to his socialism though she ran as a Democrat. With his career involving another state and era, she didn't encounter prejudice about his party or policy choices. Indeed, as she ran for office and people learned more about her father, his civil rights record became an asset, adding to the reputation she had developed in two decades at an historically black college. And her father, she told me, was proud of her public service, urged her to prepare carefully for each meeting and each constituency, and gave her great advice, including "don't eat all the food at all those lunches." Frank Zeidler had also given Jeanne a thorough childhood immersion in what a mayoral job took—enabling her to choose thoughtfully before taking it on and to succeed when she did.

Many other women found this daily involvement in politics to be essential to their development. In a phone conversation with me, Christine Todd Whitman talked about being exposed to politics all of her life, at a dinner table where the conversation often turned to current events and to the specifics of policy alternatives. And, like McCormick, Zeidler, and Whitman, Susan Molinari grew up in politics. The legend of her grandfather "loomed large, both in my household and on Staten Island." But it was Guy Molinari "who trained me for politics even before I was out of feetie pajamas." She described an early morning ritual: "At his insistence, every Sunday morning we'd sit around the breakfast table and elect a president for the day. I was expected to nominate myself and give a speech about why I wanted to be president." As she grew older, she went with her father to Republican meetings and conventions, "and I was pulled into a vortex of middle-aged men in suits arguing about tax policy and garbage collection and the stupidity of Democrats." Working with him in the U.S. House, as she volunteered in his office, she came to know "the members, the back halls, the traps and traditions." In Washington, she also worked at the Republican Governors' Association. As she wrote concerning these years of increasing involvement, "I grew up in politics the way some show-biz kids grew up in vaudeville."[18] In our phone conversation, she further stated that she would not have entered politics without this family and these experiences.

As in Susan Molinari's case, the type of support could change after the daughter entered office. When she ran for office the first time, Molinari faced in the primary an older Italian-American man, Frank Fos-sella, an incumbent and friend of her father, who pleaded with Guy Molinari to get Susan out of the race. But her father refused to take such a patriarchal step, and he told a reporter about her courageous choice: "Susan's district has the largest Italian American percentage of any district in the country. It wasn't the easiest thing for a young kid in her 20s to challenge an older male Italian." After she won this election for her father's seat, "my dad and I evolved into a kind of mini-political dynasty in the state of New York." They made "coordinated attacks" on issues they cared about: "we forged family loyalty into political teamwork."[19] At first, she called him a dozen times a day for help, a choice for which she also received the "father fixation" criticism. "Pundits disparaged me," she said of this period, "but I was acting like any kid who enters the family business or follows her dad into his profession." Later he would also ask for help, especially with issues, such as spousal abuse, affecting women and children.[20]

For the supportive parent like Guy Molinari, it could be hard to let the association end, as occurred when his daughter decided to leave the House in 1997. In a phone conversation with me, she said that leaving office was about her own priorities, about having a second child, not wanting to miss anything, as she could not insure with the endless career of Congress, a space without much flexibility. Her father understood her family concerns but was torn about her deciding not to run again: he had enjoyed their working together, and he was disappointed because he saw a future for her as governor or senator. But she had to decide on her own future.

Susan Molinari and her father Guy Molinari (© 1997 The Associated Press, photograph by Marty Lederhandler).

Power of the Name

After a politically connected woman decided to embark on a political career, one of her first decisions and one of the first complexities might come from the matter of her name. In employing this family identifier, a candidate asserted her own history, certainly, but also a center of power beyond her political party.

A positive connotation with the name can be a key element of political success for men and certainly for women who might seem like a less likely electoral choice. As Martha E. Kropf and John A. Boiney in *Women and Congress* note, "the step from recognizing a candidate's name to associating that name with some essentially positive cognition is a vital one if support for her or him is to follow"; a likeable fact or two added to an esteemed last name can create "a reasonably well-developed set of favorable cognitions."[21] Though some critics might denigrate this very public connection or label it as a father fixation, the name can matter.

Women who have taken their non-political husbands' names might also employ their birth names to make the family connection clear. In 1978, Nancy Landon Kassebaum was legally separated from her husband

Philip when she ran for the Senate from Kansas, but not yet divorced. She chose to use her full name, as she indicated, to take advantage of the political fame of her father, Alf Landon, who had been governor of the state and a presidential candidate.[22] Newspaper articles about her campaign began with titles like "Daughter of Alf Landon Enters Race"; some papers simply referred to her as "Alf's daughter" without citing her full name.[23] In her conversations with reporters, Nancy Landon Kassebaum did not shy away from the family legacy: in her first campaign, when a critic claimed that she would have been nowhere without the name, she replied that "it has been said that I am riding on the coattails of my dad, but I can't think of any better coattails to ride on."[24] To another reporter, she spoke further, "Mrs. Kassebaum candidly admitted she'll try to capitalize on whatever political value the Landon name still has in Kansas." And she said additionally of her father's name, "'I'm proud of it. I'm proud of dad's political contributions. I want to continue that tradition." In her campaign slogan, she again employed this association: "A Fresh Face, a Trusted Kansas Name." In 1984, in Kassebaum's second Senate campaign, she still employed her birth name and married name. And she wore a campaign button from her father's 1936 presidential campaign, "Deeds Not Deficits." As she said, "Dad didn't do too well with it in '36, but I think this is one of our big concerns for all of us in the next six years."[25]

Like Kassebaum, other candidates have employed the family name along with slogans that emphasized the connection. When Kathleen Brown successfully ran for state treasurer of California in 1990, for example, she used the catch phrase of "A Brown of Another Color," thus emphasizing her own priorities as well as her father and brother, Pat Brown and Jerry Brown, both governors of the state.

Nancy Landon Kassebaum and her father Alf Landon, 1997 (Kansas State Historical Society).

In recent decades and heading into the 2018 elections, another politician recognizing the power of the name has been Gwen Graham. The oldest of Bob Graham's daughters, in 1979 at age sixteen, she went with her father to Tallahassee when he was elected governor. In 2003, she worked in his campaign when he ran for president.[26] That year, she spoke for him at state party conventions, as his surrogate, declaring that "Bob Graham knows how to win Florida. He's the candidate the White House fears the most."[27] When her father dropped out of the race following a heart attack, Gwen Graham joined Howard Dean's presidential campaign. After John Kerry ultimately secured the Democratic Party's nomination, she went to work for him while also consulting on a replacement for her father in the Senate. In that campaign, as Graham's daughter, she secured attention for her own political ambitions "down the road," as other campaign workers would not.

As Gwen Graham traveled further down that road, campaigning for the U.S. House in 2013, she relied on "her father's vast network of political contacts." As a reporter wrote, "she acknowledges the huge asset of her name" and didn't mind the newspaper designations of "Bob Graham's daughter" and "the daughter of one of Florida's most famous families." She had her own record and plans, the article continued, though "name recognition, however, is an elixir in politics. And a big help in Florida."[28] As reporters noted, father and daughter campaigned together, "with the elder Graham, then 78, still a magnet for voters in his daughter's 2nd Congressional District." As her father said at the time, combining their careers, "It's wonderful to be able to watch your children perform at something you are interested in." In that election, Tea Party opponent Steve Southerland accused her of being a "liberal Washington insider," but she beat him, one of the few victories for Democrats in the state that year, the family name a well-deployed asset.[29]

Though the family name could be positive, it has to be managed carefully, especially with the press. In their first elections particularly, even as the name led to widespread coverage, women candidates might be disparaged for availing themselves of family power, for being daddy's girl, an extension of the "father fixation" accusation with which Ruth Hanna McCormick had coped.

The connection, especially to a father, can provide an easy target for an opponent when a young woman first runs for office. When Mary Landrieu ran for the Louisiana House in 1980, Republican opponent Clyde Bel made radio advertisements featuring her inexperience and her dependence on Moon Landrieu. As reporters repeated this criticism, however, they also recognized the power of the name: she was "a very young, giggly girl out of New Orleans who had a last name that people knew all over the state."[30] When Susan Molinari first ran for her father's seat in the U.S. House, she was derided as "this 35-year-old inheritor of the 'Molinari machine.'"[31] Her father was then called "an old-timer on the rubber bagel circuit," and she was labeled as "Guy's Doll." As she recalled about this judgment, "I was a nobody wannabe who everyone assumed was trading on the fact that she was Guy Molinari's daughter."[32] As the *Los Angeles Times* claimed about her experience as well as her father's influence, "Having served five years on the City Council, she had an independent reputation. But having her father, the borough boss, pushing hard didn't hurt. She handily won."[33] When Christine Todd Whitman ran for office, like Molinari, she was hindered and helped by her name and her background. In her case, as she said in my phone conversation with her, the criticism centered not on one family member, but on their economic situation: that she had garnered too much opportunity from family money, as part of a Republican elite, this response resembling "who do you think you are?" The criticism stemmed from her political connections, but this family power and name also helped her to establish a career.

Campaigning

For so many women, immersion in political issues and with politicians could lead to adopting a family campaign style. Having the chance to learn and use effective techniques, a form of education available to just the few, could create accusations of imitation but could also produce success.

Like Mary Landrieu, Ruth Hanna McCormick, Susan Molinari, Jeanne Zeidler, and so many other women, Maria Cantwell participated in the family business as a child, as her father, Paul F. Cantwell, campaigned to be a county commissioner, an Indianapolis councilman, and an Indiana state legislator. In the county commission and the state House, he worked to eliminate graff, especially in government contracts, appealing to Indianans as their champion, standing strong against entrenched interests. As a child, she campaigned door to door and registered voters: politics was such a part of life that she thought it was illegal not to vote. As a newspaper article noted, "she came from a gold mine of political experience," which involved not just her father: her mother worked as a precinct committeewoman for more than forty years; a cousin served in the Indiana House and another was a state senator.[34]

In 1986, in her first campaign at age twenty-eight, for the state House in Washington, Maria Cantwell embarked on an extensive door-knocking effort, as she had for her father. Especially when she ran for the U.S. Senate in 2000, a hard fought election, Cantwell applied lessons learned with him. By just 2,229 votes after a recount taking several weeks, she defeated an incumbent, Slade Gorton, who since 1959 had served in the state House, as the state's attorney general, and in the U.S. Senate. She created a grass-roots organization and cast her campaign as David vs. Goliath, incorporating her father's strategies, which enabled her to dodge accusations concerning her elite political family.[35] By reaching out to Native American voters and others who felt alienated from Gorton's establishment base, she was able to break his hold on the Senate seat just as her father had opposed entrenched interests in Indiana.

Working from a family center with family methods, some of these women were even able to defeat family foes. In 1986, for example, when Liz Johnston Patterson was elected to U.S. House, she defeated Bill Workman, the Republican mayor of Greenville, South Carolina, the son of W. D. Workman, Jr., a journalist who had been her father's Republican opponent in 1962 when Johnston won his last term in the U.S. Senate. Though polls favored the Greenville mayor against Patterson, she skillfully depicted him as a friend of corporations and the wealthy. In this multi-decade narrative, she depicted his candidacy as a "personal vendetta," based in their fathers' history. When Bill Workman labeled Patterson as a free-spending Democrat, she countered with television advertisements that declared, "I'm one of us"—in which she portrayed herself as a family values candidate, from a family well known and proven in the state, and even proven against her opponent's own father.[36]

Developing a Personal Style

As women availed themselves of their family's campaign techniques and relationship with voters, as they worked on many of the same issues, they also developed their own style of interaction, driven perhaps by the requirements of their gender or by changes in public rhetoric.

Maria Cantwell, U.S. senator from Washington, learned about the importance of providing personal help to constituents from her father. She says that when she was a child, someone was always calling about their problems and her father "always tried to help. I never forgot that," this engagement with constituents becoming key to her own success.[37] As a politician, she rebelled against her parents' views, moving "a little bit to the right," and she also found a rhetorical style perhaps more acceptable for her gender: while her father sought controversy and chaos, she viewed herself as a compromiser, a measured speaker and good listener.[38] Other women have demonstrated a more controlled style than their fathers. Of Liz Johnston Patterson, in her 1986 race for the U.S. House, reporter Chris Weston commented that "her quiet political style contrasts with the robust, bare-knuckled politicking in which her father excelled."[39]

Nancy Pelosi was immersed in politics as she grew up, but she would also develop her own style. She would be the first woman to become House minority leader, in 2003, and Speaker of the House, in 2007, having represented California beginning in 1987. Pelosi is the youngest of six children of Thomas D'Alesandro, Jr., a Democratic U.S. Congressman from Maryland and mayor of that city. Pelosi's brother, Thomas D'Alesandro, III, also served as mayor of that city. As a biographer commented, "Politics were a daily part of Pelosi's childhood: ground-breaking ceremonies, picnics, community events, carnivals, church gatherings, weddings, spaghetti dinners, crab feeds, dances, even funerals. Sometimes the mayor would go alone. Sometimes it was the entire family."[40] Her brother Thomas thinks of her life as an "expression of her father's keen political instincts"; her childhood, as he concluded, served as a "dress rehearsal for the big time."[41]

While she worked as a Democratic Party organizer, Pelosi began relying on family lessons. In California while she was raising five children, she became what she described as a "hardworking volunteer" and ultimately head of the state party. "Her Baltimore past was in the California air," her daughter Alexandria commented about the well-organized political center in their home: "She modeled our house in San Francisco after the house where she grew up in Baltimore."[42]

Pelosi's upbringing taught her about campaign organization, but she chose a presentation style that contrasted with her father's. She became involved in running for office when she was urged by widow Sala Burton to run for her U.S. House seat; Burton had taken her husband's seat in 1983 and was dying of cancer in 1987.[43] As a "flamboyant and legendary machine politician," her father was known for fiery rhetoric about issues and opponents. In comparison, as she ran for office in 1987 and subsequently, she chose a more mannered approach, appropriate to her gender and to national politics conducted on television. "Her style is camera-ready," as journalist Ellen Gamerman has commented. "She traded her father's fire and brimstone for a broad smile that she flashes as she coolly disarms her critics."[44]

Nancy Pelosi and her brother Thomas D'Alesandro III in 2014 (courtesy Mary Tilghman).

Moving On, Beyond a Campaign Style to an Array of Issues

In many cases, the mother and father have not just led the way into politics, but into an assessment of key legislative issues. Democrat Rosa DeLauro, a U.S. representative from Connecticut since 1991, re-elected in November of 2018, had parents with strong values concerning their neighborhood and city. Her mother, Luisa DeLauro, was elected to the New Haven Board of Aldermen in 1965 and held the position for thirty-five years, the longest-serving member in the city's history. Along with her husband Ted, she dedicated a lifetime to the neighborhood, especially attempting to help seniors, the working poor, and immigrants. Ted DeLauro had also served on the Board of Aldermen, and his wife had followed him into office when her husband took a position in the Redevelopment Agency, working to eliminate blighted and substandard housing areas.[45]

This history, involving both of her parents, made an impact on Rosa DeLauro. "I have vivid memories of my parents, sitting at the kitchen table with neighbors and new families to the neighborhood," she recalled. "My mother and father would do all that they could to help anyone who was in need." As she said further about her mother, "When I was growing up, she worked in a sweatshop, sewing shirt collars for pennies. Every day after school, she would make me come by to see the horrible, cramped conditions. It is something I will never forget.... She understood that politics was an avenue for change—a way to help people who were struggling. It is truly the blessing of a lifetime to have been able to follow in her footsteps, to serve the people of New Haven and Connecticut. All of my actions are guided by her love, encouragement and dedication."[46]

Following in these footsteps, DeLauro became one of the most liberal members of the House, dedicated to helping the poor and dispossessed. She has introduced bills aimed at improving cancer treatment and research, for the uninsured as well as insured; as chair of the appropriations subcommittee that funds the Food and Drug Administration, she has been a critic of that agency's failures to protect the public from unsafe foods and medical products. She supports full availability of abortion, along with federal subsidies to enable poor women to afford the procedure. She has also voted in support of stronger regulation of firearms, as essential to protecting inner-city neighborhoods, all choices that for her stem from the concern for others demonstrated by her parents.

In a long career, Rosa DeLauro continued with her parents' priorities while also working on an array of national issues. Other women have moved further from family in their political stances. As we have seen, Maria Cantwell

Rosa DeLauro and her mother Luisa DeLauro in 1999 (courtesy Anthony Riccio, *The Italian American Experience in New Haven* [State University of New York Press, 2006]).

thought of herself as moving "a little bit to the right." Women candidates might also move a bit to the left, especially on women's issues, facing judgment for their more independent choices as well as for their allegiance to family priorities.

During her initial campaigns and afterwards, as she told me, Susan Molinari faced accusations of both dependence and independence. Reporters have claimed that she followed the dictates of her father, her husband, or Newt Gingrich. Additionally, she faced criticism for being more conservative than her father as she attempted to work with Gingrich as well as being more liberal, especially concerning abortion. In the *Los Angeles Times,* journalist Geraldine Baum commented that "the relationship between father and daughter over the years has been a source of intense pride, competitiveness and occasional tension," with much of the tension derived from abortion law. One weekend when she was in college, as reporters have noted, she went to Washington to march for abortion rights while her father went to Buffalo for an anti-abortion rally. "I'm pro-life," her father said. "We've had some trouble with that." Father and daughter also took opposing stances on other issues. As her father would not, she voted for the Clinton assault weapons ban and backed the family medical leave bill. To assert her independence as she decided on these votes, she claimed to a *New York Times* reporter that she was "no daddy's girl who inherited her father's Congressional seat through a Machiavellian plot that left him running Staten Island and her snug in his old leather chair on Capitol Hill."[47]

Further Complications of Family and Especially Fathers

The beliefs and actions of a father or other relative could not only lead to well-publicized variations in style and approach to the issues but to greater difficulties, with the press often holding the woman candidate responsible for whatever astounding thing a man might say or do.

Though Susan Molinari and her father worked closely together, he complicated her political life. In 1992, Guy Molinari angered party officials in Washington by labeling Dan Quayle as a "liability" to President George Bush's re-election. When the press asked Susan Molinari to comment, she said that she had "mixed feelings," but she ultimately backed her father on this issue, commenting on Quayle's negative reputation: "Whether public perception is right or wrong, it is the political reality." Of the public pressure her father's comments created for her, Susan Molinari told the *New York Times* that "he called screaming. I called screaming. And after that we made up."[48]

Their public disagreements continued. In the spring 1994, Guy Molinari told reporters that his daughter might run for governor when she had not decided to do so. In a speech following a Columbus Day parade that fall, he argued that Karen Burstein, a judge, should not be elected as the New York state attorney general because she was a lesbian.[49] At first Susan Molinari avoided commenting, but eventually she supported his right to address the issue. Burstein narrowly lost. In March of 1997, he claimed to the Associated Press that the brains of partial-birth abortion doctors should be sucked out, using the same procedure by which they killed human beings, this punishment appropriate for the first-degree murder that these abortions should be deemed. Julie Wadler, a close friend of Susan Molinari, commented that "there are times that everybody's parents make them cringe. Susan's no different from anybody else. Her father just does it in public."[50]

While his declarations could lead to awkward questions from the press, Guy Molinari's views could cause even greater problems for his daughter. When Susan Molinari ran for Congress in 1990, the AFL-CIO would not endorse her because its leaders judged her father to not be sufficiently supportive of New York labor. She wasn't asked to speak at the 1992 Republican convention because of his claims about Dan Quayle.[51]

Certainly Georgia state representative Billy McKinney helped his daughter, Cynthia McKinney, as she sought to join him in the Georgia House, but they often disagreed, even vociferously, and his declarations caused her harm. In 1990, an article concerning father and daughter focused on their sometimes stark difference in beliefs: "Cynthia McKinney politely calls her father homophobic and Neanderthal, Billy McKinney affably brands his daughter a flaming liberal. She accuses him of insensitivity. He berates her for larceny." One divide, referred to here, concerned state sodomy laws, which dictated incarceration of one to twenty years. As Billy McKinney attempted to alter these laws for heterosexuals, he labeled homosexuality "an immoral, unnatural act" and opposed any extension of gay rights. His daughter, however, was attempting to eliminate the law entirely and thus its enforcement—generally reserved for gay men—and thereby take away a legal impediment to equal rights. She had seen his bill on his desk and stolen it, the basis of his half serious change of larceny; she then introduced legislation to remove the law entirely, her first bill after two years in office. "He thought I was gone crazy," she told the *Washington Post*.[52]

Cynthia McKinney and her father Billy McKinney in 2006 (© The Associated Press, photograph by Charlotte B. Teagle/Atlanta Journal & Constitution).

After Cynthia McKinney entered the U.S. House, her father caused trouble for her through other public disagreements. In 1996, her opponent John Mitnick repeatedly linked her to Nation of Islam leader Louis Farrakhan: she had appeared on a university panel with him and had voted against a resolution condemning a 1993 speech by Khalid Abdul Muhammad, one of Farrakhan's aides. Though this association hurt her with Jewish voters in Atlanta, her father worsened the situation. At Atlanta's Ebenezer Church, where Martin Luther King, Jr., had preached, Billy McKinney characterized Mitnick as a "racist Jew." Afterwards, Cynthia McKinney told reporters that her father had embarrassed her and issued a public apology. "'He's my dad, and I love him,' she said, 'but I am with him when he's right and I tell him when he's wrong.'" She also declared that "I absolutely abhor any form of racism or anti–Semitism, bigotry in general, and that is wherever it comes from, be it from Louis Farrakhan or Khalid Abdul Muhammad (a top Farrakhan aide) or John Mitnick or Billy McKinney." Here she included her opponent Mitnick as one of the bigots involved in this situation since he was trying to turn Jewish voters against her by repeating her father's comments and implying that she shared the same values.

After Cynthia McKinney repudiated her father's comments, he apologized and said that he was withdrawing as her advisor.[53] But his problematic accusations continued while she was in office in Washington. On the night before her primary vote in 2002, he claimed on an Atlanta television broadcast that she might lose that year because "Jews have bought everybody. Jews. J-E-W-S."[54] In that year's elections, Billy McKinney lost his seat in the Georgia House, and his daughter lost her U.S. House seat though she regained it in 2005 and served until 2007.[55]

Another further difficulty could arise from the complications of not just a highly opinionated father but one who was a guilty politician. Arch A. Moore, Jr., U.S. representative from West Virginia and three-term governor of the state, was the father of Shelley Moore Capito, who became a member of the West Virginia House, serving from 1996 to 2000, a U.S. representative from 2001 to 2015, and a U.S. senator from 2015 to the present. In a political family, her nephew Riley Moore and her son Moore Capito also served in the West Virginia House.[56]

In 1990, Arch A. Moore, Jr., pled guilty to five felony charges of extortion, mail and tax fraud, and obstruction of justice, stemming from claims of illegal payments accepted from Maben Energy Corporation during his 1984 and 1988 gubernatorial campaigns. He was sentenced to five years and ten months in prison and served over three years before his release. In 1995, he paid a settlement of $750,000 to the state, a year before his daughter first ran for office.[57]

Certainly in 1996 when Shelley Moore Capito ran for the West Virginia House, her political family connection was not entirely a blessing. Newspapers said in identifying her that she was the "daughter of Arch A. Moore, Jr., three-term governor convicted of extortion." In this election, Arch Moore's enemies painstakingly reviewed the specifics of the crime, but Capito also garnered sympathy for her family's misfortune. The memory in the press of his conviction, however, was not long: when Shelley Capito ran in 2000, newspapers just mentioned that her father had been a three-term governor and did not associate her with a history of felonies and prison.[58] By 2012, reporters declared that she was from a "storied West Virginia political family."[59] Throughout her political career, her father acted as an unofficial advisor to her, something that she did not discuss publicly until she spoke at his funeral.[60]

For all of these women, the family was one strong possibility of support. Fathers might prefer that their daughters not enter politics, but at least these prejudices indicated what might assail aspiring legislators, from the press and public. And even in families in which a political career was intended for men, women learned the business of legislation around the dining-room table. There they were treated as engaged citizens whose viewpoints mattered. And, within these families, they often found political mentors who took them seriously, who could forward their careers. While women in politics might need to deal with a family member's problematic record or declarations, they also gained the confidence to enter the political world—and even to cope with their own relatives. Family connections could enable a politician to move forward, with attention from the public and multiple sources of support, beyond what a party might be willing to provide.

EIGHT

What Family Members Have Achieved

Women from political families have served well at the state and national level. In governors' offices, Mary Fallin, Madeleine Kunin, Barbara Kay Roberts, Christine Whitman, and others have excelled at administering their states. In state legislatures, Anna Belle Clement O'Brien, Ophelia Ford, Jeanne Hurley Simon, Susan Fitzgerald, Frances Cleveland Axtell, Thelma Engstrom, Patricia Reid Lindner, Catherine Nora Munoz, Diane B. Snelling, Beth Kerttula, and many more members of political families have served their constituencies as have mayors through the generations, such as Mary Jo Copeland, Patricia Collins, and Jeanne Zeidler.

In the U.S. Congress, at the most basic level, women from political families have mattered because they have been there: through the 115th Congress, they have constituted 64 percent of the women elected to the Senate and 44 percent of those elected to the House.

In the congressional world of seniority, hierarchical committee structures, and two dramatically separated parties, as Michelle L. Swers states in *Women in the Club*, prejudices against women have been part of an entrenched "polarized political environment," adding to the difficulty of translating "policy preferences into legislative action."[1] Family backing can be a key factor in not just obtaining office but in effecting change, especially when a legislator's choices do not correspond with party priorities. Swers claims that women in office "may bring unique experiences and viewpoints to the policy debate and different issues to the legislative agenda," and especially women from political families have been able to forward their agendas, often standing up to members of their own party.[2] Like Frances Bolton, Lindy Boggs, Cardiss Collins, Margaret Chase Smith, Mary Bono, and other activist widows who achieved significant results in

Congress, many other women from political families have made their own mark, providing models for those that would follow.

As they have attempted to forward their own priorities, these women have certainly aided each other. Susan Collins came from Caribou, Maine, where both of her parents, Patricia M. Collins and Donald F. Collins, served as mayor; her father, as well as her grandfather and great-grandfather, also entered the Maine legislature while her uncle, Samuel W. Collins, Jr., sat on the state Supreme Court. Entering politics with family support, Collins also recognized what she gained from Margaret Chase Smith. In high school, Collins participated in the U.S. Senate Youth Program, through which she visited Washington, D.C., and engaged in a two-hour conversation with Senator Smith, discussing defense, full employment, and, as she later recalled, "other weighty issues of the day." After she entered the Senate, she noted that she had also met with Senator Edward Muskie during that trip: "Ed Muskie did what I do a zillion times a day.... I chatted briefly with him, had a picture taken, and then he was off to a meeting. But Margaret Chase Smith took me into her office and talked to me for nearly two hours." Collins recalled the difference that this attention made, adding to the effect of family on her confidence: "The meeting still fuels me. Even though my family was very encouraging of opportunities, there were a lot of mixed messages for women in that era. But I left her office that day thinking that a woman could do anything."[3]

To encourage their runs for the U.S. Senate, Margaret Chase Smith would later meet with both Susan Collins and Olympia Snowe, who had entered the Maine state legislature in 1973, elected to fill the seat vacated by the death of her husband, Peter Snowe. Reflecting on visits that occurred long after her high-school trip, Collins spoke about Smith's effect on both Snowe and herself: "Mainers for decades saw the example of the extraordinary effect and courage of a woman who, for many years, was the only woman in the U.S. Senate. There is no doubt in my mind that Margaret Chase Smith paved the way for Olympia Snowe and certainly for me. She broke the glass barrier." Both Collins and Snowe said they did not feel disadvantaged as women running for political office in Maine because of the trail that Smith blazed.[4]

Smith, Collins, Snowe, and many other women in Congress have served as models for independent decision-making, demonstrating that women can make their own way and assert their own priorities. Their family background, a separate base of support, has enabled them to frequently assert themselves not just as Republicans or Democrats following a party line, but as independent speakers and voters.

On Foreign Affairs

Many of the earliest elected women were willing to voice unpopular opinions on foreign affairs, as had Jeannette Rankin concerning war. Women in Congress may have fewer opportunities to engage in foreign policy than men because of its stereotypical association with masculinity: the House Foreign Affairs Committee has been referred to as the "big boys play pen" and defense policy as a "male-dominated sphere."[5] But, from the beginning of women's suffrage, especially women from political families have maneuvered successfully within this difficult space.

Winnifred S. Huck, the third woman elected to Congress, spent her short career in the U.S. House as a pacifist, as her father, William Mason, had been also. Indeed, he was one of the fifty representatives who, including Jeannette Rankin, voted against World War I. Not remaining silent as did many first-term legislators, Huck gave an address in the House in January 1923 in support of a constitutional amendment to hold a direct popular vote before the United States engaged in another foreign war. Huck continued her anti-war stance by pleading for the release of sixty-two men who had been imprisoned for seditious speech during World War I. She also supported separate citizenship rights for married women and restrictions on child labor. Her pacifism and other stances did not aid her as she ran in the Republican primary for a full term in 1923, an election that she lost to the more conservative Henry R. Rathbone.[6]

Like Rankin and Huck, other women from political families have taken independent action on war and foreign policy, whether operating from the left or the right of established power. Entering Congress in 1943, Clare Boothe Luce became an outspoken critic of Franklin Roosevelt's foreign policy as a member of the powerful Military Affairs Committee. During two tours of allied battlefronts in Europe during World War II, she campaigned for more support of what she considered to be America's forgotten army in Italy. In April 1945, she was present at the liberation of several Nazi concentration camps, and after V-E Day, began warning against the rise of international Communism as another form of totalitarianism.[7] During her second term in Congress, she worked to create the Atomic Energy Commission, established after the war to foster and control the development of atomic science. After leaving office in 1947, Luce returned to politics to campaign for Dwight D. Eisenhower, giving more than a hundred speeches on his behalf when he ran for president: her anti–Communist arguments helped to persuade traditionally Democratic-voting Catholics to support the military leader. For her contributions, Eisenhower appointed Luce as ambassador to Italy in 1953.

Beyond decisions about American involvement in war, women have made independent decisions concerning international human rights, their viewpoints at times conflicting with party or presidential initiatives. Nancy Landon Kassebaum, a moderate Republican, was known for her health care legislation, for the Kennedy-Kassebaum Health Insurance Portability and Accountability Act, co-sponsored by Edward Kennedy. But she also impacted foreign policy, a particular challenge for a woman, as she noted: "It's difficult for a lot of men, just relating to a woman on foreign policy or the budget or some kind of political maneuvering. There's a lot of camaraderie, the old boy network. If you know what you're talking about, you gain credibility, but for women, you have to go the extra mile to prove your credibility."[8]

As chair of the Senate Foreign Relations Committee's panel on African affairs, Kassebaum visited South Africa to inform her perspective; she then orchestrated the Senate's economic sanctions bill. In 1986, in making this choice, she was opposing President Reagan's policy of "constructive engagement" with the oppressive white minority government, and she persuaded thirty fellow Republicans to vote to override Reagan's veto. As Cokie Roberts said of this override, "The single biggest factor in that vote was the voice of Nancy Kassebaum." Roberts added that "other members of the Senate knew she had done her homework, that she had no personal political agenda, that she was motivated by what she thought was the right thing to do."[9]

Making decisions that would prove problematic for her later as a presidential candidate, in the Senate Hillary Clinton also was willing to oppose other members of her party. She strongly supported military action in Afghanistan in 2001, labeling it as a chance to combat terrorism while improving the lives of Afghan women who suffered under the Taliban government. Clinton also voted in favor of the October 2002 Iraq War Resolution. Observing that war deployments were draining regular and reserve forces, she co-introduced legislation to increase the size of the army by 80,000 soldiers. In late 2005, Clinton said that while immediate withdrawal from Iraq would be a mistake, Bush's pledge to stay "until the job is done" was also ill-advised, as it gave Iraqis "an open-ended invitation not to take care of themselves."[10] Her stance caused frustration among Democrats who favored quick withdrawal and among Republicans who wanted to give the president a free rein.

Like Hillary Clinton in the Senate and certainly as secretary of state, many women from political families have helped to shape American foreign policy. These women have been willing to take unpopular positions, to work on their own priorities, and to negotiate with national or international leaders, regardless of prejudices concerning women as preservers of national security.

Women's Rights and Civil Rights

In the U.S. Congress, some independent action taken by women from political families has concerned civil rights and women's rights, with these legislators willing to act to pursue their goals, as were widows such as Frances Bolton and Lindy Boggs. Michelle Swers wrote that female senators "are more active proponents of legislation related to women, children, and families," their commitment to these issues "derived from personal experience."[11] Swers continues by claiming that researchers have reached contradictory conclusions on whether women are generally more liberal, concerning foreign policy issues for example, but they often have a "profound commitment to the pursuit of policies for women."[12]

For many women in office, it was the commitment to women's rights that caused separation from the priorities of their party. A cousin of Franklin Roosevelt, Katharine St. George became involved in the family business of politics, serving for eighteen years in the U.S. House, beginning in 1947. A Republican, she was a fiscal conservative committed to limiting the size of government, but she also became an outspoken advocate for women's economic equality, coining the phrase "equal pay for equal work." Her 1959 proposal to outlaw sex discrimination in the payment of wages became law in the form of the Equal Pay Act of 1963, women's rights being the one area in which she dissented from her Republican colleagues.

Other women from political families have had the independence and strength to dedicate themselves to the promotion of women. Representative Martha Griffiths, for example, sponsored the Equal Rights Amendment, which passed the Congress in 1972. Many newspaper articles described her as the "Mother of the ERA." She also insisted that the classes protected from discrimination in hiring, in promotion, and in firing by Title VII of the Civil Rights Act of 1964 had to include women. Because of her insistence, Section 703 (a) of the final legislation made it unlawful for an employer to "fail or refuse to hire or to discharge any individual, or otherwise discriminate against any individual with respect to his compensation, terms, conditions or privileges or employment, because of such individual's race, color, religion, sex or national origin."[13]

Millicent Vernon Hammond Fenwick, a progressive within the Republican Party, was an outspoken in favor of the women's movement and the extension of personal freedoms. Raised in comfortable circumstances in Bernardsville, New Jersey, she attended college at Columbia University and then the New School for Social Research.[14] She married and divorced, modeled briefly for *Harper's Bazaar*, and worked as a writer and editor at *Vogue* magazine for fourteen years. In 1948 she compiled *Vogue's Book of Etiquette*, which sold a million copies. In an article written when she entered the U.S. House in 1974, she was labeled mockingly as a "67-year-old WASP-ish aristocrat and ex-Vogue writer" who smoked a pipe, but the reporter also noted her advocacy of no-fault automobile insurance, abortion rights, and the decriminalization of marijuana.[15]

During her four terms in the U.S. House, although she was a fiscal conservative, Fenwick was known as one of the most liberal Republicans in office. A founding member of the Congressional Women's Caucus, she supported issues affecting women and families, such as the ERA, federal funding for abortions, and the food stamp program. At the 1976 Republican National Convention in Kansas City, Fenwick successfully fought to keep the ERA plank in the party's platform. In 1980, when the Republican Party dropped its forty-year support for this amendment, a reporter asked Fenwick to describe her feelings: "Absurd is the only word," she claimed as she publicly opposed her party's decision.[16] She was also an early and consistent advocate for ending the marriage tax penalty, a higher income tax for two married wage earners. "Under the present law," as Fenwick argued, "if the wife decides to work to help support the family, her first dollar of income will be taxed at the same rate as the last dollar earned by her husband. In effect, her income will be taxed at a much higher rate."[17] As the *New York Times* noted concerning Fenwick's independent legislative choices for women and families, "Her views often placed her at odds with her party's leaders and seemed anomalous for the wealthy district in New Jersey's horse country that she represented."[18]

When Pat Schroeder was in Congress, she was a member of the Select Committee on Children, Youth, and Families as well as the House Armed Services Committee. Propelled by this committee work, she became a prime mover behind the Family and Medical Leave Act of 1993, requiring employers to provide job-protected leave for qualified medical and family reasons, and the Military Family Act of 1985, which included spousal employment assistance. Schroeder was also involved in reform of Congress itself, working to weaken the long-standing control of committees by their almost always male chairs, a system that lessened the opportunity for women to obtain powerful appointments and to further their own priorities.[19]

Olympia Snowe discussed her advocacy of women's rights as beginning after the death of her husband Peter Snowe and her election to her husband's seat in the Maine House: "With the devastation of Peter's death came a sensitivity to the tremendous difficulties that other women in similar situations can face—such as raising children alone. Later that was brought to bear on issues such as pension reform, child care, and displaced homemakers. And since I've served in a position that can make a difference, I have always worked to translate those lessons into a force of positive change for others."[20] Snowe became widely known for her ability to influence the outcome of close votes, for her willingness to compromise, and for her strong sense of bipartisanship. As she fought for abortion rights, gay marriage, tax reform, and gun control in schools, she was extending the commitment to family strength and safety that she made at her husband's death.

In their support of civil rights, these women have taken on the leaders of their own parties. Republican Ileana Ros-Lehtinen has been a notable Republican voice in favor of LGBTQ rights. In a 2013 interview, she stated that her support for same-sex marriage was based on "coming from Cuba, losing my homeland to communism, seeing the state control everything—I'm a person that believes in individual liberties and not having the government control everything."[21] She was one of three Republican members of the LGBT Equality Caucus, of which she is a founding member and a vice-chair. She supports anti-hate crime laws and anti-discrimination bills, and was one of fifteen Republican House members to vote in favor of the Don't Ask, Don't Tell Repeal Act of 2010 after becoming the first Republican co-sponsor of the act. In July 2012, Ros-Lehtinen became the first Republican in the House to fully support same-sex marriage. In 2013, along with Mary Bono, she was a signatory to an *amicus curiae* brief submitted to the Supreme Court in support of same-sex marriage during the *Hollingsworth v. Perry* case. A leading Republican moderate, Ros-Lehtinen opposed Donald Trump's 2016 presidential candidacy and in the 2018 election, especially in south Florida, she blamed many losses by Republicans on his anti-immigration stance.

Health Care

While women from political families have made independent decisions on foreign affairs, civil rights, women's rights, and other topics, they have also fought for American health care. Nancy Pelosi has been credited for spearheading the effort to pass President Obama's health care law when it seemed that it would go down in defeat. After Republican Scott Brown won Ted Kennedy's Senate seat in a January 2010 special election and thereby caused Senate Democrats to lose their filibuster-proof majority, Pelosi convinced the president to still go forward: she argued that this would be their only shot at real health care reform since Democratic majorities might not be sustained in 2012. She rallied her Democratic caucus as she began an "unbelievable marathon" during a two-month session to craft the health care bill, which successfully passed the House with a 219–212 vote. In Obama's remarks before signing the bill into law, he lauded Pelosi as "one of the best Speakers the House of Representatives has ever had."[22]

Another strong health-care advocate, Democrat Nicola "Niki" Sauvage Tsongas, a U.S. representative from Massachusetts, was well prepared for a legislative role but at first faced the accusation of being a poorly prepared political spouse. She earned her law degree from Boston University and started Lowell's first all-female law practice. Tsongas then worked as the dean of external affairs at Middlesex Community College, on the Lowell Civic Stadium and Arena Commission, and as a board member of Fallon Health, a provider of health insurance and health care services. In 2007, she ran in a special election in the district that her husband Paul Tsongas had served, from 1975 to 1979, prior to his being elected to the U.S. Senate. In this election, "there was grumbling that her name was her principal asset."[23] And she was smeared by her opponent with a general disgust for all things Washington, a place that she had never worked but her husband certainly had: "She presents more of the same tired Washington that continues to fail us."[24] After the election, many articles had headlines such as "Tsongas' Widow Wins." In the House, as an independent voice, strengthened by her work in health care as well as her family connections, Niki Tsongas became an advocate for universal health care and supporter of a public health insurance option. In 2010 she voted for the Patient Protection and Affordable Care Act and Health Care and Education Reconciliation Act. In 2012 Tsongas joined a Republican-led effort to repeal a 2.3 percent sales tax on medical-device manufacturers, which passed the House 270–146. Like Nancy Landon Kassebaum and others, Tsongas was putting health care first.

And Late 2017 and 2018

From the beginning of suffrage, women from political families have developed a tradition of thinking and voting independently, about foreign affairs and health care, among other key issues, and certainly about women's rights and civil rights. In the 115th Congress, in an era of party control with little cooperation between Democrats and Republicans, women from political families continued the tradition of independence and action forged in 1917 by Jeannette Rankin. These women have certainly not been the only effective legislators, but this cadre, often working together, has led the way.

In the last two years, these women from both parties have fought for civil rights. Described as one of "the last survivors of a once common species of moderate Northeastern Republican," Susan Collins has dedicated herself to the needs of women as well as to equal rights for gay Americans and other minorities, teaming with other women from political families to effect change.[25] For the last presidential election, Collins announced in August 2016 that she would not be voting for Donald Trump. In February 2017, Collins and Lisa Murkowski were the only two Republicans who voted in the Senate against Trump's selection for Secretary of Education, Betsy DeVos. In March 2017, Collins joined Murkowski in again breaking party lines, voting against a bill allowing states to defund Planned Parenthood. In July 2017, she voted against the "straight appeal" of the Affordable Care Act, the seven Republicans who joined her including Shelley Moore Capito and Lisa Murkowski. In September 2017, Collins and Kirsten Gillibrand introduced a bipartisan amendment to protect transgender service members from President Trump's plan to ban them from the military. In July 2018, Collins was one of three Republican senators, the others being Shelley Moore Capito and Lisa Murkowski, who publicly confirmed their support for the *Roe v. Wade* decision.

According to GovTrack and the *New York Times*, Lisa Murkowski is the second most moderate Republican senator, following Collins. And like Collins, Murkowski has also frequently demonstrated her independence in support of civil rights. When Republicans made an unsuccessful attempt to eliminate the Affordable Care Act in July 2017, she decided to defy her party and cast a key vote that helped to seal the repeal's defeat. Native Americans, and specifically the Alaska Natives that she represents, lauded her decision to protect their health care. In Congress, she has sponsored or co-sponsored more than a hundred acts intended to defend the rights of Native Americans, work she continued in 2017 and 2018, and she has been willing to stand against the priorities of her party in doing so. In October of 2018, she defied her party again by voting against the confirmation of Brett Kavanaugh.

In late 2017 and into 2018, these women continued their advocacy of women's rights through the #MeToo movement. In November 2017, Debbie Dingell spoke publicly about having been harassed by a high-level politician. She evoked a strong response especially among other women who had not spoken out because of the fear of losing a job or being labeled a troublemaker: "What people don't realize is there are still consequences for a lot of people [who come forward]," Dingell said. "Honestly, we're going to have to work very hard … to really change the culture. We've got to work together as men and women."[26] When the movement came to Congress, Kristen Gillibrand sponsored a bill changing the way Congress handles harassment complaints. "The way [reporting] is set up in Congress is so horrible," she said. "I mean, it is literally designed to protect perpetrators and to make sure people really don't come forward." The measure would eliminate a controversial three-month "cooling-off" period and bar lawmakers from using public money for staff settlements, among other changes. For Gillibrand, work on this act stems from a long-term advocacy of women's rights, also demonstrated in her support for federal paid family leave. In June 2018, she told NPR that she was frequently asked why she focused on women's issues. And she explained, "Well, why do you focus on issues that pertain to 52 percent of the population? It's pretty important."[27]

In their support of women's rights and civil rights, many of these women have stood up against powerful legislators as well as restrictive legislation. Kirsten Gillibrand has been a leading voice in Congress for combating sexual assault in the military. She stood up to Trump concerning sexual assault and the women who accused him. As she told CNN's Christiane Amanpour in December 2017, "President Trump has committed assault, according to these women, and those are very credible allegations of misconduct and criminal activity, and he should be fully investigated and he should resign." If he did not "immediately resign," she maintained, Congress "should have appropriate investigations of his behavior and hold him accountable."[28] Trump then attacked Gillibrand on Twitter, suggesting that she exchanged sexual favors for campaign contributions.

Other women from political families were willing to take on established powers during the 115th Congress. Catherine Cortez Masto acknowledges the impact of human-caused climate change and argues that the federal government should limit the amount of greenhouse gas emissions from power plants. She supports the growth of green jobs and funding to increase Nevada's reliance on solar power and other forms of clean energy. She opposes the use of Yucca Mountain as a nuclear waste repository. Additionally, Cortez Masto has been willing to take on the difficult issue of gun control. In response to the 2017 Las Vegas shooting, she co-sponsored a bill to ban bump stocks. She stated that, although the bill could not bring back the lives of those lost, it could be a start towards decreasing gun violence and mass shootings. President Trump ultimately banned bump stocks in December 2018.

Like Cortez Masto, other legislators from political families stood up for gun control in 2018. Kirsten Gillibrand denounced the National Rifle Association's control over lawmakers, comparing its influence to a "choke-hold on Congress." As she said on CBS's *The Late Show with Stephen Colbert*, "This is unfathomable how many deaths we've had to see over and over and over again, and Congress has done nothing,"[29] Nancy Pelosi favors increased background checks for potential gun owners, as well as the controversial banning of assault weapons. Concerning her co-sponsorship of this bill, Pelosi spokesman Drew Hammill noted that she "has always supported the ban and was part of the whip team that successfully worked to pass the original legislation in the 1990s."[30]

In 2018, these women continued to respond to and lead foreign policy. As speaker of the House and House minority leader, Nancy Pelosi has had long involvement with American foreign policy. In May and early June of 2018, a short period providing examples of a long career, she spoke out on the Trump administration's ZTE Bill, claiming that "the President continues to enrich this Chinese company after the Chinese government reportedly agreed to funnel half a billion dollars into one of his family's resorts." She also criticized Trump's withdrawal from the Paris Climate Agreement and the president's tariff decisions, which she labeled as "trade brinkmanship." About the North Korea summit, she commented that "apparently, the President handed Kim Jong-un concessions in exchange for vague promises that do not approach a clear and comprehensive pathway to denuclearization and non-proliferation." Within this short period, she also worked with other women from political families. Concerning the Harvard report on deaths of Puerto Ricans in Hurricane Maria, she lauded the "efforts led by Congresswoman Nydia Velázquez to investigate the alarming discrepancy between this report and the official death toll."[31]

From the beginning of suffrage, women from political families have developed a tradition of thinking and voting independently, about foreign affairs and health care, among other key matters, as well as women's rights and civil rights. In recent Congresses, through the 115th, in an era of party control with little cooperation between Democrats and Republicans, women these have continued the principled activist traditions forged by Jeannette Rankin in 1917.

Conclusion

In May 2018, with women planning campaigns for office in record numbers, Debbie Walsh, director of the Center for American Women and Politics at Rutgers University, declared, "We are not going to see, in one cycle, an end to the underrepresentation of women in American politics that we've seen for 250 years. The concern is we need this energy and engagement to be here for the long haul. This is a marathon, not a sprint."[1] Stories of women from political families demonstrate some of the reasons for what Walsh describes as the "long haul," even with the progress made in 2018, as well as the "energy and engagement" that can alter the political landscape in the future.

These political narratives point to many positives and victories along the way. Progress would have occurred much more slowly without the nation's political families since half of the women who have served in Congress have come from them, with the percentages similar or higher at the state and local level. And so the first great effect of widows and wives and sisters and daughters and granddaughters is that these connections have helped women to come into office and have encouraged others to follow. While these women have been criticized, as "daddy's girls" with a "father fixation," it should not be forgotten that these opportunities have helped to bring well-qualified women like Pat Schroeder, Lindy Boggs, Susan Collins, Lisa Murkowski, and Rosa DeLauro into office.

These families can provide potential candidates with an immersion in political issues and processes. Women from political families, guided by mentors, might envision themselves as leaders from childhood, able to serve their country, prepared to begin to do so.

And these stories show the power, for the elected official, of combining various forms of backing. Seeming to rely too much on the reputation of one family member, as we have seen in the case of many widows and wives, can lead to accusations of dependence and weakness. Instead of placing the focus on one partner, however, the political family can create a model involving diverse and strong allegiances. This base of support can allow a woman to work within a party without becoming subservient to it. Many women from political families, in fact, have been willing to break with party, to stand up for women's rights, for example, even when their party's platform did not. This family-fostered independence occurred in the Senate careers of Margaret Chase Smith, Nancy Landon Kassebaum, Kay Bailey Hutchison, Olympia Snowe, Susan Collins, Hillary Clinton, Lisa Murkowski, Kirsten Gillibrand, Shelley Moore Capito, and many more; and in the House careers of Frances Bolton, Lindy Boggs, Cardiss Collins, Mary Bono, Jeannette Rankin, Winnifred Huck, Ruth Hanna McCormick, Ruth Bryan Owen, Clare Booth Luce, Martha Griffiths, Pat Schroeder, Millicent Fenwick, Olympia Snowe, Nancy Pelosi, Ileana Ros-Lehtinen, Susan Molinari, Rosa DeLauro, Linda Sánchez, Niki Tsongas, Catherine Cortez Masto, and many more.

When Jeannette Rankin ran for office, she relied on her brother and fellow suffragists. She did not view herself as there to vote for every priority of the Republican Party. She stood strong against the appearance discourse that assailed her and the accusations that her brother could or should control her. And with her suffrage friends and her brother waiting for her outside the House chamber and at her home, she cast her own principled vote against World War I. In this beginning of multiple sources of support, of the resulting strength to make an independent choice, is a model for what women and men might do for whom party is part of the story but not the entire story.

In the November 2018 elections, more women ran for office than ever before. By March 2018, 575 women had declared their intention to run for the House, the Senate, or a governorship, and 277 candidates made it through the primaries to the fall election.[2] Many candidates had the motivation of the loss in 2016 of the first female major-party nominee and the election of Donald Trump. The #MeToo movement also encouraged more women to run and especially more Democrats to vote for them.

And women not only ran in November 2018: they won. Though the numbers of women elected to Congress are still far from parity, as Debbie Walsh commented, they were larger than in years past. In the U.S. House, thirty-six new women members were elected for the 116th Congress along with sixty-nine incumbents to make a total of 105, fifteen Republicans and ninety Democrats, representing 24 percent of the total. In the 115th House, there were eighty-seven women, or 20 percent. In the U.S. Senate

for the 116th Congress, there are twenty-four female senators, up one
more than in the 115th Congress, thus 24 percent, seventeen Democrats
and seven Republicans.

In this election as before, many candidates came from political
families. In the House of Representatives, for example, there were twenty-
six re-elected incumbents from political families, along with two dele-
gates: Nancy Pelosi, Rosa DeLauro, Lucille Roybal-Allard, Nydia
Velázquez, Jan Schakowsky, Linda Sánchez, Cathy McMorris-Rodgers,
Debbie Wasserman-Schultz, Kathy Castor, Yvette Clarke, Chellie Pingree,
Dina Titus, Judy Chu, Martha Roby, Terri Sewell, Suzanne Bonamici, Joyce
Beatty, Cheri Bustos, Ann McLane-Kuster, Grace Meng, Ann Wagner,
Debbie Dingell, Lisa Blunt-Rochester, Liz Cheney, Val Demings, and Doris
Matsui as well as delegates Amata Radewagen and Jenniffer González.
Continuing in the Senate in the 116th Congress, either through re-election
or a term that hadn't ended, are ten women from political families: Susan
Collins, Maria Cantwell, Lisa Murkowski, Jeanne Shaheen, Kirsten Gilli-
brand, Deb Fischer, Shelley Moore Capito, Catherine Cortez Masto,
Tammy Duckworth, and Maggie Hassan.

Some of the new members of the 116th Congress have had the backing
of political families. Mary Gay Scanlon entered office on November 13,
2018, after winning a special election to fill the vacancy created by the
resignation of Representative Pat Meehan, who left office because of sexual
harassment claims made by a former staffer. In a separate election in
November, Scanlon also won a two-year term. She is the daughter of
Daniel Scanlon, who worked for President John F. Kennedy and introduced
the president to his daughter, a memory she discussed as she campaigned:
"What struck me was that my father was so respectful." She also recalled
her father taking the family to Kennedy's graveside after the funeral to
pay their respects. After the president's death, as Mary Gay also noted,
Daniel Scanlon worked on Robert Kennedy's senatorial, then presidential,
campaigns. Her father was appointed as a part-time magistrate in 1971
and full-time U.S. federal court magistrate in 1993. As Mary Gay reminded
voters, her family's dedication to public service also came from an earlier
generation: one grandfather was a family-court judge who helped write
the juvenile justice code for New York, and the other served on a commission to plan for a bridge across the St. Lawrence River. In summarizing
the impact of these careers, Scanlon said that "I think public service was
always part of the lifestyle. That level of engagement was something I grew
up with."[3]

While some candidates in 2018 had the inspiration and example of earlier generations, others had the support of a political spouse, with the two engaging each other in civil service. In 2016, Xochitl Torres Small's husband, Nathan Small, became a Democratic member of the New Mexico House after serving for two terms as Las Cruces city councilor and chairing the City of Las Cruces Economic Development Committee. In November 2018, as he ran successfully for re-election, Xochitl Torres Small ran for a U.S. House seat, open because the incumbent, Steve Pearce, decided to instead run for governor, a race he lost to Michelle Lujan Grisham. Torres Small had worked as a field representative for Senator Tom Udall and as a federal law clerk. In May 2018, she declared that "maybe it's time for me not to be on the sidelines."[4] As her husband did in 2016, she left the sidelines in her successful 2018 race by which she entered the 116th Congress.

As in the case of women from other generations, some of these candidates faced criticism for a husband's career and had to answer publicly for his choices. In the primary campaign to replace Beto O'Rourke, in February 2018, as was reported in newspapers across Texas, Veronica Escobar claimed that congressional Democrats had abandoned Dreamers during the previous week when they voted to fund the government without securing adequate protection for immigrants. As she made this argument at one rally, a heckler yelled, "Tell that to your husband!" referring to Michael Pleters, a federal immigration judge, who presided at deportation hearings. Accusations concerning Escobar and her husband would continue to dog her and to secure press attention. Fellow Democratic candidate Dori Fenenbock was quick to highlight the "hypocrisy" of Escobar's pledge to help immigrants and their children since her husband was forcing them to leave the country. Pleters, Fenenbock claimed, served the Trump administration and his prejudices. In response, with the need to mount a defense increasing, Escobar maintained that her husband was first approached for the job by the Obama administration, that he was a lifetime Democrat and an "impartial arbiter of the law." As she commented on this situation, "I've never been in a campaign where my family has been attacked until now. And I think that it says more about those doing the attacking than it does about me. But I also wonder, when did an honorable profession such as being a jurist become a bad thing?"[5]

But although in the November 2018 elections for the 116th Congress women ran from political families, dealing with the positives and negatives experienced since the beginning of women's suffrage, for the first time the new women entering Congress were not primarily from these families. Instead, what this election signaled was the widespread adaptation,

Veronica Escobar and Michael Pleters, 2018 (*El Paso Times*/Part of the USA TODAY Network).

through other groups, of what families had offered—of the independent support that could go beyond what a party might provide.

Certainly many of these new members of Congress did not come from the traditional elite. Sharice Davids, from Kansas, is a member of the Ho-Chunk nation. She was raised by a single mother who served in the U.S. Army. Jahana Hayes grew up in public housing projects in Waterbury, Connecticut. Ayanna Pressley's father Martin Terrell struggled with addiction and was in jail during much of her childhood. She grew up on Chicago's North Side, in "a fragility of circumstance," as she described: "Coming home to an eviction notice on the door. Coming home alone. I'm an only child. My mother was raising me alone. We couldn't afford child care."[6]

Other successful candidates in 2018 had immigrated to the United States in difficult circumstances. Debbie Mucarsel-Powell, a new member of Congress from Florida, was born and raised in Guayaquil, Ecuador, immigrating when she was fourteen. She began working the early morning shift at a donut shop to help support her family, living in a one-bedroom apartment. Ilhan Omar was born in Mogadishu. After the start of a civil war there in 1991, she and her family fled the country and spent four years in a refugee camp in Kenya. In 1995, Omar and her family immigrated to Arlington, Virginia. Omar and Rashida Tlaib are the first Muslim women in Congress.

Though these women did not have the political family support of many earlier candidates, they had a level of support from activist organizations that had not occurred before. By December 2017, EMILY's List, the nation's largest resource for women in politics, announced on its web site that since the 2016 election over 25,000 women had made contact about running for office. For the 2018 election, EMILY'S List offered at unprecedented levels what women of earlier decades had secured from families: encouragement in making the choice to run, early endorsements, fundraising assistance, issue research, and training in budgeting, dealing with staff, and interacting with the press. "We're at an unprecedented time for women in politics," said Stephanie Schriock, president of EMILY's List. "This cycle, we've trained more women than ever before, endorsed more women than ever before, and we're on track to raise more for our candidates than any previous midterm cycle."[7]

Recently many other groups, with various approaches to the issues, have begun attempting to help women to run for office. They include She Should Run, National Women's Political Caucus, Women's Campaign Fund, Ignite, Running Start, Victory Institute, the National Federation of Republican Women, Our Revolution, the Center for American Women and Politics, and the Fund for the Feminist Majority.

Some groups, like political families, are also recognizing the importance of childhood immersion in politics that families have long provided. The Center for American Women and Politics' initiative, Teach a Girl to Lead, connects educators, leaders of youth organizations, parents, and students in order to engage more girls and young women in leadership. Resources listed on the CAWP web site for this initiative stress the importance of civic participation and the significant roles that women have played in American democracy.

Many of these efforts have involved women who themselves had political family support. Using more than one million dollars in unused campaign funds after she decided not to run in 2012, Olympia Snowe set up the Olympia Snowe Women's Leadership Institute, with a three-year curriculum, facilitated by women leaders to nurture tenth to twelfth grade girls. In 2015, Snowe launched this institute in Androscoggin County, Maine, where she was raised.

Kirsten Gillibrand is well-known for meeting with her top donors to appeal to them for other women candidates. In 2012, she told them that women "come from very red states and very red districts, but these are the kinds of seats that we can actually win to find that common ground, bring together and move this country forward." She further argued that more women needed to enter the House and Senate because "if we had 50 percent of women in Congress, we would not be debating contraception. We would be debating the economy, small business, jobs, national security—everything but."[8] She continued this commitment, of extending her fundraising efforts to help other candidates, in subsequent elections.

Other women from this group have established support institutes for women in their states. Carol Williams, who served in the Montana Senate from 2004 to 2012 and whose father Vern D. Griffith was a mayor of Butte and whose husband Pat Williams was in the state Senate and then the U.S. House from Montana, spoke in a phone conversation with me about the intimidation women may feel, the lack of confidence, the inability to step into the political world, even though they may be well suited to it and willing to work hard. She established Carol's List, modeled after EMILY's List, to forward the careers of Democratic women candidates in her state, to create that sense of extended family with which she began her career, winning the seat in the state Senate that her husband had held. Though she faced the criticism of just being "Pat's wife," she recognized that family support had helped her to become one of five women in the Montana Senate, and she now seeks to extend that support to other women from her state.

Beyond these organizations, women secured a form of family support in 2018 through social media. Alexandria Ocasio-Cortez's victory in New York brought recognition of a new collaborative model, involving private group chats and public Twitter posts, by which "grass-roots candidates share everything from volunteer lists to tips for handling criticism of their physical appearance."[9] When she won the primary, on Twitter, Ocasio-Cortez named other progressive candidates that should be sent to Congress, including Ayanna Pressley, who gained 5,000 Twitter followers in twenty-four hours after these tweets—as well as more than 120 volunteers. As Ocasio-Cortez claimed, such targeted appeals through social media could create name recognition, inform voters about policy initiatives, motivate volunteers and fund-raisers—and thus turn outsiders into insiders. As she came to Washington, Ocasio-Cortez narrated her experience through Instagram stories to her 642,000 followers and vowed to share her legislative plans with them. During the 2018 election, other group affiliations enabled the creation of family-like connections, as in the case of three congressional candidates who graduated from the Naval Academy—Mikie Sherrill of New Jersey, Amy McGrath of Kentucky, and Elaine Luria of Virginia—supporting each other through Twitter posts.

This election proved the power of the type of support that families have offered since Victoria Woodhull and Tennie Claflin ran for office and Jeannette Rankin entered the U.S. Congress. Politics is certainly a complex and demanding space, and successful entrance can involve so many varied challenges, such as deciding on the key issues, interacting with fundraisers, appealing to different constituencies, managing staff and an office, developing an appropriate speaking style, and withstanding press critique. Access to help with all of these priorities can foster confidence and create a huge advantage.

Subsequent elections will engage strong candidates who are members of long-term political families and of newly minted ones, continuing the power of grandparents and parents and of the single generation, whether it involves siblings or spouses. In future elections, we may also witness an increase in the ability of individual outsiders to become insiders, as activist organizations and candidates take advantage of techniques developed by political families, expanding the ranks of American elected officials through the methods that created a political elite and that gave support to generations of women as they ran for office.

Appendix

Widows and Other Members of Political Families, in the U.S. Senate and U.S. House to the 115th Congress (2017–2019)

With indication of re-election in November 2018 to the 116th Congress.

Widows Following Their Husbands into the U.S. Senate

Hattie Wyatt Caraway, 1931–45, D–AR
Rose McConnell Long, 1936–37, D–LA
Vera Cahalan Bushfield, 1948, R–SD
Maurine Brown Neuberger, 1960–67, D–OR
Maryon Pittman Allen, 1978–79, D–AL
Muriel Buck Humphrey, 1978–79, D–MN
Jocelyn Birch Burdick, 1992, D–ND
Jean Carnahan, 2001–2002, D–MO

Women in the Senate (Non-Widows) Who Came from Political Families

Rebecca Felton, 1922, D–GA
Dixie Graves, 1937–38, D–AL
Margaret Chase Smith, 1949–73, R–ME
Eva Bowring 1954, R–NE
Elaine Edwards, 1972, D–LA
Nancy Landon Kassebaum, 1978–97, R–KS
Kay Bailey Hutchison, 1993–2013, R–TX
Olympia Snowe, 1995–2013, R–ME
Susan Collins, 1997—the 115th Congress, R–ME (would next run in 2020)
Mary Landrieu, 1997–2015, D–LA
Maria Cantwell, 2001—the 115th Congress, re-elected in November 2018, D–WA

Hillary Clinton, 2001–09, D–NY
Lisa Murkowski, 2002—the 115th Congress, R–AK (would next run in 2022)
Elizabeth Dole, 2003–09, R–NC
Claire McCaskill, 2007—the 115th Congress, D–MO (defeated November 2018)
Jeanne Shaheen, 2009—the 115th Congress, D–NH (would next run in 2020)
Kay Hagan, 2009–15, D–NC
Kirsten Gillibrand, 2009—the 115th Congress, re-elected in November 2018, D–NY
Deb Fischer, 2013—the 115th Congress, re-elected in November 2018, R–NE
Heidi Hietkamp, 2013—the 115th Congress, D–ND (defeated in November 2018)
Shelley Moore Capito, 2015—the 115th Congress, R–WV (would next run in 2020)
Catherine Cortez Masto, 2017—the 115th Congress, D–NV (would run again in 2022)
Tammy Duckworth, 2017—the 115th Congress, D–IL (would run again in 2022)
Maggie Hassan, 2017—the 115th Congress, D–NH (would run again in 2022)

Widows Following Their Husbands into the U.S. House of Representatives

Mae Ella Nolan, 1923–25, R–CA
Florence Prag Kahn, 1925–37, R–CA
Edith Nourse Rogers, 1925–60, R–MA
Pearl Peden Oldfield, 1929–31, D–AR
Effiegene Locke Wingo, 1930–33, D–AR
Willa McCord Blake Eslick, 1932–33, D–TN
Marian Williams Clarke, 1934–35, R–NY
Elizabeth Hawley Gasque, 1938, D–SC
Frances Bolton, 1940–69, R–OH
Margaret Chase Smith, 1940–49, R–ME
Florence Reville Gibbs, 1940–41, D–GA
Clara Gooding McMillan, 1940–41, D–SC
Katharine Edgar Byron, 1941–43, D–MD
Veronica Grace Boland, 1942–43, D–PA
Willa Lybrand Fulmer, 1944–45, D–SC
Vera Daerr Buchanan, 1951–55, D–PA
Marguerite Stitt Church, 1951–63, R–IL
Maude Elizabeth Kee, 1951–65, D–WV
Leonor K. Sullivan, 1952–75, D–MO
Mary Elizabeth Farrington, 1954–57, R–HI
Kathryn Elizabeth Granahan, 1957–63, D–PA
Edna Oakes Simpson, 1958–61, R–IL
Catherine Dorris Norrell, 1961–63, D–AR
Louise Goff Reece, 1961–63, R–TN
Corinne Boyd Riley, 1962–63, D–SC
Irene Bailey Baker, 1964–65, R–TN
Lera Millard Thomas, 1966–67, D–TX
Elizabeth B. Andrews, 1972–73, D–AL

Corinne "Lindy" Boggs, 1973–91, D–LA
Cardiss Collins, 1973–97, D–IL
Shirley N. Pettis, 1975–79, R–CA
Beverly Barton Butcher Byron, 1979–93, D–MD
Jean Ashbrook, 1982–83, R–OH
Sala Burton, 1983–87, D–CA
Catherine S. Long, 1985–87, D–LA
Jo Ann Emerson, 1996–2013, R–MO
Lois Capps, 1998–2013, D–CA
Mary Bono, 1998–2017, R–CA
Doris Matsui, 2005—the 115th Congress, re-elected in November 2018, D–CA

Women in the House of Representatives (Non-Widows) Who Came from Political Families

Jeannette Rankin, 1917–19, 1941–43, R–MO
Winnifred Huck, 1922–23, R–IL
Katherine G. Langley, 1927–31, R–KY
Ruth Hanna McCormick, 1929–31, R–IL
Ruth Bryan Owen, 1929–33, D–FL
Kathryn O'Laughlin-McCarthy, 1933–35, D–KS
Isabella Greenway, 1933–37, D–AZ
Clare Booth Luce, 1943–47, R–CT
Emily Douglas, 1945–47, D–IL
Georgia Lusk, 1947–49, D–NM
Katharine St. George, 1947–53, 1953–63, 1963–65, R–NY
Edna F. Kelly, 1949–63, 1963–69, D–NY
Martha Griffiths, 1955–74, D–MI
Julia Hansen, 1960–74, D–WA
Louise Hicks, 1971–73, D–MA
Patricia Schroeder, 1973–97, D–CO
Millicent Fenwick, 1975–83, R–NJ
Martha Keys, 1975–79, D–KS
Helen Stevenson-Meyner, 1975–79, D–NJ
Olympia Snowe, 1979–95, R–ME
Barbara B. Kennelly, 1982–99, D–CT
Barbara Vucanovich, 1983–97, R–NV
Jan Meyers, 1985–97, R–KS
Connie Morella, 1987–2003, R–MD
Liz J. Patterson, 1987–93, D–SC
Louise Slaughter, 1987–2018, D–NY
Nancy Pelosi, 1993—the 115th Congress, re-elected November 2018, D–CA
Ileana Ros-Lehtinen, FL, 1989—the 115th Congress, R–FL (did not run in 2018)
Susan Molinari, 1990–97, R–NY
Rosa DeLauro, 1991—the 115th Congress, re-elected November 2018, D–CT
Maria Cantwell, 1993–95, D–WA
Pat Danner, 1993–2001, D–MO

Tillie K. Fowler, 1993–2001, R–FL
Jane Harman, 1993–99, 2001–2011, D–CA
Marjorie Margolies, 1993–95, D–PA
Cynthia McKinney, 1993–2003, 2005–07, D–GA
Lucille Roybal-Allard, CA, 1993—the 115th Congress, re-elected in November
    2018, D–CA
Karen Shepherd, 1993–95, D–UT
Karen Thurman, 1993–2003, D–FL
Nydia Velázquez, 1993—the 115th Congress, re-elected in November 2018, D–NY
Sue Myrick, 1995–2013, R–NC
Donna Christian-Christensen, 1997–2015, D–U.S. Virgin Islands
Loretta Sánchez, 1997–2017, D–CA
Jan Schakowsky, 1999—the 115th Congress, re-elected in November 2018, D–IL
Shelley Moore Capito, 2001–15, R–WV
Madeleine Bordallo, 2003—the 115th Congress, D–Guam (lost in the 2018
    Democratic primary)
Katherine Harris, 2003–07, R–FL
Candice Miller, 2003–17, R–MI
Linda Sánchez, 2003—the 115th Congress, re-elected in November 2018, D–CA
Stephanie Herseth-Sandlin, 2004–11, D–SD
Cathy McMorris-Rodgers, 2005—the 115th Congress, re-elected in November
    2018, R–WA
Debbie Wasserman-Schultz, 2005—the 115th Congress, re-elected in November
    2018, D–FL
Kathy Castor, 2007—the 115th Congress, re-elected in November 2018, D–FL
Yvette Clarke, 2007—the 115th Congress, re-elected in November 2018, D–NY
Mary Fallin, 2007–11, R–OK
Kristen Gillibrand, 2007–09, D–NY
Laura Richardson, 2007–13, D–CA
Betty Sutton, 2007–13, D–OH
Niki Tsongas, 2007—the 115th Congress, D–MA (did not run in 2018)
Cynthia Lummis, 2009–17, R–WY
Chellie Pingree, 2009—the 115th Congress, re-elected in November 2018, D–ME
Dina Titus, 2009–11, 2013—the 115th Congress, re-elected in November
    2018, D–NV
Judy Chu, 2009—the 115th Congress, re-elected in November 2018, D–CA
Martha Roby, 2011—the 115th Congress, re-elected in November 2018, R–AL
Terri Sewell, 2011—the 115th Congress, re-elected in November 2018, D–AL
Kathy Hochul, 2011–13, D–NY
Janice Hahn, 2011–16, D–CA
Suzanne Bonamici, 2012—the 115th Congress, re-elected in November 2018,
    D–OR
Joyce Beatty, 2013—the 115th Congress, re-elected in November 2018, D–OH
Cheri Bustos, 2013—the 115th Congress, re-elected in November 2018, D–IL
Elizabeth Esty, 2013—the 115th Congress, D–CT (resigned in 2018)
Michelle Lujan Grisham, 2013—the 115th Congress, D–NM (ran successfully
    in 2018 for governor of New Mexico)

Ann McLane-Kuster, 2013—the 115th Congress, re-elected in November
  2018, D–NH
Grace Meng, 2013—the 115th Congress, re-elected in November 2018, D–NY
Ann Wagner, 2013—the 115th Congress, re-elected in November 2018, R–MO
Debbie Dingell, 2015—the 115th Congress, re-elected in November 2018, D–MI
Gwen Graham, 2015–17, D–FL
Amata Radewagen (Aumua Amata), 2015—the 115th Congress, re-elected in
  November 2018, R–American Samoa
Lisa Blunt-Rochester, 2017—the 115th Congress, re-elected in November
  2018, D–DE
Liz Cheney, 2017—the 115th Congress, re-elected in November 2018, R–WY
Val Demings, 2017—the 115th Congress, re-elected in November 2018, D–FL
Jenniffer González, 2017—the 115th Congress, R–Puerto Rico (resident
  commissioner is a four-year term)
Claudia Tenney, 2017—the 115th Congress, R–NY (lost in the 2018 election)

Chapter Notes

Introduction

1. Kristi Andersen, *After Suffrage: Women in Partisan and Electoral Politics Before the New Deal* (Chicago: University of Chicago Press, 1996), 113; Sophonisba Breckinridge, "The Activities of Women Outside the Home," in *Recent Social Trends in the United States* (New York: McGraw-Hill, 1933), 741–744; Sophonisba Breckinridge, *Women in the Twentieth Century: A Study of Their Political, Social and Economic Activities* (New York: McGraw-Hill, 1933), 322; Doris Weatherford, *Women in American Politics: History and Milestones*, vol. 1 (Washington, D.C.: CQ Press, 2012), 38–53.

2. Quoted in Nancy Woloch, *Women and the American Experience* (New York: Knopf, 1984), 356; Kathryn Anderson, "Evolution of a Partisan: Emily Newell Blair and the Democratic Party, 1920–1932," in *We Have Come to Stay: American Women and Political Parties, 1880–1960*, ed. Melanie Gustafson, Kristie Miller, and Elisabeth I. Perry (Albuquerque: University of New Mexico Press, 1999), 109–119.

3. Emily Newell Blair, "Why I Am Discouraged About Women in Politics," *The Woman's Journal* (January 1931): 20.

4. Ellen R. Malcolm and Craig Unger, *When Women Win: EMILY's List and the Rise of Women in American Politics* (Boston: Houghton Mifflin Harcourt, 2016), 33.

5. "A Different Voice: Women in Congress," *Constitutional Rights Foundation, Bill of Rights in Action*, 9:3 and 9.4 (Summer 1993), updated July 2000, accessed November 15, 2017, www.crf-usa.org; "Women in the U.S. Congress 2017," CAWP: Center for American Women and Politics, Rutgers Eagleton Institute of Politics, accessed November 12, 2017, cawp.rutgers.edu; Marjorie

Margolies-Mezvinsky, with Barbara Feinman, *A Woman's Place … The Freshmen Women Who Changed the Face of Congress* (New York: Crown Publishers, 1994); Barbara Boxer, with Nicole Boxer, *Strangers in the Senate: Politics and the New Revolution of Women in America* (Washington, D.C.: National Press Books, 1994), 157–166.

6. Jennifer L. Lawless and Richard L. Fox, *It Takes a Candidate: Why Women Don't Run for Office* (New York: Cambridge University Press, 2005), 10.

7. Ellen Goodman, "Progress by Drip Method," *Des Moines Register*, November 8, 1986, accessed November 8, 2017, newspapers.com.

8. "Reapportionment, Redistricting and Women: The Dangers and Opportunities in California," *CAWP News & Notes* 7, no. 1 (1989): 14–15.

9. Christianna Silva, "Don't Hold Your Breath for Gender Parity In Congress—It Could Take Another 100 Years," *FiveThirtyEight*, accessed August 28, 2018, fivethirtyeight.com.

10. "Proportion of Seats Held by Women in National Parliaments," The World Bank, accessed December 12, 2017, data.worldbank.org; Nancy Cohen, *Breakthrough: The Making of America's First Woman President* (Berkeley: Counterpoint, 2016), 4, 61; Jane S. Jensen, *Women Political Leaders: Breaking the Highest Glass Ceiling* (New York: Palgrave Macmillan, 2008), 10–12.

11. Madeleine May Kunin, *Living a Political Life* (New York: Knopf, 1994), 10.

12. Susan J. Carroll, *Women as Candidates in American Politics*, 2nd ed. (Bloomington: Indiana University Press, 1994), 44; Marianne Githens, "Accounting for Women's Political Involvement: The Perennial Problem of Recruitment," in *Women and Ameri-*

can Politics: New Questions, New Directions, ed. Susan Carroll (New York: Oxford University Press, 2003), 33–52; Nancy E. McGlen, Karen O'Connor, Laura van Assendelft, and Wendy Gunther-Canada, *Women, Politics, and American Society* (New York: Longman, 2017), 102–104.

13. Susan J. Carroll, *Women as Candidates in American Politics,* 38–39.

14. Wendy Kaminer, "Crashing the Locker Room," *Atlantic* 270 (July 1992): 58–70, accessed June 12, 2018, theatlantic.com/magazine/archive.

15. Susan J. Carroll and Kira Sanbonmatsu, *More Women Can Run: Gender and Pathways to the State Legislatures* (New York: Oxford University Press, 2013), 63–122; Barbara Burrell, *Gender in Campaigns for the U.S. House of Representatives* (Ann Arbor: University of Michigan Press, 2014). See also Jennifer L. Lawless and Kathryn Pearson, "The Primary Reason for Women's Under-Representation? Re-Evaluating the Conventional Wisdom," *Journal of Politics* 70, no. 1 (2008): 78; and Anne Koenig, et al. "Are Leader Stereotypes Masculine?" *Psychological Bulletin* 137 (2011): 616–642.

16. Kristina Horn Sheeler and Karrin Vasby Anderson, *Woman President: Confronting Postfeminist Political Culture* (College Station: Texas A&M University Press, 2013), 107.

17. Clare Malone, "From 1937 to Hillary Clinton, How Americans Have Felt About a Woman President," *FiveThirtyEight,* June 9, 2016, accessed August 28, 2018; Anne Koenig, et al., "Are Leader Stereotypes Masculine?"; Todd L. Belt, "Viral Videos: Reinforcing Stereotypes of Female Candidates for President," in *Women and the White House: Gender, Popular Culture, and Presidential Politics,* ed. Justin S. Vaughn and Lilly J. Goren (Lexington: University Press of Kentucky, 2013), 206; Lori Cox Han, "Is the United States *Really* Really Ready for a Woman President?" in *Rethinking Madam President: Are We Ready for a Woman in the White House?,* ed. Lori Cox Han and Caroline Heldman (Boulder, CO: Lynne Rienner, 2007), 1–16.

18. Tim Marcin, "Nearly 60 Percent of Republicans Don't Want a Woman President in Their Lifetime, Poll Finds," *Newsweek,* April 26, 2018, accessed May 2, 2018, newsweek. com.

19. Diane Heath, "The Lipstick Watch: Media Coverage, Gender, and Presidential Campaigns," in *Anticipating Madam President,* ed. Robert P. Watson and Ann Gordon (Boulder, CO: Lynne Reinner Publishers, 2003), 123–130.

20. Teri Finneman, *Press Portrayals of Women Politicians, 1870s-2000s: From "Lunatic" Woodhull to "Polarizing" Palin* (Lanham, MD: Lexington Books, 2015), 72; Lois Duke Whitaker, "Women Politicians and the Mass Media: Does Gender Influence the News?" in *Women in Politics: Outsiders or Insiders?: A Collection of Readings,* ed. Lois Duke Whitaker, 5th ed. (Boston: Longman, 2011), 73–88; Susan A. Basow, "Evaluation of Female Leaders: Stereotypes, Prejudice and Discrimination," in *Why Congress Needs Women: Bringing Sanity to the House and Senate,* ed. Michele A. Paludi (Santa Barbara, CA: Praeger, 2016), 85–98.

21. Sylvia Bashevkin, *Women, Power, Politics: The Hidden Story of Canada's Unfinished Democracy* (New York: Oxford University Press, 2009), 88–89; Wendy Kaminer, "Crashing the Locker Room."

22. Deborah Jordan Brooks, *He Runs, She Runs: Why Gender Stereotypes Do Not Harm Women Candidates* (Princeton: Princeton University Press, 2013); Kathleen Dolan, *When Does Gender Matter?: Women Candidates and Gender Stereotypes in American Elections* (New York: Oxford University Press, 2014); Danny Hayes and Jennifer L. Lawless, *Women on the Run: Gender, Media, and Political Campaigns in a Polarized Era* (New York: Cambridge University Press, 2016).

23. Jennifer L. Lawless and Richard L. Fox, "Men Rule: The Continued Under-Representation of Women in Politics," *Women and Politics Institute,* 2012, accessed January 12, 2018, www.american.edu/spa/wpi; Mary Christine Banwart, "Gender and Candidate Communication: Effects of Stereotypes in the 2008 Election," *American Behavioral Scientist* 54, no. 3 (2010): 265–284.

24. Kathleen Jamieson, *Civility in the House of Representatives* (Philadelphia: Annenberg Center, 1999), 17–18.

25. Dana Milbank and David S. Broder, "Hopes for Civility in Washington Are Dashed; In Bush's Term, Tone Worsened, Partisans Say," *Washington Post,* January 18, 2004, accessed July 24, 2018, washingtonpost.com. Among other writers, Thomas Mann and Norman Ornstein have thoroughly investigated this decreasing civility, in *It's Even Worse Than It Looks: How the American Constitutional System Collided with the New Politics of Extremism* (New York: Basic Books, 2012) and *The Broken Branch: How Congress Is Failing Americans and How To Get It Back on Track* (New York: Oxford University Press, 2006).

26. Torey Van Oot, "For Women in Congress, the State of the Union Is a #MeToo

Moment," *Glamour*, January 30, 2018, accessed June 14, 2018, glamour.com.
27. Michael Finnegan, "Congress Is Caught Up in the Sexual Misconduct Scandals. Will It Police Its Own?," *Los Angeles Times*, November 29, 2017, accessed February 2, 2018, latimes.com; Cristina Marcos, "Women, Dems Leading Sexual Harassment Discussion in Congress," *The Hill*, November 27, 2017, accessed February 3, 2018, thehill.com.
28. Kira Sanbonmatsu and Susan J. Carroll, "Women's Decisions to Run for Office: A Relationally Embedded Model," in *The Political Psychology of Women in U.S. Politics*, ed. Angela L. Bos and Monica C. Schneider (New York: Routledge, 2017), 148–164; Barbara C. Burrell, *Gender in Campaigns for the U.S. House of Representatives*, 250.
29. Kenneth Prewitt, *The Recruitment of Political Leaders: A Study of Citizen-Politicians* (Westport, CT: Greenwood Press, 1970), 27.
30. Stephen Hess, *America's Political Dynasties: From Adams to Kennedy* (Garden City, NY: Doubleday), 1966, 3; Kenneth Prewitt, *The Recruitment of Political Leaders*, 9–11, 23–27, 39–40.
31. Stephen Hess, "Political 'Royalty' in America (or, the Son Also Rises)," *Anniston* (AL) *Star*, January 22, 1978, accessed February 15, 2018, newspapers.com; Stephen Hess, *America's Political Dynasties*; Jeane Kirkpatrick, *The New Presidential Elite: Men and Women in National Politics* (New York: Russell Sage Foundation, 1976), 61–92.
32. Stephen Hess, *America's Political Dynasties: From Adams to Clinton* (Washington, D.C.: Brookings Institution Press, 2016), 577–578.
33. Linda Witt, Karen M. Paget, and Glenna Matthews, *Running as a Woman: Gender and Power in American Politics* (New York: Free Press, 1994), 105.
34. Julie Dolan, Melissa Deckman, and Michele L. Swers, *Women and Politics: Paths to Power and Political Influence* (Upper Saddle River, NJ: Pearson Prentice Hall, 2007), 152.
35. Irwin N. Gertzog, "The Matrimonial Connection: The Nomination of Congressmen's Widows for the House of Representatives," *Journal of Politics* 42 (1980): 820–831; Irwin N. Gertzog, *Congresswomen: Their Recruitment, Treatment, and Behavior* (New York: Praeger, 1984); Irwin Gertzog, "Women's Changing Pathways to the U.S. House of Representatives: Widows, Elites, and Strategic Politicians," in *Women Transforming Congress*, ed. Cindy Simon Rosenthal (Norman: University of Oklahoma Press, 2002), 95–118.

36. Linda Witt, Karen M. Paget, and Glenna Matthews, *Running as a Woman*, 105.
37. Jennifer Lawless and Richard Fox, *It Still Takes a Candidate: Why Women Don't Run for Office* (New York: Cambridge University Press, 2010), 68.
38. Barbara Palmer and Dennis Simon, *Women and Congressional Elections: A Century of Change* (Boulder, CO: Lynne Rienner Publishers, 2012), 91–125.
39. "Robertson Letter Attacks Feminists," *New York Times*, August 26, 1992, accessed December 18, 2017, nytimes.com.

Chapter One

1. Mary Gabriel, *Notorious Victoria: The Life of Victoria Woodhull, Uncensored* (Chapel Hill, NC: Algonquin Books of Chapel Hill, 1998), 11.
2. Myra MacPherson, *The Scarlet Sisters: Sex, Suffrage, and Scandal in the Gilded Age* (New York: Twelve, 2014), 3; Mary Gabriel, *Notorious Victoria*, 9.
3. Marta Trzebiatowska and Steve Bruce, *Why Are Women More Religious Than Men?* (New York: Oxford University Press, 2012), 51.
4. Several books contain more information about spiritualism: Ruth Brandon, *The Spiritualists: The Passion for the Occult in the Nineteenth and Twentieth Centuries* (New York: Alfred A. Knopf, 1983) ; Ann Braude, *Radical Spirits: Spiritualism and Women's Rights in Nineteenth-Century America*, 2nd ed. (Urbana: Indiana University Press, 2001); Bret E. Carroll, *Spiritualism in Antebellum America* (Bloomington: Indiana University Press, 1997); and Amy Lehman, *Victorian Women and the Theatre of Trance: Mediums, Spiritualists and Mesmerists in Performance* (Jefferson, NC: McFarland, 2009).
5. Mary Gabriel, *Notorious Victoria*, 9–12.
6. Myra MacPherson, *The Scarlet Sisters*, 15.
7. "Their Ugly Past: Reviving the Record of the Claflins," *San Francisco Chronicle*, May 8, 1890, accessed March 31, 2018, newspapers.com.
8. Theodore Tilton, *Biography of Victoria C. Woodhull* (New York: Golden Age, 1871), 18.
9. Mary Gabriel, *Notorious Victoria*, 22; Myra MacPherson, *The Scarlet Sisters*, 37.
10. Edward J. Renehan, Jr., *Commodore: The Life of Cornelius Vanderbilt* (New York: Basic Books, 2009), 268.

11. Mary Gabriel, *Notorious Victoria*, 43.

12. Myra Macpherson, *The Scarlet Sisters*, 42.

13. "The Queens of Finance," *New York Herald*, January 22, 1870, accessed November 8, 2017, newspapers.com.

14. "The Female Financiers," *Tennessean* (Nashville), April 1, 1870, accessed February 21, 2018, newspapers.com.

15. "The Queens of Finance," *Reading* (PA) *Times*, February 8, 1870, accessed November 8, 2017, newspapers.com.

16. "The Petticoat Bankers," *Evening Telegraph* (Philadelphia, PA), March 26, 1870, accessed February 21, 2018, newspapers.com.

17. Susan B. Anthony, "What Can Women Do?" *Revolution* 24 (March 1870): 188; Myra Macpherson, *The Scarlet Sisters*, 49.

18. Mary Gabriel, *Notorious Victoria*, 158–159.

19. Myra Macpherson, *The Scarlet Sisters*, 50; Ellen Fitzpatrick, *The Highest Glass Ceiling: Women's Quest for the American Presidency* (Cambridge: Harvard University Press, 2016), 29–37.

20. "The Coming Woman," *New York Herald*, April 2, 1870, accessed March 31, 2018, newspapers.com.

21. "We Presume We Must Accept," *Democrat and Chronicle* (Rochester, NY), July 11, 1871, accessed January 7, 2018, newspapers.com.

22. "Tennie Claflin," *Clarion-Ledger* (Jackson, MS), April 21, 1870, accessed May 12, 2018, newspapers.com.

23. Myra Macpherson, *The Scarlet Sisters*, 52.

24. Rodger Streitmatter, *Voices of Revolution: The Dissident Press in America* (New York: Columbia University Press, 2001), 64.

25. "Letter from Hawk's Nest Peak," *Woodhull & Claflin's Weekly*, July 1, 1871, accessed July 25, 2018, victoria-woodhull.com.

26. "The Feminine Invasion of the Capitol," *Frank Leslie's Illustrated Newspaper*, 801 (February 4, 1871), 347.

27. Myra Macpherson, *The Scarlet Sisters*, 67–69.

28. Victoria Woodhull, "Tried as by Fire: Or, the True and the False, Socially," in *The Victoria Woodhull Reader*, ed. Madeleine B. Stern (Weston, MA: M&S Press, 1974), 39–40.

29. Victoria Woodhull, "Mrs. Woodhull's Own Statement," in *The Great Sensation: A Full, Complete and Reliable History of the Beecher-Tilton-Woodhull Scandal, with Biographical Sketches of the Principal Characters*, ed. Leon Oliver (Chicago: Beverly Company, 1873), 95.

30. "Female Financiers' Feuds," *Sun* (New York), May 8, 1871, accessed May 9, 2018, newspapers.com; "The Woodhull-Claflin Family," *Brooklyn Daily Eagle*, May 11, 1871, accessed March 5, 2018, newspapers.com.

31. "Blood, Be-lud!!, S-Blood!!!," *Alton* (IL) *Telegraph*, May 12, 1871, accessed May 18, 2018, newspapers.com.

32. Amanda Frisken, *Victoria Woodhull's Sexual Revolution: Political Theater and the Popular Press in Nineteenth-Century America* (Philadelphia: University of Pennsylvania Press, 2004), 30–31.

33. "The Free-Love Queen," *Charleston* (SC) *Daily News*, May 26, 1871, accessed April 1, 2018, newspapers.com.

34. Theodore Tilton, *Biography of Victoria C. Woodhull*.

35. Myra Macpherson, *The Scarlet Sisters*, 126.

36. Tennie Claflin, "The Cosmopolitical Club," *Woodhull and Claflin's Weekly*, July 8, 1871, accessed June 12, 2018, iapsop.com/archive; Mary Gabriel, *Notorious Victoria*, 126–127; "Tennie and the Germans," *Sun* (New York), August 12, 1871, accessed May 12, 2018, newspapers.com.

37. "Letter from Tennie C. Claflin," *Woodhull & Claflin's Weekly*, August 5, 1871, accessed May 12, 2018, victoria-woodhull.com.

38. Myra Macpherson, *The Scarlet Sisters*, 153–154.

39. Alesha E. Doan, *Opposition and Intimidation: The Abortion Wars and Strategies of Political Harassment* (Ann Arbor: University of Michigan, 2007), 46–47.

40. Tennie C. Claflin, "My World on Abortion, and Other Things," *Woodhull & Claflin's Weekly*, September 23, 1871, accessed May 12, 2018, victoria-woodhull.com.

41. "Tennie and the Germans."

42. "Tennie Claflin," *Athens* (PN) *Gleaner*, September 14, 1871, accessed May 12, 2018, newspapers.com; "Woodhull and Claflin Slander," *The Friends of Temperance* (Raleigh, NC), September 6, 1871, accessed March 1, 2018, newspapers.com.

43. Andrew R. Dodge and Betty K. Koed, *Biographical Directory of the United States Congress, 1774–2005* (Washington, D.C.: Government Printing Office, 2005), 714.

44. "Three Women," *Waterloo* (IO) *Press*, November 9, 1871, accessed May 12, 2018, newspapers.com; "Woodhull and Claflin at the Polls," *Harrisburg Telegraph*, November 14, 1871, accessed March 1, 2018, newspapers.com.

45. "Rule or Ruin," *Pittsburgh Daily Post*, December 18, 1871, accessed March 12, 2018, newspapers.com; "New York: The Interna-

tionalists Procession a Decided Success," *Chicago Tribune*, December 18, 1871, accessed March 12, 2018, newspapers.com.

46. "Woodhull and Claflin on the Tramp," *Burlington Free Press*, December 18, 1871, accessed March 1, 2018, newspapers.com; "The Workingmen's Voice," *Sun* (New York), December 18, 1871, accessed March 9, 2018, newspapers.com; "Her Daddy and Mamma Bother Her," *Daily Kansas Tribune*, December 16, 1871, accessed January 26, 2017, newspapers.com.

47. "The Woman's Right Women—The Irrepressible Conflict," *Star Tribune* (Minneapolis), May 18, 1872, accessed February 23, 2018, newspapers.com.

48. "Spirit of the Press; Extraordinary Politics," *Woodhull & Claflin's Weekly*, June 1, 1872, victoria-woodhull.com.

49. "A Piebald Presidency," *New York Herald*, May 11, 1872, accessed January 4, 2018, newspapers.com.

50. "Woodhull and Douglass, *Sun* (New York), May 11, 1872, accessed March 1, 2018, newspapers.com.

51. "A Piebald Presidency."

52. "Spirit of the Press; Extraordinary Politics."

53. "A Question of Clothes," *New York Times*, June 16, 1872, accessed January 21, 2018, newspapers.com.

54. "Greeley Ratified," *Daily State Journal* (Alexandria, VA), June 17, 1872, accessed June 1, 2018, newspapers.com; "The Fourth of July," *Sterling* (IL) *Standard*, July 11, 1872, accessed June 5, 2017, newspapers.com.

55. "The Congress of Internationalists," *Guardian*, September 10, 1872, accessed February 23, 2018, newspapers.com; "A Dispatch from the Hague," *Galveston Daily News*, September 8, 1872, accessed May 24, 2018, newspapers.com.

56. Debby Applegate, *The Most Famous Man in America: The Biography of Henry Ward Beecher* (New York, Doubleday, 2006), 410–423.

57. Helen Lefkowitz Horowitz, "Victoria Woodhull, Anthony Comstock, and Conflict over Sex in the United States in the 1870s," *Journal of American History* 87, no. 2 (September 2000), 406.

Chapter Two

1. "Three of a Kind: Lockwood, Anthony and Stanton, Quarreling over a Man," *St. Louis Post-Dispatch*, August 16, 1884, accessed April 2, 2018, newspapers.com.

2. "How Many of the Four Million Will Vote?" *Ladies Home Journal* 33, no.4 (1916): 12.

3. Dawn Mitchell, "Amanda Way Was Indiana's Hard-Core Anti-Booze Baroness," *Indianapolis Star*, March 20, 1917, accessed February 15, 2018, IndyStar.com.

4. "The Week," *Public Opinion* 14, no. 32 (April 3, 1902): 419.

5. "Woman Running for Congress: Miss Burkhart Making Canvass on Horseback in Kentucky," *New York Times*, March 30, 1902, accessed February 6, 2018, *New York Times* Historical Database.

6. "Mrs. Grover Announces Candidacy for Congress," *Topeka Daily Capital*, April 19, 1914, accessed March 8, 2018, newspapers.com; Jo Freeman, *We Will Be Heard: Women's Struggles for Political Power in the United States* (Lanham, MD: Rowman and Littlefield, 2008), 49–76.

7. "Today in Philadelphia," April 19, 1916, Philadelphia: The World War I Years, accessed April 7, 2018, philadelphiawwiyears.com.

8. Ethel Lloyd Patterson, "Romantic Love Will Come Only in the Future," *St. Louis Post Dispatch*, June 10, 1911, accessed May 11, 2018, newspapers.com.

9. David Burns, *The Life and Death of the Radical Historical Jesus* (New York: Oxford University Press, 2013), 190; Martha Moore Avery, "Why I Left the Socialist Movement," *Common Cause* 1 (February 1912): 14.

10. Mari Jo Buhle, *Women and American Socialism, 1870–1920* (Urbana: University of Illinois Press, 1983), 162–166.

11. "A Kansas Woman Runs for Congress," *Independent*, July 13, 1914, 66.

12. Robert E. Hennings, *James D. Phelan and the Wilson Progressives of California* (New York: Garland, 1985), 126.

13. "Dr. Eva Harding Doesn't Wait for Party Action," *Topeka Daily Capital*, January 16, 1916, accessed March 11, 2018, newspapers.com; "War on the Kansas Map," *New York Times*, February 21, 1916, accessed June 12, 2018, *New York Times* Historical Database; "Woman Not Nominated," *The Daily Gate City and Constitution-Democrat* (Keokuk, IA), August 12, 1916, accessed January 21, 2018, newspapers.com.

14. Lawrence A. Matika, *The Contributions of Frederick Albert Cleveland to the Development of a System of Municipal Accounting in the Progressive Era* (Kent, OH: Kent State University Press, 1988).

15. "Washington Woman Put Up for Congress," *St. Louis Post-Dispatch*, September 14, 1916, accessed February 27, 2018, newspapers.com.

16. Quoted in Lily Rothman, "How the

First Woman Was Elected to U.S. National Office, Exactly 100 Years Ago," *Time,* November 7, 2016, accessed April 12, 2018, news papers.com.

17. James J. Lopach and Jean A. Luckowski, *Jeannette Rankin: Political Woman* (Boulder: University Press of Colorado, 2005), 3; Peter Clark McFarlane, "Jeannette of Montana," *Colliers* (April 21, 1917): 7–8.

18. Volney Steele, *Wellington Rankin: His Family, Life and Times* (Bozeman, MT: Bridger Creek Historical Press, 2002), 46–50.

19. Volney Steele, *Wellington Rankin,* 7–9.

20. Norma Smith, *Jeannette Rankin: America's Conscience* (Helena, MT: Montana Historical Society Press, 2002), 46.

21. Ronald Schaffer, "The Montana Woman Suffrage Campaign, 1911–14," *Pacific Northwest Quarterly* 55, no. 1 (January 1964): 9–15.

22. Volney Steele, *Wellington Rankin,* 68.

23. Ronald Schaffer, "The Montana Woman Suffrage Campaign, 1911–14"; Katrina Rebecca Cheek, *The Rhetoric and Revolt of Jeannette Rankin* (masters thesis, University of Georgia, 1969), 58–60.

24. Hannah Josephson, *Jeannette Rankin: First Lady in Congress, A Biography* (Indianapolis: Bobbs-Merrill Company, 1974), 51.

25. Norma Smith, *Jeannette Rankin: America's Conscience,* 98–106.

26. Norma Smith, *Jeannette Rankin: America's Conscience,* 58.

27. Kathryn Anderson, introduction to *Jeannette Rankin: America's Conscience,* by Norma Smith (Helena, MT: Montana Historical Society Press, 2002), 18.

28. James J. Lopach and Jean A. Luckowski, *Jeannette Rankin,* 6.

29. "Equal Pay for Women," *New York Times,* November 12, 1916, accessed April 2, 2018, *New York Times* Historical Database.

30. Hannah Josephson, *Jeannette Rankin: First Lady in Congress,* 52.

31. Norma Smith, *Jeannette Rankin: America's Conscience,* 193.

32. Norma Smith, *Jeannette Rankin: America's Conscience,* 102.

33. Norma Smith, *Jeannette Rankin: America's Conscience,* 99.

34. "Election News at a Glance," *Harrisburg Telegraph,* December 2, 1916, accessed January 15, 2018, newspapers.com.

35. Kevin S. Giles, *Flight of the Dove: The Story of Jeannette Rankin* (Beaverton, OR: Touchstone Press, 1980), 70, 90.

36. Bert Lennon, "Jeannette Rankin Is Well Qualified to Serve in Congress," *Oregon Daily Journal,* December 3, 1916, accessed August 7, 2018, newspapers.com.

37. "Miss Jeannette Rankin," *Democrat and Chronicle* (Rochester, NY), October 18, 1916, accessed June 21, 2018, newspapers.com.

38. J.R. Hildebrand, "Introducing Jeannette," *Washington Times,* November 11, 1916, accessed February 21, 2018, newspapers.com.

39. Bert Lennon, "Jeannette Rankin Is Well Qualified to Serve in Congress."

40. "Who is Jeannette Rankin and What Will She Do?" *Woman's Journal and Suffrage News* (November 18, 1916): 370.

41. Maria Braden, *Women Politicians and the Media* (Lexington: University Press of Kentucky, 1996), 21.

42. "New Congresswoman Bars Picturemen," *Oakland Tribune,* November 17, 1916, accessed July 27, 2018, newspapers.com.

43. Bert Lennon, "The Lady from Montana," *Charlotte Observer,* December 24, 1916, accessed August 15, 2018, newspapers.com.

44. Norma Smith, *Jeannette Rankin: America's Conscience,* 104; Jeannette Rankin, "What We Women Should Do," *Ladies' Home Journal,* August 1917, 17.

45. "Our Busy Congresswoman," *Literary Digest* 55 (August 11, 1917): 43.

46. Kevin S. Giles, *Flight of the Dove,* 70.

47. Hannah Josephson, *Jeannette Rankin,* 73.

48. Norma Smith, *Jeannette Rankin: America's Conscience,* 107–108.

49. Wellington Rankin, interview with John Board, March 23, 1964, Wellington D. Rankin papers, Archives West, accessed December 8, 2017, archiveswest.orbiscascade.org.

50. Norma Smith, *Jeannette Rankin: America's Conscience,* 111; Jeannette Rankin, "I Would Vote 'No' Again," *Alton (IA) Democrat,* April 17, 1936, accessed February 12, 2018, newspapers.com.

51. "Seek to Explain Miss Rankin's 'No,'" *New York Times,* April 7, 1917, accessed April 15, 2018, *New York Times* Historical Database; Dave Walter, "Rebel with a Cause," *Montana* 110 (November–December 1991): 66–67.

52. Norma Smith, *Jeannette Rankin: America's Conscience,* 112; Ted Carlton Harris, *Jeannette Rankin: Suffragist, First Woman Elected to Congress, and Pacifist* (New York: Arno Press. 1982), 119; Wellington Rankin, interview with John Board; John Board, "The Lady from Montana: Jeannette Rankin" (masters thesis, University of Wyoming, 1964), 133.

53. Hannah Josephson, *Jeannette Rankin,*

74; Norma Smith, *Jeannette Rankin: America's Conscience*, 106; Wellington Rankin, interview with John Board.

54. "Seek to Explain Miss Rankin's 'No.'"

55. Hannah Josephson, *Jeannette Rankin*, 76.

56. "Strong Pressure, Failed to Influence Congresswoman's Vote on War," *Cincinnati Enquirer*, April 7, 1917, accessed February 23, 2018, newspapers.com.

57. "Jeannette Rankin Explains Peace Pacts to Outlaw War," *Havre* (MT) *Daily News*, September 4, 1928, accessed July 19, 2018, newspapers.com.

58. Volney Steele, *Wellington Rankin*, 8.

59. Norma Smith, *Jeannette Rankin: America's Conscience*, 127.

60. Maria Braden, *Women Politicians and the Media*, 25–26.

61. Hannah Josephson, *Jeannette Rankin*, 92.

62. Norma Smith, *Jeannette Rankin: America's Conscience*, 137.

63. Colonel C.B. Nolan to Thomas Walsh, August 30, 1918, Thomas James Walsh Papers, Library of Congress.

64. A.E. Spriggs to Thomas Walsh, September 2, 1918, Thomas James Walsh Papers, Library of Congress; Kevin S. Giles, *Flight of the Dove*, 118; Ronald Schaffer, "Jeannette Rankin, Progressive-Isolationist" (Ph.D. diss., Princeton, 1959), 141.

65. "Miss Rankin to Run," *The Boyden* (IA) *Reporter*, September 5, 1918, accessed January 14, 2018, newspapers.com.

66. John Morrison and Catherine Wright Morrison, *Mavericks: The Lives and Battles of Montana's Political Legends* (Helena: Montana Historical Society, 2003), 144–146.

67. *Official Abstract of Votes Cast at the General Election Held in Montana, November 5, 1918*, Montana Secretary of State, accessed December 19, 2017, sos.mt.gov; James Leonard Bates, *Senator Thomas J. Walsh of Montana: Law and Public Affairs, from TR to FDR* (Urbana: University of Illinois Press, 1999), 166.

68. "Democracy's Mental Dissolution Pictured as Nazi Goal in U.S.," *Christian Science Monitor*, July 20, 1940, 15.

69. "U.S. Now at War with Germany and Italy," *New York Times*, December 11, 1941, accessed December 15, 2017, newspapers.com.

70. "Asks Miss Rankin Recant; Montana Republican Leader Says State Deplores Anti-War Vote, *New York Times*, December 9, 1941, accessed December 5, 2017, *New York Times* Historical Database.

71. Dave Walter, *More Montana Campfire Tales: Fifteen Historical Narratives* (Helena, MT: Farcountry Press, 2002), 254.

72. "Miss Rankin, War Opponent in 1917, Hasn't Changed Mind," *Washington Post*, December 9, 1941, accessed May 16, 2018, newspapers.com; Karen Foerstel and Herbert N. Foerstel, *Climbing the Hill: Gender Conflict in Congress* (Westport, CT: Praeger, 1996), 5; Dave Walter, "Rebel with a Cause," *Montana* 110 (November–December 1991): 68–70.

73. Hannah Josephson, *Jeannette Rankin*, 171.

74. Norma Smith, *Jeannette Rankin: America's Conscience*, 193–194.

75. Wellington Rankin, interview with John Board.

76. Volney Steele, *Wellington Rankin,* 8.

Chapter Three

1. Kirsten Amundsen, *The Silenced Majority: Women and American Democracy* (Englewood Cliffs, NJ: Prentice-Hall, 1971), 68; Martin Gruberg, *Women in American Politics: An Assessment and Sourcebook* (Oshkosh, WI: Academia Press, 1968), 121; "The Widow and Familial Connections," History, Art, and Archives, U.S. House of Representatives, accessed January 23, 2018, history.house.gov; Diane D. Kincaid, "Over His Dead Body: A Positive Perspective on Widows in the U.S. Congress," *Western Political Quarterly* 31 (1978): 96.

2. Sophonisba Breckinridge, *Women in the Twentieth Century: A Study of Their Political, Social and Economic Activities* (New York: McGraw-Hill, 1933), 341.

3. Irwin N. Gertzog, *Congressional Women: Their Recruitment, Integration, and Behavior* (Westport, CT: Praeger, 1995): 19.

4. Irwin Gertzog, *Congressional Women*, 24.

5. Paul Taylor, "Political Nonpositions: Louisiana's Cathy Long Runs on Artfully Vague Race," *Washington Post*, March 30, 1985, accessed April 17, 2018, newspapers.com.

6. Lindy Boggs, with Katherine Hatch, *Washington Through a Purple Veil: Memoirs of a Southern Woman* (New York: Harcourt Brace, 1994), 262–67.

7. "Kee's Widow Wins Race for His House Seat," *Chicago Tribune*, July 18, 1951, accessed March 12, 2018, newspapers.com.

8. Irwin N. Gertzog, "Women's Changing Pathways to the U.S. House of Representatives: Widows. Elites, and Strategic Politicians," in *Women Transforming Congress*, ed. Cindy Simon Rosenthal (Norman: University

of Oklahoma Press, 2002), 98; Irwin Gertzog, *Congressional Women*, 20.

9. Diane D. Kincaid, "Over His Dead Body"; Forrest Maltzman, Lee Sigelman, and Sarah Binder, "Leaving Office Feet First," *PS: Political Science and Politics* 29, no. 4 (1996): 665–671; "Women Who Succeeded Their Husbands in Congress." 2013. Center for American Women and Politics, Rutgers Eagleton Institute of Politics, accessed February 9, 2018, cawp.rutgers.edu; Charles S. Bullock, III, and Patricia Heys, "Recruitment of Women for Congress: A Research Note," *Western Political Quarterly* 25 (1972): 416–423.

10. Emily Newell Blair, "Are Women a Failure in Politics?" *Harper's* 151 (October 1925): 516.

11. "Pro and Con," *Washington Post*, June 18, 1932, accessed November 8, 2017, newspapers.com. This article quotes from several sources about Wingo.

12. Mildred Adams, "Congresswomen Are Just Congressmen," *The New York Times Magazine*, June 19, 1932, accessed April 2, 2018, *New York Times* Historical Database.

13. Grace Adams, "Women Don't Like Themselves," *North American Review*, 247, no. 2 (Summer 1939): 291.

14. Quoted in Jodi Wilgoren, "Widows of Bono, Capps Are on Well-Worn Path to Office," *Los Angeles Times*, January 26, 1998, accessed January 2, 2018, latimes.com.

15. "Mrs. Byron Marks Victory Amid Hubbub of Congratulations and Household Duties," *Washington Post*, May 30, 1941, accessed March 1, 2018, newspapers.com; Suzanne Pullen, "First Female California Representatives from the City," *San Francisco Examiner*, November 10, 2000, A7.

16. Genevieve Reynolds, "Nation's Feminine Eyes Are on a Distaff Contingent Named as Representatives," *Washington Post*, November 12, 1944, accessed September 23, 2018, newspapers.com.

17. "Mary Bono Loses One Vote," *South Florida Sun Sentinel*, March 29, 1998, accessed September 14, 2018, newspapers.com.

18. Genevieve Reynolds, "Nation's Feminine Eyes Are on a Distaff Contingent Named as Representatives."

19. Emily Newell Blair, "Are Women a Failure in Politics?" *Harper's* 151 (October 1925): 516.

20. Lindy Boggs, with Katherine Hatch, *Washington Through a Purple Veil*, 44, 70, 263–264.

21. Elizabeth Ford, "New Rep. Reece: First Returns Were Happy Ones for Her," *Washington Post*, May 19, 1961, accessed May 17, 2018, newspapers.com.

22. F. Suzanne Bowers, *Republican, First, Last, and Always: A Biography of B. Carroll Reece* (Newcastle: Cambridge Scholars Publishing, 2010), 22, 60.

23. "Ab Hermann, Former Republican National Committee Executive Director, Honored at Luncheon," press release, September 25, 1978, Robert J. Dole Archive and Special Collections, University of Kansas, accessed April 4, 2018, dolearchivecollections.ku.edu.

24. "Education," in Census Report 2010, Chapter 10, 3–18, U.S. Census Bureau, accessed April 22, 2018, census.gov.

25. Frank Graham, Jr., *Margaret Chase Smith* (New York: John Day, 1964), 17–26; Ellen Fitzpatrick, *The Highest Glass Ceiling: Women's Quest for the American Presidency*, 68–80.

26. Nichola D. Gutgold, *Paving the Way for Madam President* (Lanham, MD: Lexington Books, 2006), 20–49.

27. "Lawmaker's Widow Will Seek His Seat," *St. Louis Post-Dispatch*, January 2, 1972, accessed May 12, 2018, newspapers.com.

28. Lera Millard Thomas, Oral History, October 11, 1968, Lyndon Baines Johnson Library, Austin, Texas, I2-19.

29. Lindy Boggs, with Katherine Hatch, *Washington through a Purple Veil*, 263.

30. Eugene L. Meyer, "Congressman Louise Reece, GOP National Chief's Widow," *Washington Post*, May 16, 1970, accessed April 27, 2018, newspapers.com.

31. "Congresswoman Clarke Finds Pleasure in Legislative Job," *Washington Post*, January 20, 1934, accessed June 18, 2018, newspapers.com.

32. William H. Hardin, "Elizabeth Kee: West Virginia's First Woman in Congress," *West Virginia History* 45 (1984): 109–112.

33. Patricia Ward Wallace, *Politics of Conscience: A Biography of Margaret Chase Smith* (Westport, CT: Praeger, 1995), 29–44.

34. "Widow of Nolan Is Winner of His Seat in Congress," *St. Louis Star and Times*, January 24, 1923, accessed January 15, 2018, newspapers.com; "Mrs. Nolan Takes Her Place in House," *Washington Post*, February 13, 1923, accessed April 17, 2018, newspapers.com.

35. "Mrs. McMillan to Carry on Husband's Work in Congress," *Washington Post*, November 9, 1939, accessed March 11, 2018, newspapers.com.

36. "Mrs. Byron Elected Maryland's First Congresswoman," *Washington Post*, May 28, 1941, accessed March 1, 2018, newspapers.com.

37. Jim Specht, "The Beat Goes On," *San*

Bernardino County Sun, January 23, 1998, accessed July 22, 2018, newspapers.com; Jim Specht, "Sonny Bono's Widow Sworn In," *Daily Journal* (Vineland, NJ), April 22, 1998, accessed December 11, 2018, newspapers. com.

38. "Mary Bono Decides to Run," *Desert Sun* (Palm Springs, CA), January 23, 1998, accessed September 27, 2018, newspapers. com.

39. "Congresswoman Clarke Finds Pleasure in Legislative Job."

40. Hattie Wyatt Caraway, *Silent Hattie Speaks: The Personal Journal of Senator Hattie Caraway*, ed. Diane D. Kincaid (Westport, CT: Greenwood Press, 1979), 119.

41. Constance Drexel, "Mrs. Nolan No 'Crusader'; Mrs. Barrett Gains Note," *Washington Post*, February 24, 1924, accessed May 2, 2018, newspapers.com.

42. Suzanne Pullen, "First Female California Representatives from the City."

43. "Mrs. Oldfield to Retire," *Los Angeles Times*, May 30, 1929, accessed April 17, 2018, newspapers.com; "Leave Politics to Men, Woman in House Says," *Washington Post*, December 31, 1929, accessed August 1, 2018, newspapers.com; "Mrs. Oldfield Decries Feminist in Politics," *New York Times*, February 19, 1931, accessed April 2, 2018, newspapers. com; "Mrs. Oldfield to Quit Congress at Term End," *New York Times*, May 30, 1929, accessed May 2, 2018, nytimes.com.

44. Lindley C. Shedd, "Effigene Wingo: An Early Congresswoman from Arkansas," *Arkansas Historical Quarterly* 62 (Spring 2008): 27–53.

45. "Mrs. McMillan to Carry on Husband's Work in Congress," *Washington Post*, November 9, 1939, accessed March 11, 2018, newspapers.com; *Youth, Jobs and Defense* (Washington, D.C.: National Youth Administration, 1941).

46. "Tennessee Area to Vote Tuesday: Rep. Baker's Widow Running for House in 2nd District," *New York Times*, March 8, 1964, accessed May 5, 2018, newspapers.com.

47. George Creel, "The Woman Who Holds Her Tongue," *Collier's* (September 18, 1937): 55.

48. R.L. Duffus, "A Woman Treads New Paths as Senator," *New York Times Magazine*, January 24, 1932, accessed February 11, 2018, *New York Times* Historical Database.

49. "Mrs. Caraway Plans Campaign," *The Courier News* (Blytheville, AK), July 14, 1932, accessed August 11, 2018, newspapers.com; David Malone, *Hattie and Huey: An Arkansas Tour* (Fayetteville: University of Arkansas Press, 1989), 17; Susan M. Hartmann, "Car-

away, Hattie Ophelia," *American National Biography*, vol. 4 (New York: Oxford University Press, 1999): 369–370.

50. David Malone, *Hattie and Huey: An Arkansas Tour* (Fayetteville: University of Arkansas Press, 1989), 20–21.

51. David Malone, *Hattie and Huey: An Arkansas Tour*, 45–98; Hermann B. Deutsch, "Hattie and Huey," *Saturday Evening Post* (October 15, 1932): 6–7, 88–92.

52. Diane D. Kincaid, "Over His Dead Body," 29; Molly A. Mayhead and Brenda DeVore Marshall, *Women's Political Discourse: A 21st-Century Perspective* (Lanham, MD: Rowman & Littlefield, 2005), 47.

53. George Creel, "The Woman Who Holds Her Tongue."

54. Jodi Wilgoren, "Widows of Bono, Capps Are on Well-Worn Path to Office."

55. Hattie Wyatt Caraway, *Silent Hattie Speaks*, 25–26.

56. George Creel, "The Woman Who Holds Her Tongue."

57. Nancy Hendricks, *Senator Hattie Caraway: An Arkansas Legacy* (Mt. Pleasant, SC: Arcadia Publishing, 2013), 67–78; Annabel Paxton, *Women in Congress* (Richmond, VA: Dietz Press, 1945), 20–24.

58. "Senator Hattie W. Caraway Rules as Arkansas' Political Matriarch," *Tampa Tribune*, September 4, 1942, accessed February 12, 2018, newspapers.com.

59. Eleanor Roosevelt, "Women in Politics, Part I," *Good Housekeeping* (January 1940): 18–19+.

60. William H. Hardin, "Elizabeth Kee: West Virginia's First Woman in Congress," *West Virginia History* 45 (1984): 109–12.

61. Frances Mangum, "Congresswoman Good Friend to War Veterans," *Washington Post*, January 23, 1934, accessed May 2, 2018, newspapers.com.

62. Bettie J. Morden, *The Women's Army Corps, 1945–1978* (Washington, D.C.: Government Printing Office, 1990), 3–34; Judith A. Bellafaire, "The Women's Army Corps: A Commemoration of World War II Service," *United States Army Center of Military History*, accessed December 15, 2017, history. army.mil.

63. Matthew A. Wasniewski, *Women in Congress, 1917–2006* (Washington: G.P.O., 2006), 75; Michael A. Bellesiles, *A People's History of the U.S. Military: Ordinary Soldiers Reflect on Their Experience of War, from the American Revolution to Afghanistan* (New York: New Press, 2012), 255–256.

64. David Loth, *A Long Way Forward, The Biography of a Congresswoman: Frances P. Bolton* (New York: Longmans, Green, 1957),

61; Susan Cramer Winters, "Enlightened Citizen: Frances Payne Bolton and the Nursing Profession" (Ph.D. diss., University of Virginia), 1997, 17–45.

65. James A. Hodges, James H. O'Donnell, and John William Oliver, *Cradles of Conscience: Ohio's Independent Colleges and Universities* (Kent, OH: Kent State University Press, 2003), 103.

66. David Loth, *A Long Way Forward*, 193.

67. David Loth, *A Long Way Forward*, 216; Beatrice J. Kalisch and Philip A. Kalisch, "Nurses in American History The Cadet Nurse Corps-in World War II," *American Journal of Nursing* 76, no. 2 (1976): 240–242; *United States Cadet Nurse Corps [1943–1948] and Other Federal Nursing Programs*, U.S. Public Health Service, 38 (1950), accessed August 11, 2018, usphs.gov; David Loth, *A Long Way Forward*, 216; Susan Cramer Winters, "Enlightened Citizen," 259–314.

68. David Loth. *A Long Way Forward*, 3; Susan Cramer Winters, "Enlightened Citizen," 315–360.

69. Margaret Chase Smith, "No Place for a Woman," *Ladies Home Journal* (February 1952): 50; Patricia L. Schmidt, *Margaret Chase Smith: Beyond Convention* (Orono: University of Maine Press, 1996), 137–138.

70. Kay Bailey Hutchison, *American Heroines: The Spirited Women Who Shaped Our Country* (New York: Morrow, 2004), 214.

71. Rhodri Jeffreys-Jones, *Changing Differences: Women and the Shaping of American Foreign Policy, 1917–1994* (New Brunswick: Rutgers University Press, 1997), 109.

72. Gregory P. Gallant, *Hope and Fear in Margaret Chase Smith's America: A Continuous Tangle* (Lanham, MD: Lexington, 2014), 16; Josephine Ripley, "The Surprising Mrs. Smith," *Christian Science Monitor* (November 10, 1950): 5; Margaret Chase Smith, "Declaration of Conscience," June 1, 1950, *American Rhetoric*, accessed August 3, 2018, americanrhetoric.com.

73. Margaret Chase Smith, "Declaration of Conscience"; Frank Graham, Jr., *Margaret Chase Smith*, 175–179; Eric R. Crouse, *An American Stand: Senator Margaret Chase Smith and the Communist Menace, 1948–1972* (Lanham, MD: Lexington Books, 2010), 19–48.

74. Patricia Ward Wallace, *Politics of Conscience: A Biography of Margaret Chase Smith* (Westport, CT: Praeger, 1995), 105–112; James Cross Giblin, *The Rise and Fall of Senator Joe McCarthy* (New York: Houghton Mifflin Harcourt, 2009), 109–111, 244–258.

75. Hope Chamberlin, *A Minority of Members: Women in the U.S. Congress* (New York: Praeger, 1973), 236.

76. Susan Tolchin, *Women in Congress* (Washington, D.C.: Government Printing Office, 1976), 106; Irwin N. Gertzog, *Congressional Women: Their Recruitment, Integration, and Behavior* (Westport, CT: Praeger, 1995): 166–167; "Leonor K. Sullivan," *Los Angeles Times*, September 2, 1988, accessed August 18, 2018, newspapers.com; "Leonor K. Sullivan," *Washington Post*, September 2, 1988, accessed August 18, 2018, newspapers.com.

77. Marcy Kaptur, *Women of Congress: A Twentieth-Century Odyssey* (Washington, D.C.: Congressional Quarterly Press, 1996), 108.

78. Lindy Boggs, with Katherine Hatch, *Washington Through a Purple Veil*, 267–271.

79. Thomas H. Ferrell and Judith Haydel, "Hale and Lindy Boggs: Louisiana's National Democrats," *Louisiana History* 35 (Fall 1994): 389–402.

Chapter Four

1. Rainbow Murray, "Conclusion: A New Comparative Framework," in *Cracking the Highest Glass Ceiling: A Global Comparison of Women's Campaigns for Executive Office*, ed. Rainbow Murray (Santa Barbara: Praeger, 2010), 237.

2. Patricia Lyn Scott and Linda Thatcher, *Women in Utah History: Paradigm or Paradox?* (Logan: Utah State University Press, 2005), 24, 66.

3. Mari Grana, *Dr. Martha: The Life of a Pioneer Physician, Politician, and Polygamist* (Guilford, CT: TwoDot, 2015), 45.

4. Quoted in Janath Cannon, "Taking the Great Plan into Consideration" in *Heroines of the Restoration*, ed. Barbara B. Smith and Blythe Darlyn Thatcher (Salt Lake City: Bookcraft, 1997), 242–246.

5. "Our Morning Contemporary," *Salt Lake Tribune*, November 1, 1896, accessed December 23, 2018, newspapers.com.

6. "Women Office Seekers," *New York Times*, November 1, 1896, accessed January 20, 2018, *New York Times* Historical Database; Mari Grana, *Dr. Martha: The Life of a Pioneer Physician, Politician, and Polygamist*, 1.

7. Mari Grana, *Dr. Martha: The Life of a Pioneer Physician, Politician, and Polygamist*, 90–106.

8. Robynn Tysver, "Ann Ferlic Ashford Considering a Run for Husband's Old Seat in 2nd Congressional District," *Omaha World-Herald*, March 13, 2017, accessed July 12,

2018, omaha.com; Kristina Peterson, "Dear, Are You Running for Congress?" *Wall Street Journal*, June 1, 2017, A1+; Joseph Morton, "Brad Ashford Will Run Again for Nebraska's 2nd District Seat," *Omaha World-Herald*, June 19, 2017, accessed December 28, 2018, omaha.com.

9. John Corry, "Wallace Ponders a New Strategy for Retaining His Power in Alabama," *New York Times*, October 31, 1965, accessed March 26, 2018, *New York Times* Historical Database; Don Wasson, "Big Foot-Stomping Rally Climaxes Wallace Swing," *Montgomery Advertiser*, October 25, 1966, accessed March 26, 2018, newspapers.com.

10. Carol O'Keefe Wilson, *In the Governor's Shadow: The True Story of Ma and Pa Ferguson* (Denton: University of North Texas Press, 2014), 124–130.

11. Carol O'Keefe Wilson, *In the Governor's Shadow*, 149–154.

12. Karen L. Owen, *Women Officeholders and the Role Models Who Pioneered the Way* (Lanham, MD: Lexington Books, 2017), 26–27.

13. F.A. Behymer, "How Mrs. Langley, with Her Husband in Prison, Was Elected to Congress," *St. Louis Post Dispatch*, September 26, 1926, accessed January 12, 2018, newspapers.com.

14. Daisy Fitzhugh Ayers, "Katherine Langley Is Equal to the Task, Writer Declares," *Indianapolis Star*, November 14, 1926, accessed May 4, 2018, newspapers.com.

15. "Kentucky's First Congresswoman," *Literary Digest* (August 21, 1926): 14; Karen Foerstel, *Biographical Dictionary of Congressional Women* (Westport, CT: Greenwood Press, 1999), 155.

16. Duff Gilfond, "Gentlewomen of the House," *American Mercury* (October 1929): 151; Karen Foerstel, *Biographical Dictionary of Congressional Women*, 155.

17. Hope Chamberlin, *A Minority of Members: Women in the U.S. Congress* (New York: Praeger, 1973), 63–65.

18. "Mrs. Langley to Retire from Politics in 1930," *Washington Post*, December 25, 1928, accessed July 12, 2018, newspapers.com; "Langley May Return to Politics," *Washington Post*, January 2, 1929, accessed July 12, 2018, newspapers.com.

19. John Kass, "Schakowsky Ire Phony as Kited Checks," *Chicago Tribune*, April 7, 2006, accessed December 2, 2017, newspapers.com.

20. Daniella Diaz and Drew Griffin, "Dem Operative 'Stepping Back' after Video Suggests Group Incited Violence at Trump Rallies," CNN Politics, October 18, 2016, accessed January 22, 2018, cnn.com.

21. "Choices for U.S. House," *Chicago Tribune*, January 15, 2008, accessed March 23, 2018, newspapers.com.

22. "Change the Illinois House," *Chicago Tribune*, November 6, 2016, accessed June 2, 2018, newspapers.com.

23. Anne Firor Scott, *Making the Invisible Woman Visible* (Urbana: University of Illinois Press, 1984), 319.

24. For more information on this senator for a day, see John E. Talmadge, *Rebecca Latimer Felton* (Athens: University of Georgia Press, 1960); Rebecca Felton, *My Memoirs of Georgia Politics* (Atlanta, GA: Index Print Company, 1911); and Matthew Hild, *Greenbackers, Knights of Labor, and Populists: Farmer-Labor Insurgency in the Late-Nineteenth-Century South* (Athens: University of Georgia Press, 2007), 35–37.

25. "Nebraska Woman Named to Griswold Senate Seat," *New York Times*, April 17, 1954, accessed February 11, 2018, newspapers.com.

26. Todd Spangler and Kathleen Gray, "Michigan Losing Political Clout," *Livingston County* (MI) *Daily Press and Argus*, August 13, 2014, accessed June 3, 2018, newspapers.com.

27. Andrea Chambers, "Congressman John Dingell Makes Washington Quake, but Not His Executive Wife, Debbie," *People*, June 23, 1986, accessed January 14, 2018, people.com.

28. "New Congress Boasts Record Number of Women," *Chillicothe* (OH) *Gazette*, December 14, 1954, accessed December 14, 2018, newspapers.com.

29. A.F. Mahan, "Washington Letter: Rep. Martha Griffiths (D–Michigan)," *The Robesonian* (Lumberton, NC), December 1, 1954, accessed August 14, 2018, newspapers.com.

30. Pat Schroeder, *24 Years of House Work ... and the Place Is Still a Mess: My Life in Politics* (Kansas City: Andrews McMeel Publishing, 1998), 4.

31. Pat Schroeder, *Champion of the Great American Family* (New York: Random House, 1989), 26.

32. "Congressman Knows Plenty About Hart," *Muncie* (IN) *Evening Press*, March 13, 1984, accessed May 7, 2018, newspapers.com.

33. John C. Braden and Hortense Myers, "Love Is Great for the Poets, but Not All Roses for Voters," *Brownsville* (TX) *Herald*, October 17, 1976, accessed January 12, 2018, newspapers.com.

34. Kristie Hill, "Rep. Keys, Jacobs Retain Independence," *Kansas City* (MO) *Times*,

November 5, 1976, accessed March 12, 2018, newspapers.com.

35. Bob Mercer, "Some Things We Learned About Ourselves Tuesday," *Black Hills Pioneer* (Spearfish, SD), June 14, 2010, accessed February 17, 2018, newspapers.com.

36. "Herseth Sandlin: Touts Work with Moderates," *Argus-Leader* (Sioux Falls, SD), October 10, 2010, accessed February 1, 2017, newspapers.com.

Chapter Five

1. Sheryl Gay Stolberg, "A Second Act in Washington for Half of Power Couple," *Star Tribune* (Minneapolis), November 27, 2014, accessed January 14, 2018, newspapers.com.

2. Molly Meijer Wertheimer and Nichola D. Gutgold, *Elizabeth Hanford Dole: Speaking from the Heart* (Westport, CT: Praeger Publishers, 2004), 108; Julia Malone, "First Lady Facing Tough Task at Convention," *Rocky Mountain News*, August 25, 1996, accessed March 16, 2018, newspapers.com; Kelly Dittmar, "Turning the Tables: Behind Every Successful Woman," in *Women and Executive Office: Pathways and Performance*, ed. Melody Rose (Boulder: Lynne Rienner Publishers, 2013), 232–234.

3. Bob Dole and Elizabeth Dole, with Richard Norton Smith, *The Doles, Unlimited Partners* (New York: Simon and Schuster, 1988), 73.

4. Nichola D. Gutgold, *Paving the Way for Madam President* (Lanham, MD: Lexington Books, 2006), 104–133; Bob Dole and Elizabeth Dole, with Richard Norton Smith, *The Doles, Unlimited Partners*, 134, 140.

5. Maureen Dowd, "Elizabeth Dole Is Leaving Labor Post," *New York Times*, October 24, 1990, accessed March 26, 2018, nytimes.com.

6. Alec Gallup and Frank Newport, *The Gallup Poll: Public Opinion 2005* (Lanham, MD: Rowman & Littlefield, 2006), 94; Rachel B. Friedman and Ronald E. Lee, *The Style and Rhetoric of Elizabeth Dole: Public Persona and Political Discourse* (Lanham, MD: Lexington Books, 2013), 8.

7. Karrin Vasby Anderson, "From Spouses to Candidates: Hillary Rodham Clinton, Elizabeth Dole, and the Gendered Office of U.S. President," *Rhetoric and Public Affairs* 5 (Spring 2002), 114.

8. Caroline Heldman, Susan J. Carroll, and Stephanie Olson, "'She Brought Only a Skirt': Media Coverage of Elizabeth Dole's Bid for the Republican Presidential Nomina-

tion," *Political Communication* 22, no. 3 (August 2006): 315–335.

9. Caroline Heldman, Susan J. Carroll, and Stephanie Olson, "'She Brought Only a Skirt'"; Sean Aday and James Devitt, "Style over Substance: Newspaper Coverage of Elizabeth Dole's Presidential Bid," *International Journal of Press/Politics* 6, no. 2 (2001): 52–73; Arianna Huffington, "This Dole Is Getting a Free Ride," *Los Angeles Times*, March 16, 1999, accessed March 9, 2018, newspapers.com.

10. Maureen Dowd, "Discipline Us, Please," *New York Times*, January 6, 1999, accessed April 23, 2018, nytimes.com.

11. Caroline Heldman, Susan J. Carroll, and Stephanie Olson, "'She Brought Only a Skirt.'"

12. Michael Kramer, "Liddy Without Tears," *New York Daily News*, October 24, 1999, accessed May 5, 2018, nydailynews.com.

13. Arianna Huffington, "This Dole Is Getting a Free Ride."

14. "Mrs. Dole, President, of U.S., Not Red Cross?," *Pittsburgh Post-Gazette*, January 4, 1999, accessed March 1, 2018, newspapers.com.

15. "Could He Add Stand-Up Comic to His Résumé?," *Star Press* (Munice, IN), February 4, 1999, accessed December 12, 2017, newspapers.com.

16. Geraldine Ferraro, "Bob, Some Things Should Just Remain Private," *Chicago Tribune*, April 1, 1999, accessed January 11, 2017, newspapers.com.

17. Ellen Goodman, "Ads Make Candidate's Sex Life a Topic for Debate," *Tampa Tribune*, April 5, 1999, accessed January 15, 2018, newspapers.com.

18. Gail Collins, "Politics: Taking the 'Help' out of 'Helpmate': Bob Dole Shows How Not to Be a Supportive Spouse," *New York Times*, May 18, 1999, accessed December 12, 2017, nytimes.com.

19. Deborah Orin, "Bob: I'd Be Happy as First Man as Long as 'I Go to Bed with Her,'" *New York Post*, March 11, 1999, accessed April 11, 2018, newspapers.com.

20. Joan Silverman, "The New Bob Dole, Viagra Spokesman," *Journal of Commerce*, March 15, 1999, accessed May 29, 2018, newspapers.com.

21. Ellen Goodman, "Ads Make Candidate's Sex Life a Topic for Debate."

22. David M. Schribman, "Bob Dole Eager to Play Second Fiddle to His Wife," *Salina* (KS) *Journal*, April 1, 1999, accessed January 12, 2018, newspapers.com.

23. Richard L. Berke, "As Political Spouse,

Bob Dole Strays From Campaign Script," *New York Times*, May 17, 1999, accessed March 11, 2018, nytimes.com.

24. Gail Collins, "Politics: Taking the 'Help' Out of 'Helpmate': Bob Dole Shows How Not to Be a Supportive Spouse."

25. Richard L. Berke, "I'm Your No. 1 Fan, Hon. Really," *New York Times*, May 23, 1999, accessed March 12, 2018, nytimes.com; "Elizabeth Dole Exiles Mate to Woodshed," *New York Times*, May 19, 1999, accessed March 17, 2018, nytimes.com.

26. Maureen Dowd, "Bile in Bloom," *New York Times*, May 23, 1999, accessed May 21, 2018, nytimes.com.

27. Kenneth T. Walsh and Gloria Borger, "Psst, Bob Dole Beats His Wife," *U.S. News & World Report*, May 31, 1999, accessed March 18, 2018, Lexis Nexis Academic Universe.

28. Deborah Orin, "Bob: I'd Be Happy as First Man as Long as 'I Go to Bed with Her,'" *New York Post*, March 11, 1999, accessed April 11, 2018, newspapers.com.

29. Richard Berke, "I'm Your No. 1 Fan, Hon. Really," *New York Times*, May 23, 1999, accessed March 12, 2018, nytimes.com.

30. "Liddy Dole Has a Problem with a Prominent Politician," *Portland* (ME) *Press Herald*, May 30, 1999, accessed October 12, 2017, newspapers.com.

31. Maureen Dowd, "Political Husbandry in Iowa," *New York Times*, August 8, 1999, accessed December 7, 2017, nytimes.com.

32. Jay Tokasz, "Bob Dole Still Plays Politics," *Democrat and Chronicle* (Rochester, NY), September 15, 1999, accessed October 7, 2018, newspapers.com.

33. Mary McGrory, "It's Not the Money, Honey," *Washington Post*, October 24, 1999, accessed September 10, 2018, newspapers.com.

34. Bonnie Erbe, "Elizabeth Dole Overreached," *News Journal* (Wilmington, DE), October 30, 1999, accessed July 12, 2018, newspapers.com.

35. Richard L. Berke, "As Political Spouse, Bob Dole Strays from Campaign Script."

36. Kenneth R. Bazinet, "Campaign Divides Doles—He Won't Drop McCain," *Daily News* (NY), January 10, 2000, accessed September 12, 2018, newspapers.com.

37. "Does Name Recognition Really Count? You Bet It Does," *Asheville Citizen-Times*, April 13, 2002, accessed November 12, 2018, newspapers.com.

38. "Bob Dole Anticipating Rematch with Clinton," *Pensacola* (FL) *News Journal*, April 29, 2002, accessed December 8, 2017, newspapers.com.

39. Jill Lawrence, "Dole Turns from Sticky

Senate to Bully Pulpit," *Indiana Gazette*, February 21, 2002, accessed July 2, 2018, newspapers.com.

40. Patrick S. Halley, *On the Road with Hillary: A Behind-the-Scenes Look at the Journey from Arkansas to the U.S. Senate* (New York: Viking, 2002), 290–292; Michael Tomasky, *Hillary's Turn: Inside Her Improbable, Victorious U.S. Senate Campaign* (New York: Free Press, 2001), 19.

41. Sandy Grady, "'Hillary,' Just 'Hillary,' Has Dropped Her Surname and First Lady Role in NY Race," *Clarion-Ledger* (Jackson, MS), February 10, 2000, accessed February 8, 2018, newspapers.com; Karrin Vasby Anderson, "From Spouses to Candidates," 114.

42. Michael Tomasky, *Hillary's Turn*, 117.

43. Sandy Grady, "'Hillary,' Just 'Hillary,' Has Dropped Her Surname and First Lady Role in NY Race."

44. Patrick Halley, *On the Road with Hillary*, 300.

45. Harry Levins, "Relationship Roulette," *St-Louis Dispatch*, December 4, 1999, accessed August 9, 2018, newspapers.com.

46. Michael Tomasky, *Hillary's Turn*, 18, 39.

47. Lucinda Franks, "The Intimate Hillary," *Talk* 1, no.1 (September 1999): 173+.

48. Bill Press, "Hillary, Please Shut Up Now," *News Journal* (Wilmington, DE), August 7, 1999, accessed July 12, 2018, newspapers.com.

49. Herb Brock, "Some Left Over Political Scraps from the Thanksgiving Table," *Advocate Messenger* (Danville, KY), November 29, 1999, accessed May 11, 2018, newspapers.com.

50. DeWayne Wickham, "Broaddrick's Back with Old Charges," *Asheville Citizen-Times*, November 1, 2000, accessed January 12, 2018, newspapers.com.

51. Patrick Healy, "Politics Means Sometimes Having to Say You're Sorry," *New York Times*, March 4, 2007, accessed February 4, 2018, *New York Times* Historical Database.

52. William A. Orme, Jr., "While Mrs. Clinton Looks On, Palestinian Officials Criticize Israel," *New York Times*, November 12, 1999, accessed February 19, 2018, nytimes.com; "Hillary Clinton Rebukes Arafat's Wife," *Los Angeles Times*, November 13, 1999, accessed February 18, 2018, newspapers.com.

53. Cal Thomas, "Peace Negotiators Blind to Truth about PLO," *News-Press* (Ft. Myers, FL), November 22, 1999, accessed June 11, 2018, newspapers.com.

54. "Guiliani Slams Hillary Clinton for Arafat Hug after Israel Slap," *New York Times*, November 13, 1999, accessed January 3, 2018, newspapers.com.

55. Hugh Dellios, "Hillary Clinton in a Pickle: Arafat's Wife Puts First Lady in Middle," *Chicago Tribune*, November 12, 1999, accessed March 28, 2018, newspapers.com.

56. Michael Tomasky, *Hillary's Turn*, 173.

57. Elisabeth Bumiller, "The Mayor's Separation: The Overview," *New York Times*, May 11, 2000, accessed March 26, 2018, *New York Times* Historical Database; Michael Tomasky, *Hillary's Turn*, 306.

58. Patrick S. Halley, *On the Road with Hillary*, 306; Theodore F. Sheckels, *Cracked but Not Shattered: Hillary Rodham Clinton's Unsuccessful Campaign for the Presidency* (Lanham, MD: Lexington Books, 2009), 119.

59. Matt Towery, "Hang It Up, Obama— It's Hillary's Nomination," *Human Events Online*, January 18, 2007, lexisnexis.com.

60. Lori Cox Han, *In It to Win*, 86; Nancy Cohen, *Breakthrough: The Making of America's First Woman President* (Berkeley: Counterpoint, 2016), 119.

61. "Her Latest Incarnation: Presidential Front-Runner," *Economist*, May 17, 2007, accessed March 22, 2018, economist.com.

62. Robin Givhan, "Hillary Clinton's Tentative Dip into New Neckline Territory," *Washington Post*, July 20, 2007, accessed February 12, 2018, washingtonpost.com; Howard Kurtz, "Hillary Chuckles; Pundits Snort; Clinton's Robust Yuks Leads to Analysis of Appeal of Laughter," *Washington Post*, October 3, 2007, accessed February 12, 2018, washingtonpost. com; Kathleen Henehan and Jeremy Holden, "Taking Lead from Drudge, Conservative Echo Chamber Hypes Clinton Photo," December 18, 2007, Media Matters, accessed April 22, 2018, mediamatters.org.

63. "Does Our Looks-Obsessed Culture Want to Stare at an Aging Woman?," *The Rush Limbaugh Show*, December 17, 2007, accessed March 22, 2018, rushlimbaugh.com; Diana B. Carlin and Kelly L. Winfrey, "Have You Come a Long Way, Baby? Hillary Clinton, Sarah Palin, and Sexism in 2008 Campaign Coverage," *Communication Studies* 60, no. 4 (September–October 2009), 331–332; Kathleen Henehan and Jeremy Holden, "Taking Lead from Drudge."

64. Rebecca Traister, *Big Girls Don't Cry: The Election that Changed Everything for American Women* (New York: Free Press, 2010), 69–71.

65. Mary Lou Finlay, "There's Always Next Time," *Ottawa Citizen*, June 5, 2008, lexisnexis.com.

66. Rebecca Traister, *Big Girls Don't Cry*, 70; Joshua Green, "The Front-Runner's Fall," *Atlantic*, September 2008, accessed March 23, 2018, theatlantic.com/archive.

67. Jonathan Allen and Amie Parnes, *Shattered*, 2.

68. Jennifer Senior, "The First: Female President, Male First Lady, Former President in the White House," *New York Magazine*, September 30, 2007, accessed February 12, 2018, nymag.com; Lori Cox Han, *In It to Win*, 76–77.

69. Kelly Dittmar, *Navigating Gendered Terrain: Stereotypes and Strategy in Political Campaigns*, 2; Dan Balz, "Union in Clinton's Corner—and Ready for a Fight," *Washington Post*, November 1, 2007, accessed April 24, 2018, washingtonpost.com.

70. Lori Cox Han, *In It to Win*, 26, 116; Rebecca Traister, *Big Girls Don't Cry*, 72.

71. Calvin Woodward, "On the Road to Denver, St. Paul: Obama Audaciously Overcame Huge Favorite," *Decatur* (IL) *Daily*, August 25, 2008, accessed January 22, 2018, decaturdaily.com.

72. Rebecca Traister, *Big Girls Don't Cry*, 60.

73. Rebecca Traister, *Big Girls Don't Cry*, 61.

74. "The Republican Debate," *New York Times*, January 24, 2008, accessed April 16, 2018, nytimes.com.

75. Jennifer Senior, "The First: Female President, Male First Lady, Former President in the White House."

76. Kathleen Parker, "Let's Give JFK, Reagan a Rest," *Baltimore Sun*, January 31, 2008, accessed January 21, 2018, newspapers.com; Nichola D. Gutgold, *Almost Madam President: Why Hillary Clinton 'Won' in 2008* (Lanham, MD: Lexington Books, 2009), 89–91.

77. Rebecca Traister, *Big Girls Don't Cry*, 121–122.

78. Jonathan Alter, "A Catharsis in Denver?," *Newsweek*, August 8, 2008, accessed April 11, 2018, newsweek.com.

79. Cynthia Tucker, "Whiny Recriminations Don't Suit Clinton Supporters, So Stop Them," *Atlanta Constitution*, June 7, 2008, accessed February 17, 2018, newspapers.com.

80. Tim Jones and Mike Dorning, "Texas Too Close to Call," *Chicago Tribune*, March 5, 2008, accessed February 4, 2018, newspapers.com.

81. "Wolf Blitzer Interview with Cokie Roberts," CNN Politics, April 14, 2008, accessed February 1, 2018, politicalticker.blogs. cnn.com; Jonathan Mann, "Bill Clinton's Gaffes Stump Hillary," CNN Politics, April 17, 2008, accessed December 5, 2017, cnn. com; Rebecca Traister, *Big Girls Don't Cry*, 123.

82. "Bill's Gaffe Shows He's Clueless," *Des Moines* (IA) *Register*, January 31, 2008, ac-

cessed February 2, 2018, newspapers.com; Michael Tackett, "Bill Clinton Emerges as Polarizing Figure in S.C.," *Santa Fe New Mexican,* January 27, 2008, accessed February 1, 2018, newspapers.com.

83. Rekha Basu, "Idealism Trumped Clinton's Hubris," *Marion* (OH) *Star,* June 17, 2008, accessed December 7, 2017, newspapers.com.

84. Rebecca Traister, *Big Girls Don't Cry,* 205.

85. Nicholas Kristof, "Hillary Clinton, Free to Speak Her Mind," *New York Times,* April 8, 2017, accessed January 2, 2018, nytimes.com.

86. Hillary Rodham Clinton, *What Happened* (New York: Simon and Schuster, 2017), 413–415.

87. Heidi M. Przybyla, "Bill Clinton Comes Off Sidelines of 2016 Campaign," *USA Today,* October 8, 2015, accessed March 14, 2018, usatoday.com.

88. Gary Bauer, "Bill Clinton Would Lose 2016 Democratic Primary," *USA Today,* April 5, 2016, accessed February 5, 2018, usatoday.com.

89. Heidi M. Przybyla, "Bill Clinton Comes Off Sidelines of 2016 Campaign," *USA Today,* October 8, 2015, accessed March 14, 2018, usatoday.com; "Bill Clinton Returns to the Campaign Trail," *Newsmax,* October 3, 2015, accessed March 14, 2018, newsmax.com.

90. David Jackson, "Hillary Clinton's Test: A Third Straight Democratic Term," *USA Today,* April 10, 2015, accessed January 22, 2018, newspapers.com.

91. Dan Merica, "Bill Clinton: Hillary Can 'Put the Awful Legacy of the Last Eight Years Behind Us,'" CNN Politics, March 22, 2016, accessed March 11, 2018, cnn.com.

92. Jonathan Allen and Amie Parnes, *Shattered,* 168.

93. "Peace and Freedom: Policy and World Ideas," accessed December 29, 2018, johnib. wordpress.com.

94. John Kass, "GOP Fight Hogs Spotlight, Doing Clinton a Favor," *Chicago Tribune,* February 28, 2016, accessed February 6, 2018, newspapers.com; Sam Sanders, "Bill Clinton Gets into Heated Exchange With Black Lives Matter Protester," NPR, April 7, 2016, accessed March 15, 2018, npr.com.

95. Paul Solotaroff, "Trump Seriously: On the Trail with the GOP's Tough Guy," *Rolling Stone,* September 9, 2015, accessed March 11, 2018, rollingstone.com.

96. Ruth Marcus, "Trump is Right: Bill Clinton's Sordid Sexual History Is Fair Game," *Washington Post,* December 28, 2015, accessed April 19, 2018, washingtonpost.com.

Chapter Six

1. Kenneth Prewitt, *The Recruitment of Political Leaders: A Study of Citizen-Politicians* (Westport, CT: Greenwood Press, 1970).

2. Judith Horstman, "When Politics Is the Family Business," *Times Herald* (Port Huron, MI), January 19, 1984, accessed February 27, 2018, newspapers.com; Debra L. Dodson, *The Impact of Women in Congress* (New York: Oxford University Press, 2006), 53–64.

3. Stephen Hess, *America's Political Dynasties: From Adams to Kennedy* (Garden City, NY: Doubleday, 1966), 2, 5.

4. Stephen Hess, *America's Political Dynasties: From Adams to Clinton* (Washington, D.C.: Brookings Institution Press, 2016), 3.

5. "The Power of Wealth," *American Dynasties: The Kennedys,* episode 1, directed by Peter W. Kunhardt., aired March 11, 2018 (New York: CNN, 2018).

6. Amy Schapiro, *Millicent Fenwick: Her Way* (New Brunswick: Rutgers University Press, 2003), 118–119.

7. Amy Schapiro, *Millicent Fenwick: Her Way,* 161; Leslie Wayne, "Millicent Fenwick: 'Power Has No Charm,'" *Philadelphia Inquirer,* November 24, 1974, accessed January 3, 2018, newspapers.com; Lorraine Pelter, "Fenwick Welcomes Challenge," *Echoes Sentinel* (Warren Township, NJ), April 11, 1974, accessed June 22, 2018, newspapers.com; Ann Blackman, "Women Seeking Office Find Special Problems," *Louisville Courier-Journal,* October 13, 1974, accessed March 26, 2018, newspapers.com.

8. Chas Sisk, "In a 'Man's World,' O'Brien Was Political Pioneer," *Tennessean* (Nashville), September 2, 2009, accessed February 12, 2018, newspapers.com.

9. Ken Whitehouse, "Annabelle Clement O'Brien Passes Away at 86; Former State Senator Was Stalwart of Tennessee Democratic Politics," *Nashville Post,* September 1, 2009, accessed March 9, 2018, newspapers. com.

10. Sam Roberts, "Gillibrand's Grandmother Also Wielded Political Power, but from the Wings," *New York Times,* January 31, 2009, accessed April 15, 2018, *New York Times* Historical Database; Brian Tumulty, "Political Novice Brings New Ideas," *Democrat and Chronicle* (Rochester, NY), January 24, 2009, accessed June 12, 2018, newspapers.com.

11. Kirsten Gillibrand, "A Reflection of My

First Year in Congress," *The Hill,* December 14, 2007, accessed April 4, 2018, thehill.com.

12. "Katherine Harris Ponders Senate Race," *South Florida Sun Sentinel,* November 7, 2003, accessed June 2, 2018, newspapers.com.

13. Jennifer Yachnin, "In New Mexico, It's Good to Be a Luján," *E&E Daily,* June 26, 2015, accessed May 12, 2018, eenews.net; Christopher Snow Hopkins, "New Mexico, 1st House District: Michelle Lujan Grisham (D)," *Atlantic,* November 6, 2012, accessed May 13, 2018, theatlantic.com.

14. "Michelle Lujan Grisham for U.S. House District 1," *Albuquerque Journal,* October 28, 2012, accessed February 7, 2018, newspapers.com.

15. "Death of a Patriarch," *Statesman Journal* (Salem, OR), November 1, 1993, accessed April 11, 2018, newspapers.com.

16. Rob Crow, "A Literal Legacy," *Southern Illinoisan* (Carbondale), December 26, 2010, accessed April 11, 2018, newspapers.com.

17. Sean Murphy, "Should Being a Mother Matter?," *Indianapolis Star,* October 24, 2010, accessed April 12, 2018, newspapers.com.

18. Susan Molinari, *Representative Mom: Balancing Budgets, Bill and Baby in the U.S. Congress* (New York: Doubleday, 1998), 270.

19. "Mrs. Huck for Congress; Mason's Daughter, Mother of Four, a Candidate to Succeed Him," *New York Times,* July 1, 1921, accessed March 22, 2018, newspapers.com.

20. Matthew A. Wasniewski, *Women in Congress, 1917–2006* (Washington: G.P.O., 2006), 49.

21. "Alaska Governor Appoints Daughter for His Senate Spot," *Post Crescent* (Appleton, WI), December 21, 2002, accessed May 11, 2018, newspapers.com.

22. "It's All in the Family in Alaska Politics," *Los Angeles Times,* December 21, 2002, accessed April 6, 2018, newspapers.com.

23. "Name Recognition No Help in Alaska Race," *Los Angeles Times,* October 3, 2004, accessed April 2, 2018, newspapers.com.

24. Kay Bailey Hutchison, *American Heroines: The Spirited Women Who Shaped Our Country.* (New York: Morrow, 2004), 84.

25. Joanne Kaufman and Barbara Kleban Mills, "While Nebraska Governor Kay Orr Makes Policy, Husband Bill, Her 'First Gentleman,' Bakes Meat Loaf," *People,* December 12, 1988, accessed February 12, 2018, people.com.

26. Joseph Lyons, *Clare Boothe Luce, Author and Diplomat* (New York: Chelsea House, 1989), 19–51.

27. Ronald Gary Willis, "The Persuasion of Clare Boothe Luce" (Ph.D. diss., Indiana University, 1993), 56–58; "Mrs. Luce Wins Another Term," *Press and Sun Bulletin* (Binghamton, NY), November 8, 1944, accessed April 2, 2018, newspapers.com.

28. Sylvia Jukes Morris, *Rage for Fame: The Ascent of Clare Boothe Luce* (New York: Random House, 1997); 459–473; "Attacks Man for Backing Clare Booth," *Palladium Item* (Richmond, IN), September 5, 1942, accessed April 3, 2018, newspapers.com.

29. Carol Hardy-Fanta, et al., *Contested Transformation: Race, Gender, and Political Leadership in 21st Century America* (New York: Cambridge University Press, 2016), 155–157.

30. Dana Milbank, "Family Ties Playing a Big Role on the Hill: Some Offices Appear Inherited, Not Elected," *Washington Post,* January 23, 2005, accessed July 17, 2018, washingtonpost.com; Cindy Hooper, *Conflict: African American Women and the New Dilemma of Race and Gender Politics* (Santa Barbara, CA: Praeger, 2012), 117–118.

31. Guy Clifton, "UNR Grad Cortez Masto Has Sights on Attorney General Seat," *Reno Gazette-Journal,* October 23, 2005, accessed February 2, 2018, newspapers.com.

32. "33rd Congressional Race to Represent Downtown," *Los Angeles Times,* May 27, 1992, accessed March 12, 2018, newspapers.com.

33. "New Hispanic Congresswomen Face Tough Challenges, Reflect Trend of More Women in Congress," *Santa Fe New Mexican,* February 8, 1993, accessed November 24, 2018, newspapers.com.

34. Maria Newman, "From Puerto Rico to Congress, a Determined Path," *New York Times,* September 27, 1992, accessed February 6, 2018, *New York Times* Historical Database.

35. Chelsea J. Carter, "Sister Act May Be Coming to Congress," *Indianapolis Star,* October 27, 2002, accessed January 15, 2018, newspapers.com; Barbara Burrell, *Women and Political Participation: A Reference Handbook* (Santa Barbara, CA: ABC-CLIO, 2004), 133–135.

Chapter Seven

1. Sarah Pauline Vickers, *The Life of Ruth Bryan Owen: Florida's First Congresswoman and America's First Woman Diplomat* (Tallahassee, FL: Sentry Press, 2009), 40–41, 47–48; Ruth Bryan Owen Rohde, "Let's Live with Our Careers," Bess Furman Papers, Library of Congress, Manuscript Division; Michael

Kazin, *A Godly Hero: The Life of William Jen-nings Bryan* (New York: Anchor Books, 2007), 170–171.

2. "Daughters of the Fire-Eaters," *Santa Ana Register*, April 29, 1928, accessed April 4, 2018, newspapers.com.

3. Ruby Black, "The Case of Ruth Bryan Owen," *Equal Rights*, April 5, 1930, 67–69.

4. Brisa Usher, "Political Progress of Women Impresses Even Men in the GOP," *Akron* (Ohio) *Beacon Journal*, July 15, 1984, accessed May 19, 2018, newspapers.com.

5. "Nancy Hopes to Become a Chip off Landon Block," *Iola* (KS) *Register*, March 23, 1978, accessed January 2, 2018, newspapers. com.

6. Maeve Reston, "Louisiana Sen. Mary Landrieu Teams Up with Father for Cam-paign Ad," *Los Angeles Times*, May 13, 2014, accessed January 5, 2018, newspapers.com.

7. Lisa L. Roland, "Family, Women's Is-sues at Heart of Landrieu Campaign," *Times* (Shreveport. LA), September 1, 1996, ac-cessed October 12, 2018, newspapers.com.

8. "Washington's Luckiest Kids: The Children of Congressmen Live in a World of Open Doors, Famous People, and Big Goings-On," *Life*, June 6, 1949, 146–152.

9. Sally Saunders, "It Was a Shock When Liz Said She Wouldn't Run," *Greenville* (SC) *News*, April 13, 1978, accessed February 22, 2018, newspapers.com.

10. Kate Moore, "Elizabeth Johnston Pat-terson: Following a Family Tradition," *A Capitol Blog*, April 1, 2015, accessed Febru-ary 12, 2018, library.sc.edu/blogs.

11. Susan Molinari, *Representative Mom*, 36.

12. "Daughters of the Fire-Eaters," *Santa Ana Register*, April 29, 1928, accessed April 4, 2018, newspapers.com.

13. "Mark Hanna's Daughter Puts Vim into Anti-Hoover Camp," *Indianapolis Star*, June 8, 1928, accessed September 27, 2018, newspapers.com; Kristie Miller, *Ruth Hanna McCormick: A Life in Politics, 1880–1944* (Albuquerque: University of New Mexico Press, 1992), 17–31.

14. "Running for Office," *Outlook and In-dependent*, January 23, 1929, 126.

15. Karen Hasara, "McCormick Unsung Heroine in U.S. Politics," *Illinois Issues*, 19, no. 7 (July 1993): 28.

16. "Daughters of the Fire-Eaters."

17. Dan Parsons, "Zeidler Looks Back on Career as Williamsburg's First Female Mayor," *Daily Press* (Williamsburg, VA), June 29, 2010, accessed January 22, 2018, articles.daily press.com; Will Molineux, "High Profile: Jeanne Zeidler: Leading Williamsburg into

Its Tercentenary," *Daily Press* (Williamsburg, VA), April 26, 1999, accessed January 22, 2018, articles.dailypress.com.

18. Susan Molinari, *Representative Mom*, 16–26, 69–78.

19. Geraldine Baum, "A Rising Voice in the Revolution: Politics," *Los Angeles Times*, March 6, 1995, accessed February 11, 2018, latimes.com.

20. Susan Molinari, *Representative Mom*, 272–278.

21. Martha E. Kropf and John A. Boiney, "The Electoral Glass Ceiling? Gender, Via-bility, and the News in U.S. Senate Cam-paigns," in *Women and Congress: Running, Winning, and Ruling* (New York: Haworth Press, 2001), 82, 91–92; Kim Fridkin Kahn, *The Political Consequences of Being a Woman: How Stereotypes Influence the Conduct and Consequences of Political Campaigns* (New York: Columbia University Press, 1996), 92–94.

22. "Nancy Landon Kassebaum Intends to Use Dad's Name," *Fort Scott* (KS) *Tribune*, March 22, 1978, accessed January 22, 2018, newspapers.com.

23. "Nancy Hopes to Become a Chip off Landon Block," *Iola* (KS) *Register*, March 23, 1978, accessed January 2, 2018, newspapers. com.

24. "Nancy Landon Kassebaum," *Current Biography* (New York: H.W. Wilson, 1982), 191; Karen L. Owen, *Women Officeholders and the Role Models Who Pioneered the Way*, 48.

25. "Kassebaum to Seek Second Term," *Salina* (KS) *Journal*, March 18, 1994, ac-cessed January 2, 2018, newspapers.com..

26. Carol Pugh, "Gwen Graham Thinks Her Father Might Run for President," *News-Press* (Ft. Myers, FL), January 9, 1979, ac-cessed January 2, 2018, newspapers.com.

27. "Delegates Unanimous: 'Anybody but Bush,'" *Star Tribune* (Minneapolis), June 15, 2003, accessed April 14, 2018, newspapers. com.

28. "Gwen Graham Eyes Politics: Sena-tor's Daughter Has Name Recognition, Con-tacts," *News Press* (Ft. Myers, FL), June 14, 2004, accessed January 9, 2018, newspapers. com.

29. Margie Menzel, "Graham: Daughter Will Work for Constituents," *Palm Beach* (FL) *Post*, January 11, 2015, accessed October 14, 2018, newspapers.com; William E. Gib-son, "Gwen Graham Rides into Congress with 'Independent Voice,'" *South Florida Sun Sentinel*, December 28, 2014, accessed March 23, 2018, sun-sentinel.com.

30. "Landrieu Follows Long Political Tra-

dition," *The Times* (Shreveport, LA), December 1, 2002, accessed January 11, 2018, newspapers.com.

31. Catherine S. Manegold, "Her Father's Daughter and Her Party's Luminary," *New York Times*, May 18, 1993, accessed September 1, 2018, nytimes.com.

32. Susan Molinari, *Representative Mom: Balancing Budgets, Bill and Baby in the U.S. Congress* (New York: Doubleday, 1998), 39.

33. Geraldine Baum, "A Rising Voice in the Revolution: Politics," *Los Angeles Times*, March 6, 1995, accessed February 11, 2018, latimes.com.

34. Melissa Harris, "Seattle Senator Retains Hoosier Ties," *Indianapolis Star*, January 1, 2001, accessed January 9, 2018, newspapers.com.

35. Melissa Harris, "Seattle Senator Retains Hoosier Ties."

36. Chris Weston, "Workman Fails to Get Showdown with Patterson," *Greenville* (SC) *News*, January 30, 1986, accessed January 14, 2018, newspapers.com.

37. Melissa Harris, "Seattle Senator Retains Hoosier Ties."

38. Melissa Harris, "Cantwell Merges Father's Tactics into Race," *Indianapolis Star*, November 5, 2000, accessed January 15, 2018, newspapers.com.

39. Chris Weston, "Workman Fails to Get Showdown with Patterson."

40. Marc Sandalow, *Madam Speaker: Nancy Pelosi's Life, Times, and Rise to Power* (New York: Modern Times, 2008), 25.

41. Ellen Gamerman, "Democratic Leader's Instincts Sewn in Baltimore," *Orlando Sentinel*, January 4, 2003, accessed May 20, 2018, newspapers.com; "Minority Leader Had Early Taste for Politics," *Lansing State Journal*, January 5, 2003, accessed July 29, 2018, newspapers.com.

42. Ellen Gamerman, "Democratic Leader's Instincts Sewn in Baltimore"; "Pelosi Prizes Loyalty and Partisanship," *Baltimore Sun*, October 27, 2006, accessed June 14, 2018, newspapers.com; "Political Family Inspired Pelosi," *Argus Leader* (Sioux Falls, SD), November 12, 2006, accessed November 28, 2017, newspapers.com.

43. Barbara Burrell, *Women and Political Participation: A Reference Handbook* (Santa Barbara, CA: ABC-CLIO, 2004), 152–153.

44. Ellen Gamerman, "Child of Politics, All Grown Up"; Barbara Burrell, *Women and Political Participation*, 152–153.

45. Mary O'Leary, "Luisa DeLauro, Mother of Rosa, Dies at 103," *New Haven Register*, September 11, 2017, accessed February 28, 2018, nhregister.com.

46. "Honoring Luisa DeLauro on Her 100th Birthday," Press Release, Rosa DeLauro Web Site, December 24, 2013, accessed January 22, 2018, delauro.house.gov; Mary O'Leary, "Luisa DeLauro, Mother of Rosa, Dies at 103."

47. Catherine S. Manegold, "Her Father's Daughter and Her Party's Luminary," *New York Times*, May 18, 1993, accessed September 1, 2018, nytimes.com.

48. Catherine S. Manegold, "Her Father's Daughter and Her Party's Luminary."

49. Geraldine Baum, "A Rising Voice in the Revolution: Politics"; David Bauder, "Vacco Refuses to Criticize Remarks Against Burstein," *The Post-Star* (Glen Falls, NY), October 12, 1994, accessed February 2, 2018, newspapers.com; Maureen Dowd, "Live from New York: It's Susan Molinari," *Salina* (KS) *Journal*, June 2, 1997, accessed February 19, 2018, newspapers.com.

50. Geraldine Baum, "A Rising Voice in the Revolution: Politics."

51. Mimi Hall, "Republican Women: A 'Contrast' with America," *USA Today*, December 27, 1994, accessed March 11, 2018, newspapers.com.

52. Mary T. Schmich, "Georgia Sodomy Law a Family Matter," *Chicago Tribune*, February 2, 1990, accessed March 12, 2018, newspapers.com; Kim Masters, "The Woman in the Hot Seat," *Washington Post*, July 5, 1995, accessed March 12, 2018, washingtonpost.com.

53. "Father's Slur Irks Black Rep," *Philadelphia Daily News*, October 17, 1996, accessed June 12, 2018, newspapers.com; Donna Britt, "A Happy Ending in Black and White," *Los Angeles Times*, November 17, 1996, accessed December 31, 2017, latimes.com.

54. "Rift between Blacks, Jews Worries Democrats for Fall," *Baltimore Sun*, August 26, 2002, accessed September 29, 2018, newspapers.com.

55. "Is 'the Old Cynthia' Back?" *Democrat and Chronicle* (Rochester, NY), April 6, 2006, accessed March 9, 2018, newspapers.com.

56. Mary Lynn F. Jones, "A Slow, Steady Climb Up Capitol Hill," *Chicago Tribune*, October 4, 2000, accessed March 19, 2018, newspapers.com.

57. "Ex-West Virginia Governor Admits Corruption Schemes," *New York Times*, April 13, 1990, accessed March 12, 2018, nytimes.com.

58. Mary Lynn F. Jones, "A Slow, Steady Climb Up Capitol Hill."

59. "Meet the Freshmen," *Burlington Free Press*, November 6, 2014, accessed January 19, 2018, newspapers.com.

60. "Former W. Va. Gov. Arch Moore Dies

at 91," *News Journal* (Wilmington, DE), January 9, 2015, accessed April 22, 2018, newspapers.com.

Chapter Eight

1. Michele L. Swers, *Women in the Club: Gender and Policy Making in the Senate* (Chicago: University of Chicago Press, 2013), 232, 246; Michele L. Swers, *The Difference Women Make: The Policy Impact of Women in Congress* (Chicago: University of Chicago Press, 2002), 10.

2. Michele L. Swers, *The Difference Women Make*, 3.

3. Martha Sherrill, "The Sisters of Maine," *Washington Post*, May 6, 2011, accessed January 12, 2018, newspapers.com; Karen L. Owen, *Women Officeholders and the Role Models Who Pioneered the Way* (Lanham, MD: Lexington Books, 2017), 3; Jerry Markavy, "Two Women from One New England State Stand Out in the Senate," *Star-Democrat* (Easton, MD), June 27, 2005, accessed September 22, 2018, newspapers.com; Barbara Mikulski, et al., *Nine and Counting: The Women of the Senate* (New York: HarperCollins, 2000), 36–38.

4. Kevin Miller, "Margaret Chase Smith Paved the Way, but Will the Governor's Mansion Remain Elusive?," *Bangor* (ME) *Daily News*, July 30, 2010, accessed March 25, 2018, bangordailynews.com; Barbara Mikulski, et al., *Nine and Counting: The Women of the Senate* (New York: HarperCollins, 2000), 69.

5. Sara Angevine, "Representing All Women: An Analysis of Congress, Foreign Policy, and the Boundaries of Women's Surrogate Representation," *Political Research Quarterly* 70, no. 1 (2017): 100; Michele L. Swers, *Women in the Club*, 234.

6. Matthew A. Wasniewski, *Women in Congress, 1917–2006* (Washington: G.P.O., 2006), 49.

7. "Mrs. Luce Wins Another Term," *Press and Sun Bulletin* (Binghamton, NY), November 8, 1944, accessed April 2, 2018, newspapers.com.

8. Steven V. Roberts, "From 'Nice Little Nancy' to 'Effective,'" *New York Times*, July 11, 1983, accessed April 18, 2018, nytimes.com.

9. Rhonda Holman, "Kassebaum Pushed for Anti-Apartheid Sanctions," *Wichita* (KS) *Eagle*, December 11, 2013, accessed March 25, 2018, kansas.com.

10. Jim Fitzgerald, "Clinton Fails to Endorse Immediate Withdrawal," *Lincoln Journal Star* (Lincoln, NE), November 22, 2005,

accessed December 18, 2018, newspapers.com.

11. Michele L. Swers, *Women in the Club*, 232–233; Michele L. Swers, *The Difference Women Make*.

12. Michele L. Swers, *The Difference Women Make*, 8–10, 132.

13. Emily George, *Martha W. Griffiths* (Washington, D.C.: University Press of America, 1982), 149–150.

14. "Parents of Mrs. Fenwick: Ambassador Hammond Lost Wife on Lusitania," *Bernardsville* (NJ) *News*, August 22, 1974, accessed April 11, 2018, newspapers.com.

15. Leslie Wayne, "Millicent Fenwick: 'Power Has No Charm,'" *Philadelphia Inquirer*, November 24, 1974, accessed January 3, 2018, newspapers.com.

16. Lorraine Pelter, "Fenwick Welcomes Challenge," *Echoes Sentinel* (Warren Township, NJ), April 11, 1974, accessed June 22, 2018, newspapers.com; Ann Blackman, "Women Seeking Office Find Special Problems," *Louisville Courier-Journal*, October 13, 1974, accessed August 12, 2018, newspapers.com; Leslie Bennetts, "Republicans and Women's Issues: For Some, A Painful Conflict," *New York Times*, September 2, 1980, accessed March 30, 2018, *New York Times* Historical Database.

17. Amy Schapiro, *Millicent Fenwick* (New Brunswick: Rutgers University Press, 2003), 153, 193; Edward C. Burks, "Rep. Fenwick: Basics Her Forte," *New York Times*, May 13, 1979, accessed May 17, 2018, nytimes.com; Edward C. Burks, "Mrs. Fenwick Sees Marriage Tax's End," *New York Times*, March 1, 1981, accessed May 17, 2018, nytimes.com; Spencer Rich, "GOP Panel Adopts a Pro–ERA Plank," *Washington Post*, August 13, 1976, accessed July 12, 2018, washingtonpost.com; Leslie Bennetts, "Republicans and Women's Issues."

18. Bruce Lambert, "Millicent Fenwick, 82, Dies; Gave Character to Congress," *New York Times*, September 17, 1992, accessed March 14, 2018, nytimes.com.

19. Michele L. Swers, *The Difference Women Make*, 124.

20. Barbara Mikulski, et al., *Nine and Counting: The Women of the Senate* (New York: HarperCollins, 2000), 70.

21. "Vote My Conscience, " Ileana Ros-Lehtinen Interview with the *Human Rights Campaign*, Winter 2013, accessed March 12, 2017, hrc.org.

22. Sheryl Gay Stolberg, Jeff Zenley, and Carl Hulse, "Health Vote Caps a Journey Back From the Brink," *New York Times*, March 20, 2010, accessed March 15, 2018, nytimes.

com; Carrie Budoff Brown and Glenn Thrush, "Nancy Pelosi Steeled White House for Health Push," *Politico,* March 20, 2010, accessed March 15, 2018, politico.com.

23. E.J. Dionne, Jr., "Special Election Squeaker Shakes Dem Confidence," *Albuquerque Journal,* October 22, 2007, accessed June 23, 2018, newspapers.com.

24. "Kin of 9/11 Pilot Runs for House," *Philadelphia Inquirer,* September 6, 2007, accessed March 26, 2018, newspapers.com.

25. Stephen Ward, "Susan Collins: Most Likely to Make You Wish You Had Ninety-Nine More of Her in the Senate (Alternatively: Perfect Attendance)," *BYU Political Review,* December 2, 2017, accessed February 16, 2018, politicalreview.byu.edu.

26. Torey Van Oot, "For Women in Congress, the State of the Union Is a #MeToo Moment," *Glamour,* January 30, 2018, accessed June 14, 2018, glamour.com.

27. Scott Detrow, "With Women's Rights As A Focus, Attention Turns To Gillibrand," NPR, December 26, 2017, accessed June 14, 2018, npr.org.

28. Mick Krever and Sophie Tatum, "Sen. Kirsten Gillibrand Calls on Trump to Resign," CNN Politics, December 11, 2017, accessed February 7, 2018, cnn.com.

29. Max Greenwood, "Gillibrand Laments NRA's 'Chokehold' on Congress," *The Hill,* February 21, 2018, accessed July 11, 2018, thehill.com.

30. Christopher Ingraham, "The Two Assault Weapons Bans before Congress Are Co-sponsored by 195 Democrats and 0 Republicans," *Washington Post,* February 28, 2018, accessed June 15, 2018, washingtonpost.com.

31. Nancy Pelosi Web Site, accessed December 18, 2018, https://pelosi.house.gov/.

Is Narrowing," *New York Times News,* May 15, 2018, accessed August 11, 2018, nytimes.com.

2. Heather Caygle, "Record-Breaking Number of Women Run for Office," March 8, 2018, *Politico,* accessed December 19, 2018, politico.com; Alex Schroeder, "Putting the Record-Setting Election for Women in Context," WBUR On Point, November 7, 2018, accessed December 19, 2018, wbur.org.

3. Kathleen E. Carey, "Year of Woman in 5th: Longtime Education Advocate Mary Gay Scanlon Carries Dem Banner," *U.S. News and World Report,* July 25, 2018, accessed December 16, 2018, usnews.com.

4. Angela Kocherga, "Democrats Look to Flip Pearce's Seat," *Albuquerque Journal,* May 7, 2018, accessed December 20, 2018, abqjournal.com.

5. Julián Aguilar, "Six Democrats Vying for O'Rourke's El Paso Seat," *Austin American-Statesman* (Austin, TX), February 18, 2018, accessed December 17, 2018, newspapers.com.

6. Katharine Q. Seelye and Astead W. Herndon, "Ayanna Pressley Seeks Her Political Moment in a Changing Boston," *New York Times,* September 1, 2018, accessed December 21, 2018, nytimes.com.

7. "By the Numbers: EMILY's List + the 2018 Midterms," Emily's List, September 24, 2018, accessed December 22, 2018, emilys list.org.

8. Ed O'Keefe, "Gillibrand Works to Elect More Women," *Washington Post,* August 1, 2012, accessed December 22, 2018, washingtonpost.com.

9. Vivian Wang, "Ocasio-Cortez's Next Task: Empowering Other Female Outsiders to Win," *New York Times,* July 6, 2018, accessed December 23, 2018, nytimes.com.

Conclusion

1. Kate Zernike and Denise Lu, "Women Run for Congress in Droves, but Their Path

Bibliography

"Ab Hermann, Former Republican National Committee Executive Director, Honored at Luncheon." Press Release. September 25, 1978. Robert J. Dole Archive and Special Collections, University of Kansas. Accessed April 4, 2018, dolearchivecollections.ku. edu.

Adams, Grace. "Women Don't Like Themselves." *North American Review* 247, no. 2 (Summer 1939): 288–295.

Adams, Mildred. "Congresswomen Are Just Congressmen." *New York Times.* June 19, 1932. Accessed April 2, 2018, *New York Times* Historical Database.

Aday, Sean, and James Devitt. "Style over Substance: Newspaper Coverage of Elizabeth Dole's Presidential Bid." *International Journal of Press/Politics* 6, no. 2 (2001): 52–73.

Aguilar, Julián. "Six Democrats Vying for O'Rourke's El Paso Seat." *Austin American-Statesman* (Austin, TX). February 18, 2018. Accessed December 17, 2018, newspapers.com.

"Alaska Governor Appoints Daughter for His Senate Spot." *Post Crescent* (Appleton, WI). December 21, 2002. Accessed May 11, 2018, newspapers.com.

Allen, Jonathan, and Amie Parnes. *Shattered: Inside Hillary Clinton's Doomed Campaign.* New York: Crown, 2017.

Alter, Jonathan. "A Catharsis in Denver?" *Newsweek.* August 8, 2008. Accessed April 11, 2018, newsweek.com.

Amundsen, Kirsten. *The Silenced Majority: Women and American Democracy.* Englewood Cliffs, NJ: Prentice-Hall, 1971.

Andersen, Kristi. *After Suffrage: Women in Partisan and Electoral Politics before the New Deal.* Chicago: University of Chicago Press, 1996.

Anderson, Karrin Vasby. "From Spouses to Candidates: Hillary Rodham Clinton, Elizabeth Dole, and the Gendered Office of US President." *Rhetoric and Public Affairs* 5 (Spring 2002): 105–132.

Anderson, Kathryn. "Evolution of a Partisan: Emily Newell Blair and the Democratic Party, 1920–1932." In *We Have Come to Stay: American Women and Political Parties, 1880–1960,* 109–119. Edited by Melanie Gustafson, Kristie Miller, and Elisabeth I. Perry. Albuquerque: University of New Mexico Press, 1999.

_____. Introduction to *Jeannette Rankin: America's Conscience,* by Norma Smith, 5–22. Helena, MT: Montana Historical Society Press, 2002.

Angevine, Sara. "Representing All Women: An Analysis of Congress, Foreign Policy, and the Boundaries of Women's Surrogate Representation." *Political Research Quarterly* 70, no. 1 (2017): 98–110.

Anthony, Susan B. "What Can Women Do?" *Revolution* (March 24, 1870): 188.

Applegate, Debby. *The Most Famous Man in America: The Biography of Henry Ward Beecher.* New York: Doubleday, 2006.

"Attacks Man for Backing Clare Booth." *Palladium Item* (Richmond, IN). September 5, 1942. Accessed April 3, 2018, newspapers.com.

Avery, Martha Moore. "Why I Left the Socialist Movement." *Common Cause* 1 (February 1912): 14.

Ayers, Daisy Fitzhugh. "Katherine Langley Is Equal to the Task, Writer Declares." *Indianapolis Star.* November 14, 1926. Accessed May 4, 2018, newspapers.com.

Balz, Dan. "Union in Clinton's Corner—and Ready for a Fight." *Washington Post.* November 1, 2007. Accessed April 24, 2018, washingtonpost.com.

Banwart, Mary Christine. "Gender and Candidate Communication: Effects of Stereotypes in the 2008 Election." *American Behavioral Scientist* 54, no. 3 (2010): 265–284.

Bashevkin, Sylvia. *Women, Power, Politics: The Hidden Story of Canada's Unfinished Democracy.* New York: Oxford University Press, 2009.

Basow, Susan A. "Evaluation of Female Leaders: Stereotypes, Prejudice and Discrimination." In *Why Congress Needs Women: Bringing Sanity to the House and Senate*, 85–98. Edited by Michele A. Paludi. Santa Barbara, CA: Praeger, 2016.

Basu, Rekha. "Idealism Trumped Clinton's Hubris. " *Marion* (OH) *Star.* June 17, 2008. Accessed December 7, 2017, newspapers.com.

Bates, James Leonard. *Senator Thomas J. Walsh of Montana: Law and Public Affairs, from TR to FDR.* Urbana: University of Illinois Press, 1999.

Bauder, David. "Vacco Refuses to Criticize Remarks against Burstein." *The Post-Star* (Glen Falls, NY). October 12, 1994. Accessed February 2, 2018, newspapers.com.

Bauer, Gary. "Bill Clinton Would Lose 2016 Democratic Primary." *USA Today.* April 5, 2016. Accessed February 5, 2018, usatoday.com.

Baum, Geraldine. "A Rising Voice in the Revolution: Politics." *Los Angeles Times.* March 6, 1995. Accessed February 11, 2018, latimes.com.

Bazinet, Kenneth R. "Campaign Divides Doles—He Won't Drop McCain." *Daily News* (NY). January 10, 2000. Accessed September 12, 2018, newspapers.com.

Behymer, F.A. "How Mrs. Langley, with Her Husband in Prison, Was Elected to Congress." *St. Louis Post Dispatch.* September 26, 1926. Accessed January 12, 2018, newspapers.com.

Bellafaire, Judith A. "The Women's Army Corps: A Commemoration of World War II Service." *United States Army Center of Military History.* Accessed December 15, 2017, history.army.mil.

Bellesiles, Michael A. *A People's History of the US Military: Ordinary Soldiers Reflect on Their Experience of War, from the American Revolution to Afghanistan.* New York: New Press, 2012.

Belt, Todd L. "Viral Videos: Reinforcing Stereotypes of Female Candidates for President." In *Women and the White House: Gender, Popular Culture, and Presidential Politics*, 205–226. Edited by Justin S. Vaughn and Lilly J. Goren. Lexington: University Press of Kentucky, 2013.

Bennetts, Leslie. "Republicans and Women's Issues: For Some, a Painful Conflict." *New York Times.* September 2, 1980. Accessed March 30, 2018, *New York Times* Historical Database.

Berke, Richard L. "As Political Spouse, Bob Dole Strays from Campaign Script." *New York Times.* May 17, 1999. Accessed March 11, 2018, nytimes.com.

_____. "I'm Your No. 1 Fan, Hon. Really." *New York Times.* May 23, 1999. Accessed March 12, 2018, nytimes.com.

"Bill's Gaffe Shows He's Clueless." *Des Moines Register.* January 31, 2008. Accessed February 2, 2018, newspapers.com.

Black, Ruby. "The Case of Ruth Bryan Owen." *Equal Rights* (April 5, 1930): 67–69.

Blackman, Ann. "Women Seeking Office Find Special Problems." *Louisville Courier-Journal.* October 13, 1974. Accessed August 12, 2018, newspapers.com.

Blair, Emily Newell. "Are Women a Failure in Politics?" *Harper's* 151 (October 1925): 513–522.

_____. "Why I Am Discouraged about Women in Politics." *The Woman's Journal* (January 1931): 20–22.

"Blood, Be-lud!!, S-Blood!!!" *Alton* (IL) *Telegraph.* May 12, 1871. Accessed May 18, 2018, newspapers.com.

Board, John. "The Lady from Montana: Jeannette Rankin." Masters thesis, University of Wyoming, 1964.

"Bob Dole Anticipating Rematch with Clinton." *Pensacola News Journal.* April 29, 2002. Accessed December 8, 2017, newspapers.com.

Boggs, Lindy, with Katherine Hatch. *Washington Through a Purple Veil: Memoirs of a Southern Woman.* New York: Harcourt Brace, 1994.

Bowers, F. Suzanne. *Republican, First, Last, and Always: A Biography of B. Carroll Reece.* Newcastle: Cambridge Scholars Publishing, 2010.

Boxer, Barbara, with Nicole Boxer. *Strangers in the Senate: Politics and the New Revolution of Women in America.* Washington, D.C.: National Press Books, 1994.

Braden, John C., and Hortense Myers. "Love Is Great for the Poets, but Not All Roses for Voters." *Brownsville* (TX) *Herald.* October 17, 1976. Accessed January 12, 2018, news papers.com.

Braden, Maria. *Women Politicians and the Media.* Lexington: University Press of Kentucky, 1996.

Brandon, Ruth. *The Spiritualists: The Passion for the Occult in the Nineteenth and Twentieth Centuries.* New York: Alfred A. Knopf, 1983.

Braude, Ann. *Radical Spirits: Spiritualism and Women's Rights in Nineteenth-Century America.* Bloomington: Indiana University Press, 2001.

Breckinridge, Sophonisba P. "The Activities of Women Outside the Home." In *Recent Social Trends in the United States,* 709–750 (New York: McGraw-Hill, 1933).

_____. *Women in the Twentieth Century: A Study of Their Political, Social and Economic Activities.* New York: McGraw-Hill, 1933.

Britt, Donna. "A Happy Ending in Black and White." *Los Angeles Times.* November 17, 1996. Accessed December 31, 2017, latimes.com.

Brock, Herb. "Some Left Over Political Scraps from the Thanksgiving Table." *Advocate Messenger* (Danville, KY). November 29, 1999. Accessed May 11, 2018, newspapers. com.

Brooks, Deborah Jordan. *He Runs, She Runs: Why Gender Stereotypes Do Not Harm Women Candidates.* Princeton: Princeton University Press, 2013.

Brown, Carrie Budoff, and Glenn Thrush. "Nancy Pelosi Steeled White House for Health Push." *Politico,* March 20, 2010. Accessed March 15, 2018, politico.com.

Buhle, Mari Jo. *Women and American Socialism, 1870–1920.* Urbana: University of Illinois Press, 1983.

Bullock, Charles S., III, and Patricia Heys. "Recruitment of Women for Congress: A Research Note." *Western Political Quarterly* 25 (1972): 416–423.

Bumiller, Elisabeth. "The Mayor's Separation: The Overview." *New York Times.* May 11, 2000. Accessed March 26, 2018, *New York Times* Historical Database.

Burks, Edward C. "Mrs. Fenwick Sees Marriage Tax's End." *New York Times.* March 1, 1981. Accessed May 17, 2018, nytimes.com.

_____. "Rep. Fenwick: Basics Her Forte." *New York Times.* May 13, 1979. Accessed May 17, 2018, nytimes.com.

Burns, David. *The Life and Death of the Radical Historical Jesus.* New York: Oxford University Press, 2013.

Burrell, Barbara C. *Gender in Campaigns for the U.S. House of Representatives.* Ann Arbor: University of Michigan Press, 2014.

_____. *Women and Political Participation: A Reference Handbook.* Santa Barbara, CA: ABC-CLIO, 2004.

"By the Numbers: EMILY's List + the 2018 Midterms." Emily's List. September 24, 2018. Accessed December 22, 2018, emilyslist.org.

Cannon, Janath. "Taking the Great Plan into Consideration." In *Heroines of the Restoration,* 242–258. Edited by Barbara B. Smith and Blythe Darlyn Thatcher. Salt Lake City: Bookcraft, 1997.

Caraway, Hattie Wyatt. *Silent Hattie Speaks: The Personal Journal of Senator Hattie Caraway.* Edited by Diane D. Kincaid. Westport, CT: Greenwood Press, 1979.

Carey, Kathleen E. "Year of Woman in 5th: Longtime Education Advocate Mary Gay Scanlon Carries Dem Banner." *U.S. News and World Report.* July 25, 2018. Accessed December 16, 2018, usnews.com.

Carlin, Diana B., and Kelly L. Winfrey. "Have You Come a Long Way, Baby? Hillary Clinton,

Sarah Palin, and Sexism in 2008 Campaign Coverage." *Communication Studies* 60, no. 4 (September–October 2009): 326–343.
Carroll, Bret E. *Spiritualism in Antebellum America.* Bloomington: Indiana University Press, 1997.
Carroll, Susan J. *Women as Candidates in American Politics.* 2nd ed. Bloomington: Indiana University Press, 1994.
Carroll, Susan J., and Kira Sanbonmatsu. *More Women Can Run: Gender and Pathways to the State Legislatures.* New York: Oxford University Press, 2013.
Carter, Chelsea J. "Sister Act May Be Coming to Congress." *Indianapolis Star.* October 27, 2002. Accessed January 15, 2018, newspapers.com.
Caygle, Heather. "Record-Breaking Number of Women Run for Office." March 8, 2018. *Politico.* Accessed December 19, 2018, politico.com.
Chamberlin, Hope. *A Minority of Members: Women in the U.S. Congress.* New York: Praeger, 1973.
Chambers, Andrea. "Congressman John Dingell Makes Washington Quake, but Not His Executive Wife, Debbie." *People.* June 23, 1986. Accessed January 14, 2018, people.com.
"Change the Illinois House." *Chicago Tribune.* November 6, 2016. Accessed June 2, 2018, newspapers.com.
Cheek, Katrina Rebecca. *The Rhetoric and Revolt of Jeannette Rankin.* Masters thesis, University of Georgia, 1969.
"Choices for U.S. House." *Chicago Tribune.* January 15, 2008. Accessed March 23, 2018, newspapers.com.
Claflin, Tennie C. "My Word on Abortion, and Other Things." *Woodhull & Claflin's Weekly.* September 23, 1871. Accessed May 12, 2018, victoria-woodhull.com.
Clifton, Guy. "UNR Grad Cortez Masto Has Sights on Attorney General." *Reno Gazette-Journal.* October 23, 2005. Accessed February 2, 2018, newspapers.com.
Clinton, Hillary Rodham. *Living History.* New York: Simon & Schuster, 2004.
_____. *What Happened.* New York: Simon & Schuster, 2017.
Cohen, Nancy. *Breakthrough: The Making of America's First Woman President.* Berkeley: Counterpoint, 2016.
Collins, Gail. "Politics: Taking the 'Help' Out of 'Helpmate': Bob Dole Shows How Not to Be a Supportive Spouse." *New York Times.* May 18, 1999. Accessed December 12, 2017, nytimes.com.
"The Coming Woman." *New York Herald.* April 2, 1870. Accessed March 31, 2018, newspapers.com.
"The Congress of Internationalists." *Guardian.* September 10, 1872. Accessed February 23, 2018, newspapers.com.
"Congressman Knows Plenty About Hart." *Muncie* (IN) *Evening Press.* March 13, 1984. Accessed May 7, 2018, newspapers.com.
"Congresswoman Clarke Finds Pleasure in Legislative Job." *Washington Post.* January 20, 1934. Accessed June 18, 2018, newspapers.com.
Corry, John. "Wallace Ponders a New Strategy for Retaining His Power in Alabama." *New York Times.* October 31, 1965. Accessed March 26, 2018, *New York Times* Historical Database.
"Could He Add Stand-Up Comic to His Résumé?" *Star Press* (Muncie, IN). February 4, 1999. Accessed December 12, 2017, newspapers.com.
Creel, George. "The Woman Who Holds Her Tongue." *Collier's.* September 18, 1937: 22+.
Crouse, Eric R. *An American Stand: Senator Margaret Chase Smith and the Communist Menace, 1948–1972.* Lanham, MD: Lexington Books, 2010.
Crow, Rob. "A Literal Legacy." *Southern Illinoisan* (Carbondale). December 26, 2010. Accessed April 11, 2018, newspapers.com.
"Daughters of the Fire-Eaters." *Santa Ana Register.* April 29, 1928. Accessed April 4, 2018, newspapers.com.
"Death of a Patriarch." *Statesman Journal* (Salem, OR). November 1, 1993. Accessed April 11, 2018, newspapers.com.
"Delegates Unanimous: 'Anybody but Bush.'" *Star Tribune* (Minneapolis). June 15, 2003. Accessed April 14, 2018, newspapers.com.

Dellios, Hugh. "Hillary Clinton in a Pickle: Arafat's Wife Puts First Lady in Middle." *Chicago Tribune.* November 12, 1999. Accessed March 28, 2018, newspapers.com.
"Democracy's Mental Dissolution Pictured as Nazi Goal in US." *Christian Science Monitor.* July 20, 1940, 15.
Detrow, Scott. "With Women's Rights as a Focus, Attention Turns to Gillibrand." NPR. December 26, 2017. Accessed June 14, 2018, npr.org.
Deutsch, Hermann B. "Hattie and Huey." *Saturday Evening Post* (October 15, 1932): 6–7, 88–92.
Diaz, Daniella, and Drew Griffin. "Dem Operative 'Stepping Back' after Video Suggests Group Incited Violence at Trump Rallies." CNN Politics. October 18, 2016. Accessed January 22, 2018, cnn.com.
"A Different Voice: Women in Congress." *Constitutional Rights Foundation. Bill of Rights in Action.* 9:3 and 9.4 (Summer 1993). Updated July 2000. Accessed November 15, 2017, www.crf-usa.org.
Dionne, E.J., Jr. "Special Election Squeaker Shakes Dem Confidence." *Albuquerque Journal.* October 22, 2007. Accessed June 23, 2018, newspapers.com.
"A Dispatch from the Hague." *Galveston Daily News.* September 8, 1872. Accessed May 24, 2018, newspapers.com.
Dittmar, Kelly. *Navigating Gendered Terrain: Stereotypes and Strategy in Political Campaigns.* Philadelphia: Temple University Press, 2015.
_____. "Turning the Tables: Behind Every Successful Woman." In *Women and Executive Office: Pathways and Performance,* 231–256. Edited by Melody Rose. Boulder: Lynne Rienner Publishers, 2013.
Doan, Alesha E. *Opposition and Intimidation: The Abortion Wars and Strategies of Political Harassment.* Ann Arbor: University of Michigan, 2007.
"Dr. Eva Harding Doesn't Wait for Party Action." *Topeka Daily Capital.* January 16, 1916. Accessed March 11, 2018, newspapers.com.
Dodge Andrew R., and Betty K. Koed. *Biographical Directory of the United States Congress, 1774–2005.* Washington, D.C.: Government Printing Office, 2005.
Dodson, Debra L. *The Impact of Women in Congress.* New York: Oxford University Press, 2006.
"Does Name Recognition Really Count? You Bet It Does." *Asheville Citizen-Times.* April 13, 2002. Accessed November 12, 2018, newspapers.com.
"Does Our Looks-Obsessed Culture Want to Stare at an Aging Woman?" *The Rush Limbaugh Show.* December 17, 2007. Accessed March 22, 2018, rushlimbaugh.com.
Dolan, Julie, Melissa Deckman, and Michele L. Swers. *Women and Politics: Paths to Power and Political Influence.* Upper Saddle River, NJ: Pearson Prentice Hall, 2007.
Dolan, Kathleen A. *When Does Gender Matter?: Women Candidates and Gender Stereotypes in American Elections.* New York: Oxford University Press, 2014.
Dole, Bob, and Elizabeth Dole, with Richard Norton Smith. *The Doles, Unlimited Partners.* New York: Simon & Schuster, 1988.
Dowd, Maureen. "Bile in Bloom." *New York Times.* May 23, 1999. Accessed May 21, 2018, nytimes.com.
_____. "Discipline Us, Please." *New York Times.* January 6, 1999. Accessed April 23, 2018, nytimes.com.
_____. "Elizabeth Dole Is Leaving Labor Post." *New York Times.* October 24, 1990. Accessed March 26, 2018, nytimes.com.
_____. "Live from New York: It's Susan Molinari." *Salina* (KS) *Journal.* June 2, 1997. Accessed February 19, 2018, newspapers.com.
_____. "Political Husbandry in Iowa." *New York Times.* August 8, 1999. Accessed December 7, 2017, nytimes.com.
Drexel, Constance. "Mrs. Nolan No 'Crusader'; Mrs. Barrett Gains Note." February 24, 1924. *Washington Post.* Accessed May 2, 2018, newspapers.com.
Duffus, R.L. "A Woman Treads New Paths as Senator." *New York Times Magazine.* January 24, 1932. Accessed February 11, 2018, *New York Times* Historical Database.
"Education." In Census Report 2010, Chapter 10, 3–18. US Census Bureau. Accessed April 22, 2018, census.gov.

"Election News at a Glance." *Harrisburg Telegraph.* December 2, 1916. Accessed January 15, 2018, newspapers.com.

"Elizabeth Dole Exiles Mate to Woodshed." *New York Times.* May 19, 1999. Accessed March 17, 2018, nytimes.com.

"Equal Pay for Women." *New York Times.* November 12, 1916. Accessed April 2, 2018, *New York Times* Historical Database.

Erbe, Bonnie. "Elizabeth Dole Overreached." *News Journal* (Wilmington, DE). October 30, 1999. Accessed July 12, 2018, newspapers.com.

"Ex-West Virginia Governor Admits Corruption Schemes." *New York Times.* April 13, 1990. Accessed March 12, 2018, nytimes.com.

"Father's Slur Irks Black Rep." *Philadelphia Daily News.* October 17, 1996. Accessed June 12, 2018, newspapers.com.

Felton, Rebecca. *My Memoirs of Georgia Politics.* Atlanta, GA: Index Print Company, 1911.

"The Female Financiers." *Tennessean* (Nashville). April 1, 1870. Accessed February 21, 2018, newspapers.com.

"Female Financiers' Feuds." *Sun* (New York). May 8, 1871. Accessed May 9, 2018, newspapers. com.

"The Feminine Invasion of the Capitol." *Frank Leslie's Illustrated Newspaper.* 801 (February 4, 1871): 347.

Ferraro, Geraldine. "Bob, Some Things Should Just Remain Private." *Chicago Tribune.* April 1, 1999. Accessed January 11, 2017, newspapers.com.

Ferrell, Thomas H., and Judith Haydel. "Hale and Lindy Boggs: Louisiana's National Democrats." *Louisiana History* 35 (Fall 1994): 389–402.

Finlay, Mary Lou. "There's Always Next Time." *Ottawa Citizen.* June 5, 2008. Accessed July 11, 2018, lexisnexis.com.

Finnegan, Michael. "Congress Is Caught Up in the Sexual Misconduct Scandals. Will It Police Its Own?" *Los Angeles Times.* November 29, 2017. Accessed February 2, 2018, latimes.com.

Finneman, Teri. *Press Portrayals of Women Politicians, 1870s-2000s: From "Lunatic" Woodhull to "Polarizing" Palin.* Lanham, MD: Lexington Books, 2015.

Fitzgerald, Jim. "Clinton Fails to Endorse Immediate Withdrawal." *Lincoln Journal Star* (Lincoln, NE). November 22, 2005. Accessed December 18, 2018, newspapers.com.

Fitzpatrick, Ellen. *The Highest Glass Ceiling: Women's Quest for the American Presidency.* Cambridge: Harvard University Press, 2016.

Foerstel, Karen. *Biographical Dictionary of Congressional Women.* Westport, CT: Greenwood Press, 1999.

Foerstel, Karen, and Herbert N. Foerstel. *Climbing the Hill: Gender Conflict in Congress.* Westport, CT: Praeger, 1996.

Ford, Elizabeth. "New Rep. Reece: First Returns Were Happy Ones for Her." *Washington Post.* May 19, 1961. Accessed May 17, 2018, newspapers.com.

"Former W. Va. Gov. Arch Moore Dies at 91." *News Journal* (Wilmington, DE). January 9, 2015. Accessed April 22, 2018, newspapers.com.

"The Fourth of July." *Sterling* (IL) *Standard.* July 11, 1872. Accessed June 5, 2017, newspapers. com.

Franks, Lucinda. "The Intimate Hillary." *Talk.* 1, no. 1 (September 1999): 173+.

"The Free-Love Queen." *Charleston Daily News.* May 26, 1871. Accessed April 1, 2018, news papers.com.

Freeman, Jo. *We Will Be Heard: Women's Struggles for Political Power in the United States.* Lanham, MD: Rowman and Littlefield, 2008.

Friedman, Rachel B., and Ronald E. Lee. *The Style and Rhetoric of Elizabeth Dole: Public Persona and Political Discourse.* Lanham, MD: Lexington Books, 2013.

Frisken, Amanda. *Victoria Woodhull's Sexual Revolution: Political Theater and the Popular Press in Nineteenth-Century America.* Philadelphia: University of Pennsylvania Press, 2004.

Gabriel, Mary. *Notorious Victoria: The Life of Victoria Woodhull, Uncensored.* Chapel Hill, NC: Algonquin Books of Chapel Hill, 1998.

Gallant, Gregory P. *Hope and Fear in Margaret Chase Smith's America: A Continuous Tangle.* Lanham, MD: Lexington, 2014.

Gallup, Alec, and Frank Newport. *The Gallup Poll: Public Opinion 2005.* Lanham, MD: Rowman & Littlefield, 2006.

Gamerman, Ellen. "Child of Politics, All Grown Up." *Baltimore Sun.* November 14, 2002. Accessed February 3, 2018, newspapers.com.

_____. "Democratic Leader's Instincts Sewn in Baltimore." *Orlando Sentinel.* January 4, 2003. Accessed May 20, 2018, newspapers.com.

George, Emily. *Martha W. Griffiths.* Washington, D.C.: University Press of America, 1982.

Gertzog, Irwin N. *Congressional Women: Their Recruitment, Integration, and Behavior.* 2nd ed., Revised and Updated. Westport, CT: Praeger, 1995.

_____. *Congresswomen: Their Recruitment, Treatment, and Behavior.* New York: Praeger, 1984.

_____. "The Matrimonial Connection: The Nomination of Congressmen's Widows for the House of Representatives." *Journal of Politics* 42 (1980): 820–831.

_____. "Women's Changing Pathways to the U.S. House of Representatives: Widows, Elites, and Strategic Politicians." In *Women Transforming Congress,* 95–118. Edited by Cindy Simon Rosenthal. Norman: University of Oklahoma Press, 2002.

Giblin, James Cross. *The Rise and Fall of Senator Joe McCarthy.* New York: Houghton Mifflin Harcourt, 2009.

Gibson, William E. "Gwen Graham Rides into Congress with 'Independent Voice.'" *South Florida Sun Sentinel.* December 28, 2014. Accessed March 23, 2018, Sun-Sentinel.com.

Giles, Kevin S. *Flight of the Dove: The Story of Jeannette Rankin.* Beaverton, OR: Touchstone Press, 1980.

Gilfond, Duff. "Gentlewomen of the House." *American Mercury* (October 1929): 151.

Gillibrand, Kirsten. "A Reflection of My First Year in Congress." *The Hill.* December 14, 2007. Accessed April 4, 2018, thehill.com.

Githens, Marianne. "Accounting for Women's Political Involvement: The Perennial Problem of Recruitment." In *Women and American Politics: New Questions, New Directions,* 33–52. Edited by Susan Carroll. New York: Oxford University Press, 2003.

Givhan, Robin. "Hillary Clinton's Tentative Dip into New Neckline Territory." *Washington Post.* July 20, 2007. Accessed February 12, 2018, washingtonpost.com.

Goodman, Ellen. "Ads Make Candidate's Sex Life a Topic for Debate." *Tampa Tribune.* April 5, 1999. Accessed January 15, 2018, newspapers.com.

_____. "Progress by Drip Method." *Des Moines Register.* November 8, 1986. Accessed November 8, 2017, newspapers.com.

Grady, Sandy. "'Hillary,' Just 'Hillary,' Has Dropped Her Surname and First Lady Role in NY Race." *Clarion-Ledger* (Jackson, MS). February 10, 2000. Accessed February 8, 2018, newspapers.com.

Graham, Frank, Jr. *Margaret Chase Smith.* New York: John Day, 1964.

Grana, Mari. *Dr. Martha: The Life of a Pioneer Physician, Politician, and Polygamist.* Guilford, CT: TwoDot, 2015.

"Greeley Ratified." *Daily State Journal* (Alexandria, VA). June 17, 1872. Accessed June 1, 2018, newspapers.com.

Green, Joshua. "The Front-Runner's Fall." *Atlantic* September 2008. Accessed March 23, 2018, theatlantic.com/archive.

Greenwood, Max. "Gillibrand Laments NRA's 'Chokehold' on Congress." *The Hill.* February 21, 2018. Accessed July 11, 2018, thehill.com.

Gruberg, Martin. *Women in American Politics: An Assessment and Sourcebook.* Oshkosh, WI: Academia Press, 1968.

"Guiliani Slams Hillary Clinton for Arafat Hug After Israel Slap." *New York Times.* November 13, 1999. Accessed January 3, 2018, newspapers.com.

Gutgold, Nichola D. *Almost Madam President: Why Hillary Clinton 'Won' in 2008.* Lanham, MD: Lexington Books, 2009.

_____. *Paving the Way for Madam President.* Lanham, MD: Lexington Books, 2006.

"Gwen Graham Eyes Politics: Senator's Daughter Has Name Recognition, Contacts." *News Press* (Ft. Myers, FL). June 14, 2004. Accessed January 9, 2018, newspapers.com.

Hall, Mimi. "Republican Women: A 'Contrast' with America." *USA Today*. December 27, 1994. Accessed March 11, 2018, newspapers.com.

Halley, Patrick S. *On the Road with Hillary: A Behind-the-Scenes Look at the Journey from Arkansas to the U.S. Senate*. New York: Viking, 2002.

Han, Lori Cox. *In It to Win: Electing Madam President*. New York: Bloomsbury Academic, 2015.

_____. "Is the United States *Really* Really Ready for a Woman President?" In *Rethinking Madam President: Are We Ready for a Woman in the White House?*, 1–16. Edited by Lori Cox Han and Caroline Heldman. Boulder, CO: Lynne Rienner, 2007.

Hardin, William H. "Elizabeth Kee: West Virginia's First Woman in Congress." *West Virginia History* 45 (1984): 109–123.

Hardy-Fanta, Carol, Pei-te Lien, Dianne Pinderhughes, and Christine Marie Sierra. *Contested Transformation: Race, Gender, and Political Leadership in 21st Century America*. New York: Cambridge University Press, 2016.

Harris, Melissa. "Cantwell Merges Father's Tactics into Race." *Indianapolis Star*. November 5, 2000. Accessed January 15, 2018, newspapers.com.

_____. "Seattle Senator Retains Hoosier Ties." *Indianapolis Star*, January 1, 2001. Accessed January 9, 2018, newspapers.com.

Harris, Ted Carlton. *Jeannette Rankin: Suffragist, First Woman Elected to Congress, and Pacifist*. New York: Arno Press. 1982.

Hartmann, Susan M. "Caraway, Hattie Ophelia." In *American National Biography*, vol. 4, 369–370. New York: Oxford University Press, 1999.

Hayes, Danny, and Jennifer L. Lawless. *Women on the Run: Gender, Media, and Political Campaigns in a Polarized Era*. New York: Cambridge University Press, 2016.

Healy, Patrick. "Politics Means Sometimes Having to Say You're Sorry." *New York Times*. March 4, 2007. Accessed February 4, 2018, *New York Times* Historical Database.

Heith, Diane. "The Lipstick Watch: Media Coverage, Gender, and Presidential Campaigns." In *Anticipating Madam President*, 123–130. Edited by Robert P. Watson and Ann Gordon. Boulder, CO: Lynne Rienner Publishers, 2003.

Heldman, Caroline, Susan J. Carroll, and Stephanie Olson. "'She Brought Only a Skirt': Media Coverage of Elizabeth Dole's Bid for the R Presidential Nomination." *Political Communication* 22, no. 3 (August 2006): 315–335.

Hendricks, Nancy. *Senator Hattie Caraway: An Arkansas Legacy*. Mt. Pleasant, SC: Arcadia Publishing, 2013.

Henehan, Kathleen, and Jeremy Holden, "Taking Lead from Drudge, Conservative Echo Chamber Hypes Clinton Photo." December 18, 2007. Media Matters. Accessed April 22, 2018, mediamatters.org.

Hennings, Robert E. *James D. Phelan and the Wilson Progressives of California*. New York: Garland, 1985.

"Her Daddy and Mamma Bother Her." *Daily Kansas Tribune*. December 16, 1871. Accessed January 26, 2017, newspapers.com.

"Her Latest Incarnation: Presidential Front-Runner." *Economist*. May 17, 2007. Accessed March 22, 2018, economist.com.

"Herseth Sandlin: Touts Work with Moderates. " *Argus-Leader* (Sioux Falls, SD). October 10, 2010. Accessed February 1, 2017, newspapers.com.

Hess, Stephen. *America's Political Dynasties: From Adams to Clinton*. Washington, D.C.: Brookings Institution Press, 2016.

_____. *America's Political Dynasties: From Adams to Kennedy*. Garden City, NY: Doubleday, 1966.

_____. "Political 'Royalty' in America (or, the Son Also Rises)." *Anniston* (AL) *Star*. January 22, 1978. Accessed February 15, 2018, newspapers.com.

Hild, Matthew. *Greenbackers, Knights of Labor, and Populists: Farmer-Labor Insurgency in the Late-Nineteenth-Century South*. Athens: University of Georgia Press, 2007.

Hildebrand, J.R. "Introducing Jeannette." *Washington Times*. November 11, 1916. Accessed February 21, 2018, newspapers.com.

Hill, Kristie. "Rep. Keys, Jacobs Retain Independence." *Kansas City* (MO) *Times*. November 5, 1976. Accessed March 12, 2018, newspapers.com.

"Hillary Clinton Rebukes Arafat's Wife." *Los Angeles Times.* November 13, 1999. Accessed February 18, 2018, newspapers.com.
Hodges, James A., James H. O'Donnell, and John William Oliver. *Cradles of Conscience: Ohio's Independent Colleges and Universities.* Kent, OH: Kent State University Press, 2003.
Holman, Rhonda. "Kassebaum Pushed for Anti-Apartheid Sanctions." *Wichita Eagle.* December 11, 2013. Accessed March 25, 2018, kansas.com.
"Honoring Luisa DeLauro on Her 100th Birthday." Press Release. Rosa DeLauro Web Site. December 24, 2013. Accessed January 22, 2018, delauro.house.gov.
Hooper, Cindy. *Conflict: African American Women and the New Dilemma of Race and Gender Politics.* Santa Barbara, CA: Praeger, 2012.
Hopkins, Christopher Snow. "New Mexico, 1st House District: Michelle Lujan Grisham (D)." *Atlantic.* November 6, 2012. Accessed May 13, 2018, theatlantic.com.
Horowitz, Helen Lefkowitz. "Victoria Woodhull, Anthony Comstock, and Conflict Over Sex in the United States in the 1870s." *Journal of American History* 87, no. 2 (September 2000): 403–434.
Horstman, Judith. "When Politics Is the Family Business." *Times Herald* (Port Huron, MI). January 19, 1984. Accessed February 27, 2018, newspapers.com.
Huffington, Arianna. "This Dole Is Getting a Free Ride." *Los Angeles Times.* March 16, 1999. Accessed March 9, 2018, newspapers.com.
Hutchison, Kay Bailey. *American Heroines: The Spirited Women Who Shaped Our Country.* New York: Morrow, 2004.
Ingraham, Christopher. "The Two Assault Weapons Bans Before Congress Are Co-sponsored by 195 Democrats and 0 Republicans." *Washington Post.* February 28, 2018. Accessed June 15, 2018, washingtonpost.com.
"Is 'the Old Cynthia' Back?" *Democrat and Chronicle* (Rochester, NY). April 6, 2006. Accessed March 9, 2018, newspapers.com.
"It's All in the Family in Alaska Politics." *Los Angeles Times.* December 21, 2002. Accessed April 6, 2018, newspapers.com.
Jackson, David. "Hillary Clinton's Test: A Third Straight Democratic Term." *USA Today.* April 10, 2015. Accessed January 22, 2018, newspapers.com.
Jamieson, Kathleen Hall. *Civility in the House of Representatives.* Philadelphia: Annenberg Center, 1999.
"Jeannette Rankin Explains Peace Pacts to Outlaw War." *Havre* (MT) *Daily News.* September 4, 1928. Accessed July 19, 2018, newspapers.com.
Jeffreys-Jones, Rhodri. *Changing Differences: Women and the Shaping of American Foreign Policy, 1917–1994.* New Brunswick: Rutgers University Press, 1997.
Jensen, Jane S. *Women Political Leaders: Breaking the Highest Glass Ceiling.* New York: Palgrave Macmillan, 2008.
Jones, Mary Lynn F. "A Slow, Steady Climb Up Capitol Hill." *Chicago Tribune.* October 4, 2000. Accessed March 19, 2018, newspapers.com.
Jones, Tim, and Mike Dorning. "Texas Too Close to Call." *Chicago Tribune.* March 5, 2008. Accessed February 4, 2018, newspapers.com.
Josephson, Hannah. *Jeannette Rankin: First Lady in Congress, A Biography.* Indianapolis: Bobbs-Merrill Company, 1974.
Kahn, Kim Fridkin. *The Political Consequences of Being a Woman: How Stereotypes Influence the Conduct and Consequences of Political Campaigns.* New York: Columbia University Press, 1996.
Kalisch, Beatrice J., and Philip A. Kalisch. "Nurses in American History The Cadet Nurse Corps in World War II." *American Journal of Nursing* 76, no. 2 (1976): 240–242.
Kaminer, Wendy. "Crashing the Locker Room." *Atlantic* 270 (July 1992): 58–70. Accessed June 12, 2018, theatlantic.com/magazine/archive.
"A Kansas Woman Runs for Congress." *Independent* (July 13, 1914): 66.
Kaptur, Marcy. *Women of Congress: A Twentieth-Century Odyssey.* Washington, D.C.: Congressional Quarterly Press, 1996.
Kass, John. "GOP Fight Hogs Spotlight, Doing Clinton a Favor." *Chicago Tribune.* February 28, 2016. Accessed February 6, 2018, newspapers.com.

_____. "Schakowsky Ire Phony as Kited Checks." *Chicago Tribune.* April 7, 2006. Accessed December 2, 2017, newspapers.com.
"Kassebaum to Seek Second Term." *Salina Journal.* March 18, 1994. Accessed January 2, 2018, newspapers.com.
"Katherine Harris Ponders Senate Race." *South Florida Sun Sentinel.* November 7, 2003. Accessed June 2, 2018, newspapers.com.
Kaufman, Joanne, and Barbara Kleban Mills. "While Nebraska Governor Kay Orr Makes Policy, Husband Bill, Her 'First Gentleman,' Bakes Meat Loaf." *People.* December 12, 1988. Accessed February 12, 2018, people.com.
Kazin, Michael. *A Godly Hero: The Life of William Jennings Bryan.* New York: Anchor Books, 2007.
"Kee's Widow Wins Race for His House Seat." *Chicago Tribune.* July 18, 1951. Accessed March 12, 2018, newspapers.com.
"Kentucky's First Congresswoman." *Literary Digest* (August 21, 1926): 14.
"Kin of 9/11 Pilot Runs for House." *Philadelphia Inquirer.* September 6, 2007. Accessed March 26, 2018, newspapers.com.
Kincaid, Diane. "Over His Dead Body: A Positive Perspective on Widows in the U.S. Congress." *Western Political Quarterly* 31 (1978): 96–104.
Kirkpatrick, Jeane. *The New Presidential Elite: Men and Women in National Politics.* New York: Russell Sage Foundation, 1976.
Kocherga, Angela. "Democrats Look to Flip Pearce's Seat." *Albuquerque Journal.* May 7, 2018. Accessed December 20, 2018, abqjournal.com.
Kramer, Michael. "Liddy Without Tears." *New York Daily News.* October 24, 1999. Accessed December 5, 2018, nydailynews.com.
Krever, Mick, and Sophie Tatum. "Sen. Kirsten Gillibrand Calls on Trump to Resign." CNN Politics. December 11, 2017. Accessed February 7, 2018, cnn.com.
Kristof, Nicholas. "Hillary Clinton, Free to Speak Her Mind." *New York Times.* April 8, 2017. Accessed January 2, 2018, nytimes.com.
Kropf, Martha E., and John A. Boiney. "The Electoral Glass Ceiling? Gender, Viability, and the News in U.S. Senate Campaigns." In *Women and Congress: Running, Winning, and Ruling,* 79–103. Edited by Karen O'Connor. New York: Haworth Press, 2001.
Kunin, Madeleine May. *Living a Political Life.* New York: Knopf, 1994.
Kurtz, Howard. "Hillary Chuckles; Pundits Snort; Clinton's Robust Yuks Leads to Analysis of Appeal of Laughter." *Washington Post.* October 3, 2007. Accessed February 12, 2018, washingtonpost.com.
Lambert, Bruce. "Millicent Fenwick, 82, Dies; Gave Character to Congress." *New York Times.* September 17, 1992. Accessed March 14, 2018, nytimes.com.
"Landrieu Follows Long Political Tradition." *Times* (Shreveport, LA). December 1, 2002. Accessed January 11, 2018, newspapers.com.
"Langley May Return to Politics." *Washington Post.* January 2, 1929. Accessed July 12, 2018, newspapers.com.
Lawless, Jennifer L., and Richard L. Fox. *It Still Takes A Candidate: Why Women Don't Run for Office.* New York: Cambridge University Press, 2010.
_____. *It Takes a Candidate: Why Women Don't Run for Office.* New York: Cambridge University Press, 2005.
_____. "Men Rule: The Continued Under-Representation of Women in Politics." Women and Politics Institute, Washington, D.C.: 2012. Accessed January 12, 2018, www.american.edu/spa/wpi.
"Lawmaker's Widow Will Seek His Seat." *St. Louis Post-Dispatch.* January 2, 1972. Accessed May 12, 2018, newspapers.com.
Lawrence, Jill. "Dole Turns from Sticky Senate to Bully Pulpit." *Indiana Gazette.* February 21, 2002. Accessed July 2, 2018, newspapers.com.
"Leave Politics to Men, Woman in House Says." *Washington Post.* December 31, 1929. Accessed August 1, 2018, newspapers.com.
Lehman, Amy. *Victorian Women and the Theatre of Trance: Mediums, Spiritualists and Mesmerists in Performance.* Jefferson, NC: McFarland, 2009.

Lennon, Bert. "Jeannette Rankin Is Well Qualified to Serve in Congress." *Oregon Daily Journal.* December 3, 1916. Accessed August 7, 2018, newspapers.com.
_____. "The Lady from Montana." *Charlotte Observer.* December 24, 1916. Accessed August 15, 2018, newspapers.com.
"Leonor K. Sullivan." *Los Angeles Times.* September 2, 1988. Accessed August 18, 2018, news papers.com.
_____. *Washington Post.* September 2, 1988. Accessed August 18, 2018, newspapers.com.
"Letter from Hawk's Nest Peak." *Woodhull & Claflin's Weekly.* July 1, 1871. Accessed July 25, 2018, victoria-woodhull.com.
"Letter from Tennie C. Claflin." *Woodhull & Claflin's Weekly.* August 5, 1871. Accessed May 12, 2018, victoria-woodhull.com.
Levins, Harry. "Relationship Roulette." *St-Louis Dispatch.* December 4, 1999. Accessed August 9, 2018, newspapers.com.
"Liddy Dole Has a Problem with a Prominent Politician." *Portland* (ME) *Press Herald.* May 30, 1999. Accessed October 12, 2017, newspapers.com.
Lopach, James J., and Jean A. Luckowski. *Jeannette Rankin: Political Woman.* Boulder: University Press of Colorado, 2005.
Loth, David. *A Long Way Forward, The Biography of a Congresswoman: Frances P. Bolton.* New York: Longmans, Green, 1957.
Lyons, Joseph. *Clare Boothe Luce, Author and Diplomat.* New York: Chelsea House, 1989.
MacPherson, Myra. *The Scarlet Sisters: Sex, Suffrage, and Scandal in the Gilded Age.* New York: Twelve, 2014.
Mahan, A.F. "Washington Letter: Rep. Martha Griffiths (D–Michigan)." *The Robesonian* (Lumberton, NC). December 1, 1954. Accessed August 14, 2018, newspapers.com.
Malcolm, Ellen R., and Craig Unger. *When Women Win: EMILY's List and the Rise of Women in American Politics.* Boston: Houghton Mifflin Harcourt, 2016.
Malone, Clare. "From 1937 To Hillary Clinton, How Americans Have Felt About a Woman President." June 9, 2016. *FiveThirtyEight.* Accessed August 28, 2018, fivethirtyeight. com/features.
Malone, David. *Hattie and Huey: An Arkansas Tour.* Fayetteville: University of Arkansas Press, 1989.
Malone, Julia. "First Lady Facing Tough Task at Convention." *Rocky Mountain News.* August 25, 1996. Accessed March 16, 2018, newspapers.com.
Maltzman, Forrest, Lee Sigelman, and Sarah Binder. "Leaving Office Feet First." *PS: Political Science and Politics* 29, no. 4 (1996): 665–671.
Manegold, Catherine S. "Her Father's Daughter and Her Party's Luminary." *New York Times.* May 18, 1993. Accessed September 1, 2018, nytimes.com.
Mangum, Frances. "Congresswoman Good Friend to War Veterans." *Washington Post.* January 23, 1934. Accessed May 2, 2018, newspapers.com.
Mann, Jonathan. "Bill Clinton's Gaffes Stump Hillary." CNN Politics. April 17, 2008. Accessed December 5, 2018, cnn.com.
Mann, Thomas, and Norman Ornstein. *The Broken Branch: How Congress Is Failing American and How To Get It Back on Track.* New York: Oxford University Press, 2006.
_____. *It's Even Worse than It Looks: How the American Constitutional System Collided with the New Politics of Extremism.* New York: Basic Books, 2012.
Marcin, Tim. "Nearly 60 Percent of Republicans Don't Want a Woman President in Their Lifetime, Poll Finds." *Newsweek.* April 26, 2018. Accessed May 2, 2018, newsweek.com.
Marcos, Cristina. "Women, Dems Leading Sexual Harassment Discussion in Congress." November 27, 2017. *The Hill.* Accessed February 3, 2018, thehill.com.
Marcus, Ruth. "Trump is Right: Bill Clinton's Sordid Sexual History Is Fair Game." *Washington Post.* December 28, 2015. Accessed April 19, 2018, washingtonpost.com.
Margolies-Mezvinsky, Marjorie, with Barbara Feinman. *A Woman's Place ... The Freshmen Women Who Changed the Face of Congress.* New York: Crown Publishers, 1994.
"Mark Hanna's Daughter Puts Vim into Anti-Hoover Camp." *Indianapolis Star.* June 8, 1928. Accessed September 27, 2018, newspapers.com.
Markavy, Jerry. "Two Women from One New England State Stand Out in the Senate." *Star-Democrat* (Easton, MD). June 27, 2005. Accessed September 22, 2018, newspapers.com.

"Mary Bono Decides to Run." *Desert Sun* (Palm Springs, CA). January 23, 1998. Accessed September 27, 2018, newspapers.com.
"Mary Bono Loses One Vote." *South Florida Sun Sentinel.* March 29, 1998. Accessed September 14, 2018, newspapers.com.
Masters, Kim. "The Woman in the Hot Seat." *Washington Post.* July 5, 1995. Accessed March 12, 2018, washingtonpost.com.
Matika, Lawrence A. *The Contributions of Frederick Albert Cleveland to the Development of a System of Municipal Accounting in the Progressive Era.* Kent, OH: Kent State University Press, 1988.
Mayhead, Molly A., and Brenda DeVore Marshall. *Women's Political Discourse: A 21st-Century Perspective.* Lanham, MD: Rowman & Littlefield, 2005.
McFarlane, Peter Clark. "Jeannette of Montana." *Colliers* (April 21, 1917): 7–8+.
McGlen, Nancy E., Karen O'Connor, Laura van Assendelft, and Wendy Gunther-Canada. *Women, Politics, and American Society.* New York: Longman, 2017.
McGrory, Mary. "It's Not the Money, Honey." *Washington Post.* October 24, 1999. Accessed September 10, 2018, newspapers.com.
"Meet the Freshmen." *Burlington Free Press.* November 6, 2014. Accessed January 19, 2018, newspapers.com.
Menzel, Margie. "Graham: Daughter Will Work for Constituents." *Palm Beach Post.* January 11, 2015. Accessed October 14, 2018, newspapers.com.
Mercer, Bob. "Some Things We Learned about Ourselves Tuesday." *Black Hills Pioneer* (Spearfish, SD). June 14, 2010. Accessed February 17, 2018, newspapers.com.
Merica, Dan. "Bill Clinton: Hillary Can 'Put the Awful Legacy of the Last Eight Years Behind Us.'" CNN Politics. March 22, 2016. Accessed March 11, 2018, cnn.com.
Meyer, Eugene L. "Congressman Louise Reece, GOP National Chief's Widow." *Washington Post.* May 16, 1970. Accessed April 27, 2018, newspapers.com.
"Michelle Lujan Grisham for U.S. House District I." *Albuquerque Journal.* October 28, 2012. Accessed February 7, 2018, newspapers.com.
Mikulski, Barbara, Kay Bailey Hutchison, Diane Feinstein, Barbara Boxer, Patty Murray, Olympia Snowe, Susan Collins, Mary Landrieu, and Blanche L. Lincoln. *Nine and Counting: The Women of the Senate.* New York: HarperCollins, 2000.
Milbank, Dana. "Family Ties Playing a Big Role on the Hill: Some Offices Appear Inherited, Not Elected." *Washington Post.* January 23, 2005. Accessed July 17, 2018, washingtonpost.com.
Milbank, Dana, and David S. Broder. "Hopes for Civility in Washington Are Dashed; In Bush's Term, Tone Worsened, Partisans Say." *Washington Post.* January 18, 2004. Accessed July 24, 2018, washingtonpost.com.
Miller, Kevin. "Margaret Chase Smith Paved the Way, but Will the Governor's Mansion Remain Elusive?" *Bangor* (ME) *Daily News.* July 30, 2010. Accessed March 25, 2018, bangordailynews.com.
Miller, Kristie. *Ruth Hanna McCormick: A Life in Politics, 1880–1944.* Albuquerque: University of New Mexico Press, 1992.
"Minority Leader Had Early Taste for Politics." *Lansing State Journal.* January 5, 2003. Accessed July 29, 2018, newspapers.com.
"Miss Jeannette Rankin." *Democrat and Chronicle* (Rochester, NY). October 18, 1916. Accessed June 21, 2018, newspapers.com.
"Miss Rankin to Run." *The Boyden* (IA) *Reporter.* September 5, 1918. Accessed January 14, 2018, newspapers.com.
"Miss Rankin, War Opponent in 1917, Hasn't Changed Mind." *Washington Post.* December 9, 1941. Accessed May 16, 2018, newspapers.com.
Mitchell, Dawn. "Amanda Way Was Indiana's Hard-Core Anti-Booze Baroness." *Indianapolis Star.* March 20, 1917. Accessed February 15, 2018, IndyStar.com.
Molinari, Susan. *Representative Mom: Balancing Budgets, Bill and Baby in the U.S. Congress.* New York: Doubleday, 1998.
Molineux, Will. "High Profile: Jeanne Zeidler: Leading Williamsburg Into Its Tercentenary." *Daily Press* (Williamsburg, VA). April 26, 1999. Accessed January 22, 2018, articles.dailypress.com.

Moore, Kate. "Elizabeth Johnston Patterson: Following a Family Tradition." April 1, 2015. A Capitol Blog. Accessed February 12, 2018, library.sc.edu/blogs.

Morden, Bettie J. *The Women's Army Corps, 1945–1978.* Washington, D.C.: Government Printing Office, 1990.

Morris, Sylvia Jukes. *Rage for Fame: The Ascent of Clare Boothe Luce.* New York: Random House, 1997.

Morrison, John, and Catherine Wright Morrison. *Mavericks: The Lives and Battles of Montana's Political Legends.* Helena, MT: Montana Historical Society, 2003.

Morton, Joseph. "Brad Ashford Will Run Again for Nebraska's 2nd District Seat." *Omaha World-Herald.* June 19, 2017. Accessed December 28, 2018, omaha.com.

"Mrs. Byron Elected Maryland's First Congresswoman." *Washington Post.* May 28, 1941. Accessed March 1, 2018, newspapers.com.

"Mrs. Byron Marks Victory Amid Hubbub of Congratulations and Household Duties." *Washington Post.* May 30, 1931. Accessed March 1, 2018, newspapers.com.

"Mrs. Caraway Plans Campaign." *The Courier News* (Blytheville, AK). July 14, 1932. Accessed August 11, 2018, newspapers.com.

"Mrs. Dole, President, of U.S., not Red Cross?" *Pittsburgh Post-Gazette.* January 4, 1999. Accessed March 1, 2018, newspapers.com.

"Mrs. Grover Announces Candidacy for Congress." *Topeka Daily Capital.* April 19, 1914. Accessed March 8, 2018, newspapers.com.

"Mrs. Huck for Congress; Mason's Daughter, Mother of Four, a Candidate to Succeed Him." *New York Times.* July 1, 1921. Accessed March 22, 2018, newspapers.com.

"Mrs. Langley to Retire From Politics in 1930." *Washington Post.* December 25, 1928. Accessed July 12, 2018, newspapers.com.

"Mrs. Luce Wins Another Term." *Press and Sun Bulletin* (Binghamton, NY). November 8, 1944. Accessed April 2, 2018, newspapers.com.

"Mrs. McMillan to Carry on Husband's Work in Congress." *Washington Post.* November 9, 1939. Accessed March 11, 2018, newspapers.com.

"Mrs. Nolan Takes Her Place in House." *Washington Post.* February 13, 1923. Accessed April 17, 2018, newspapers.com.

"Mrs. Oldfield Decries Feminist in Politics." *New York Times.* February 19, 1931. Accessed April 2, 2018, newspapers.com.

"Mrs. Oldfield to Quit Congress at Term End." *New York Times.* May 30, 1929. Accessed December 12, 2017, newspapers.com.

"Mrs. Oldfield to Retire." *Los Angeles Times.* May 30, 1929. Accessed April 17, 2018, newspapers.com.

Murphy, Sean. "Should Being a Mother Matter?" *Indianapolis Star.* October 24, 2010. Accessed April 12, 2018, newspapers.com.

Murray, Rainbow. "Conclusion: A New Comparative Framework." In *Cracking the Highest Glass Ceiling: A Global Comparison of Women's Campaigns for Executive Office,* 223–248. Edited by Rainbow Murray. Santa Barbara: Praeger, 2010.

"Name Recognition No Help in Alaska Race." *Los Angeles Times.* October 3, 2004. Accessed April 2, 2018, newspapers.com.

"Nancy Hopes to Become a Chip Off Landon Block." *Iola* (KS) *Register.* March 23, 1978. Accessed January 2, 2018, newspapers.com.

"Nancy Landon Kassebaum Intends to Use Dad's Name." *Fort Scott* (KS) *Tribune.* March 22, 1978. Accessed January 22, 2018, newspapers.com.

Nancy Pelosi Web Site, accessed June 14, 2018, https://pelosi.house.gov/.

Nast, Thomas. "Get Thee Behind Me, Mrs. Satan." *Harpers Weekly,* February 17, 1872, HarpWeek: Cartoon of the Day, accessed September 11, 2017, harpweek.com.

"Nebraska Woman Named to Griswold Senate Seat." *New York Times.* April 17, 1954. Accessed February 11, 2018, newspapers.com.

"New Congress Boasts Record Number of Women." *Chillicothe* (OH) *Gazette.* December 14, 1954. Accessed December 14, 2018, newspapers.com.

"New Congresswoman Bars Picturemen." *Oakland Tribune.* November 17, 1916. Accessed July 27, 2018, newspapers.com.

"New Hispanic Congresswomen Face Tough Challenges, Reflect Trend of More Women in

Congress." *Santa Fe New Mexican.* February 8, 1993. Accessed November 24, 2017, newspapers.com.
"New York: The Internationalists Procession a Decided Success." *Chicago Tribune.* December 18, 1871. Accessed March 12, 2018, newspapers.com.
Newman, Maria. "From Puerto Rico to Congress, a Determined Path." *New York Times.* September 27, 1992. Accessed February 6, 2018, *New York Times* Historical Database.
Official Abstract of Votes Cast at the General Election Held in Montana, November 5, 1918. Montana Secretary of State. Accessed December 19, 2017, sos.mt.gov.
O'Keefe, Ed. "Gillibrand Works to Elect More Women." *Washington Post.* August 1, 2012. Accessed December 22, 2018, washingtonpost.com.
O'Leary, Mary. "Luisa DeLauro, Mother of Rosa, Dies at 103." *New Haven Register.* September 11, 2017. Accessed February 28, 2018, nhregister.com.
Orin, Deborah. "Bob: I'd Be Happy as First Man as Long as 'I Go to Bed with Her.'" *New York Post.* March 11, 1999. Accessed April 11, 2018, newspapers.com.
Orme, William A., Jr. "While Mrs. Clinton Looks On, Palestinian Officials Criticize Israel." *New York Times.* November 12, 1999. Accessed February 19, 2018, nytimes.com.
"Our Busy Congresswoman." *Literary Digest* 55 (August 11, 1917): 43.
"Our Morning Contemporary." *Salt Lake Tribune.* November 1, 1896. Accessed December 23, 2018, newspapers.com.
Owen, Karen L. *Women Officeholders and the Role Models Who Pioneered the Way.* Lanham, MD: Lexington Books, 2017.
Palmer, Barbara, and Dennis Simon. *Women and Congressional Elections: A Century of Change.* Boulder, CO: Lynne Rienner Publishers, 2012.
"Parents of Mrs. Fenwick: Ambassador Hammond Lost Wife on Lusitania." *Bernardsville (NJ) News.* August 22, 1974. Accessed April 11, 2018, newspapers.com.
Parker, Kathleen. "Let's Give JFK, Reagan a Rest." *Baltimore Sun.* January 31, 2008. Accessed January 21, 2018, newspapers.com.
Parsons, Dan. "Zeidler Looks Back on Career as Williamsburg's First Female Mayor." *Daily Press* (Williamsburg, VA). June 29, 2010. Accessed January 22, 2018, articles.dailypress.com.
Patterson, Ethel Lloyd. "Romantic Love Will Come Only in the Future." *St. Louis Post Dispatch.* June 10, 1911. Accessed May 11, 2018, newspapers.com.
Paxton, Annabel. *Women in Congress.* Richmond, VA: Dietz Press, 1945.
"Peace and Freedom: Policy and World Ideas." Accessed December 29, 2018, johnib.wordpress.com.
"Pelosi Prizes Loyalty and Partisanship." *Baltimore Sun.* October 27, 2006. Accessed June 14, 2018, newspapers.com.
Pelter, Lorraine. "Fenwick Welcomes Challenge." *Echoes Sentinel* (Warren Township, NJ). April 11, 1974. Accessed June 22, 2018, newspapers.com.
Peterson, Kristina. "Dear, Are You Running for Congress?" *Wall Street Journal.* June 1, 2017: A1+.
"The Petticoat Bankers." *Evening Telegraph* (Philadelphia, PA). March 26, 1870. Accessed February 21, 2018, newspapers.com.
"A Piebald Presidency." *New York Herald.* May 11, 1872. Accessed January 4, 2018, newspapers.com.
"Political Family Inspired Pelosi." *Argus Leader* (Sioux Falls, SD). November 12, 2006. Accessed November 28, 2017, newspapers.com.
"The Power of Wealth." *American Dynasties: The Kennedys.* Episode 1. Directed by Peter W. Kunhardt. Aired March 11, 2018. New York: CNN, 2018.
Press, Bill. "Hillary, Please Shut Up Now." *News Journal* (Wilmington, DE). August 7, 1999. Accessed July 12, 2018, newspapers.com.
Prewitt, Kenneth. *The Recruitment of Political Leaders: A Study of Citizen-Politicians.* Westport, CT: Greenwood Press, 1970.
"Pro and Con." *Washington Post.* June 18, 1932. Accessed November 8, 2017, newspapers.com.
"Proportion of Seats Held by Women in National Parliaments." The World Bank. Accessed December 12, 2017, data.worldbank.org.

Przybyla, Heidi M. "Bill Clinton Comes Off Sidelines of 2016 Campaign." *USA Today*. October 8, 2015. Accessed March 14, 2018, usatoday.com.

Pugh, Carol. "Gwen Graham Thinks Her Father Might Run for President." *News-Press* (Ft. Myers, FL). January 9, 1979. Accessed January 2, 2018, newspapers.com.

Pullen, Suzanne. "First Female California Representatives from the City." *San Francisco Examiner*. November 10, 2000. A7.

"The Queens of Finance." *New York Herald*. January 22, 1870. Accessed November 8, 2017, newspapers.com.

"The Queens of Finance." *Reading* (PA) *Times*. February 8, 1870. Accessed November 8, 2017, newspapers.com.

"A Question of Clothes." *New York Times*. June 16, 1872. Accessed January 21, 2018, news papers.com.

Rankin, Jeannette. "I Would Vote 'No' Again." *The Alton* (IO) *Democrat*. April 17, 1936. Accessed February 12, 2018, newspapers.com.

_____. "What We Women Should Do." *Ladies Home Journal*. August 1917: 17.

Rankin, Wellington. Interview with John Board. University of Montana. March 23, 1964. Wellington D. Rankin papers. Archives West. Accessed December 8, 2017, archives west.orbiscascade.org.

"Reapportionment, Redistricting and Women: The Dangers and Opportunities in California." *CAWP News & Notes* 7, no. 1 (1989): 14–15.

Renehan, Edward J., Jr. *Commodore: The Life of Cornelius Vanderbilt*. New York: Basic Books, 2009.

"The Republican Debate." *New York Times*. January 24, 2008. Accessed April 16, 2018, nytimes.com.

Reston, Maeve. "Louisiana Sen. Mary Landrieu Teams Up with Father for Campaign Ad." *Los Angeles Times*. May 13, 2014. Accessed January 5, 2018, newspapers.com.

Reynolds, Genevieve. "Nation's Feminine Eyes Are on a Distaff Contingent Named as Representatives." *Washington Post*. November 12, 1944. Accessed September 23, 2018, newspapers.com.

"Rift between Blacks, Jews Worries Democrats for Fall." *Baltimore Sun*. August 26, 2002. Accessed September 29, 2018, newspapers.com.

Ripley, Josephine. "The Surprising Mrs. Smith," *Christian Science Monitor* (November 10, 1950): 5.

Roberts, Sam. "Gillibrand's Grandmother Also Wielded Political Power, but from the Wings." *New York Times*. January 31, 2009. Accessed April 15, 2018, *New York Times* Historical Database.

Roberts, Steven V. "From 'Nice Little Nancy' to 'Effective.'" *New York Times*. July 11, 1983. Accessed April 18, 2018, nytimes.com.

"Robertson Letter Attacks Feminists." *New York Times*. August 26, 1992. Accessed December 18, 2017, nytimes.com.

Rohde, Ruth Bryan Owen. "Let's Live with Our Careers." Bess Furman Papers. Library of Congress, Manuscript Division.

Roland, Lisa L. "Family, Women's Issues at Heart of Landrieu Campaign." *Times* (Shreveport, LA). September 1, 1996. Accessed October 12, 2018, newspapers.com.

Roosevelt, Eleanor. "Women in Politics, Part I." *Good Housekeeping* (January 1940): 18–19+.

Rothman, Lily. "How the First Woman Was Elected to US National Office, Exactly 100 Years Ago." *Time*. November 7, 2016. Accessed April 12, 2018, newspapers.com.

"Rule or Ruin." *Pittsburgh Daily Post*. December 18, 1871. Accessed March 12, 2018, news papers.com.

Sanbonmatsu, Kira, and Susan J. Carroll. "Women's Decisions to Run for Office: A Relationally Embedded Model." In *The Political Psychology of Women in US Politics*, 148–164. Edited by Angela L. Bos and Monica C. Schneider. New York: Routledge, 2017.

Sandalow, Marc. *Madam Speaker: Nancy Pelosi's Life, Times, and Rise to Power*. New York: Modern Times, 2008.

Sanders, Sam. "Bill Clinton Gets into Heated Exchange With Black Lives Matter Protester." NPR. April 7, 2016. Accessed March 15, 2018, npr.com.

Saunders, Sally. "It Was a Shock When Liz Said She Wouldn't Run." *Greenville* (SC) *News.* April 13, 1978. Accessed February 22, 2018, newspapers.com.
Schaffer, Ronald. "Jeannette Rankin, Progressive-Isolationist." Ph.D. diss., Princeton, 1959.
_____. "The Montana Woman Suffrage Campaign, 1911–14." *Pacific Northwest Quarterly* 55, no. 1 (January 1964): 9–15.
Schapiro, Amy. *Millicent Fenwick: Her Way.* New Brunswick: Rutgers University Press, 2003.
Schmich, Mary T. "Georgia Sodomy Law a Family Matter." *Chicago Tribune.* February 2, 1990. Accessed March 12, 2018, newspapers.com.
Schmidt, Patricia L. *Margaret Chase Smith: Beyond Convention.* Orono: University of Maine Press, 1996.
Schribman, David M. "Bob Dole Eager to Play Second Fiddle to His Wife." *Salina* (KS) *Journal.* April 1, 1999. Accessed January 12, 2018, newspapers.com.
Schroeder, Alex. "Putting the Record-Setting Election for Women in Context." WBUR On Point. November 7, 2018. Accessed December 19, 2018, wbur.org.
Schroeder, Pat. *Champion of the Great American Family.* New York: Random House, 1989.
_____. *24 Years of House Work ... and the Place Is Still a Mess: My Life in Politics.* Kansas City: Andrews McMeel Publishing, 1998.
Scott, Anne Firor. *Making the Invisible Woman Visible.* Urbana: University of Illinois Press, 1984.
Scott, Patricia Lyn, and Linda Thatcher. *Women in Utah History: Paradigm or Paradox?* Logan: Utah State University Press, 2005.
"Seek to Explain Miss Rankin's 'No.'" *New York Times.* April 7, 1917. Accessed April 15, 2018, *New York Times* Historical Database.
Seelye, Katharine Q., and Astead W. Herndon. "Ayanna Pressley Seeks Her Political Moment in a Changing Boston." *New York Times.* September 1, 2018. Accessed December 21, 2018, nytimes.com.
"Senator Hattie W. Caraway Rules as Arkansas' Political Matriarch." *Tampa Tribune.* September 4, 1942. Accessed February 12, 2018, newspapers.com.
Senior, Jennifer. "The First: Female President, Male First Lady, Former President in the White House; Contemplating Clinton II." *New York Magazine.* September 30, 2007. Accessed February 12, 2018, nymag.com.
Sheckels, Theodore F. *Cracked but Not Shattered: Hillary Rodham Clinton's Unsuccessful Campaign for the Presidency.* Lanham, MD: Lexington Books, 2009.
Shedd, Lindley C. "Effiegene Wingo: An Early Congresswoman from Arkansas." *Arkansas Historical Quarterly* 67, no. 1 (2008): 27–53.
Sheeler, Kristina Horn, and Karrin Vasby Anderson. *Woman President: Confronting Postfeminist Political Culture.* College Station: Texas A&M University Press, 2013.
Sherrill, Martha. "The Sisters of Maine." *Washington Post.* May 6, 2011. Accessed January 12, 2018, newspapers.com.
Silva, Christianna. "Don't Hold Your Breath for Gender Parity in Congress—It Could Take Another 100 Years." *FiveThirtyEight.* October 3, 2016. Accessed August 28, 2018, fivethirtyeight.com.
Silverman, Joan. "The New Bob Dole, Viagra Spokesman." *Journal of Commerce.* March 15, 1999. Accessed May 29, 2018, newspapers.com.
Sisk, Chas. "In a 'Man's World,' O'Brien Was Political Pioneer." *Tennessean* (Nashville). September 2, 2009. Accessed February 12, 2018, newspapers.com.
Smith, Margaret Chase. "Declaration of Conscience." June 1, 1950. *American Rhetoric.* Accessed August 3, 2018, americanrhetoric.com.
_____. "No Place for a Woman." *Ladies Home Journal* (February 1952): 50.
Smith, Norma. *Jeannette Rankin: America's Conscience.* Helena, MT: Montana Historical Society Press, 2002.
Solotaroff, Paul. "Trump Seriously: On the Trail with the GOP's Tough Guy." *Rolling Stone.* September 9, 2015. Accessed March 11, 2018, rollingstone.com.
Spangler, Todd, and Kathleen Gray. "Michigan Losing Political Clout." *Livingston County* (MI) *Daily Press and Argus.* August 13, 2014. Accessed June 3, 2018, newspapers.com.
Specht, Jim. "The Beat Goes On." *San Bernardino County Sun.* January 23, 1998. Accessed July 22, 2018, newspapers.com.

_____. "Sonny Bono's Widow Sworn In." *The Daily Journal* (Vineland, NJ). April 22, 1998. Accessed December 11, 2018, newspapers.com.
"Spirit of the Press; Extraordinary Politics." *Woodhull & Claflin's Weekly.* June 1, 1872. Accessed February 4, 2018, victoria-woodhull.com.
Spriggs, A.E. Letter to Thomas Walsh. September 2, 1918. Thomas James Walsh Papers. Library of Congress.
Steele, Volney. *Wellington Rankin: His Family, Life and Times.* Bozeman, MT: Bridger Creek Historical Press, 2002.
Stolberg, Sheryl Gay. "A Second Act in Washington for Half of Power Couple." *Star Tribune* (Minneapolis). November 27, 2014. Accessed January 14, 2018, newspapers.com.
Stolberg, Sheryl Gay, Jeff Zenley, and Carl Hulse. "Health Vote Caps a Journey Back From the Brink." *New York Times.* March 20, 2010. Accessed March 15, 2018, nytimes.com.
Streitmatter, Rodger. *Voices of Revolution: The Dissident Press in America.* New York: Columbia University Press, 2001.
"Strong Pressure, Failed to Influence Congresswoman's Vote on War." *Cincinnati Enquirer.* April 7, 1917. Accessed February 23, 2018, newspapers.com.
Swers, Michele L. *The Difference Women Make: The Policy Impact of Women in Congress.* Chicago: University of Chicago Press, 2002.
_____. *Women in the Club: Gender and Policy Making in the Senate.* Chicago: University of Chicago Press, 2013.
Tackett, Michael. "Bill Clinton Emerges as Polarizing Figure in S.C." *Santa Fe New Mexican.* January 27, 2008. Accessed February 1, 2018, newspapers.com.
Talmadge, John E. *Rebecca Latimer Felton.* Athens: University of Georgia Press, 1960.
Taylor, Paul. "Political Nonpositions: Louisiana's Cathy Long Runs on Artfully Vague Race." *Washington Post.* March 30, 1985. Accessed April 17, 2018, newspapers.com.
"Tennessee Area to Vote Tuesday: Rep. Baker's Widow Running for House in 2nd District." *New York Times.* March 8, 1964. Accessed May 5, 2018, newspapers.com.
"Tennie and the Germans." *Sun* (New York). August 12, 1871. Accessed May 12, 2018, newspapers.com.
"Tennie Claflin." *Athens* (PN) *Gleaner.* September 14, 1871. Accessed May 12, 2018, newspapers.com.
_____. *Clarion-Ledger* (Jackson, MS). April 21, 1870. Accessed May 12, 2018, newspapers.com.
"Their Ugly Past: Reviving the Record of the Claflins." *San Francisco Chronicle.* May 8, 1890. Accessed March 31, 2018, newspapers.com.
"33rd Congressional Race to Represent Downtown." *Los Angeles Times.* May 27, 1992. Accessed March 12, 2018, newspapers.com.
Thomas, Cal. "Peace Negotiators Blind to Truth about PLO." *News-Press* (Ft. Myers, FL). November 22, 1999. Accessed June 11, 2018, newspapers.com.
Thomas, Lera Millard. Oral History. October 11, 1968. Lyndon Baines Johnson Library, Austin, Texas.
"Three of a Kind: Lockwood, Anthony and Stanton, Quarreling over a Man." *St. Louis Post-Dispatch.* August 16, 1884. Accessed April 2, 2018, newspapers.com.
"Three Women." *Waterloo* (IO) *Press.* November 9, 1871. Accessed May 12, 2018, newspapers.com.
Tilton, Theodore. *Biography of Victoria C. Woodhull.* New York: Golden Age, 1871.
"Today in Philadelphia." April 19, 1916. Philadelphia: The World War I Years. Accessed April 7, 2018. philadelphiawwiyears.com.
Tokasz, Jay. "Bob Dole Still Plays Politics. " *Democrat and Chronicle* (Rochester, NY). September 15, 1999. Accessed October 7, 2018, newspapers.com.
Tolchin, Susan. *Women in Congress.* Washington, D.C.: Government Printing Office, 1976.
Tomasky, Michael. *Hillary's Turn: Inside Her Improbable, Victorious U.S. Senate Campaign.* New York: Free Press, 2001.
Towery, Matt. "Hang It Up, Obama—It's Hillary's Nomination." *Human Events Online.* January 18, 2007, lexisnexis.com.
Traister, Rebecca. *Big Girls Don't Cry: The Election that Changed Everything for American Women.* New York: Free Press, 2010.

Trzebiatowska, Marta, and Steve Bruce. *Why are Women More Religious Than Men?* New York: Oxford University Press, 2012.
Tucker, Cynthia. "Whiny Recriminations Don't Suit Clinton Supporters, So Stop Them." *Atlanta Constitution.* June 7, 2008. Accessed February 17, 2018, newspapers.com.
Tumulty, Brian. "Political Novice Brings New Ideas." *Democrat and Chronicle* (Rochester, NY). January 24, 2009. Accessed June 12, 2018, newspapers.com.
Tysver, Robynn. "Ann Ferlic Ashford Considering a Run for Husband's Old Seat in 2nd Congressional District." *Omaha World-Herald.* March 13, 2017. Accessed July 12, 2018, omaha.com.
United States Cadet Nurse Corps [1943–1948] and Other Federal Nursing Programs. U.S. Public Health Service. 38 (1950). Accessed August 11, 2018, usphs.gov.
"U.S. Now at War with Germany and Italy." *New York Times.* December 11, 1941. Accessed December 15, 2017, newspapers.com.
Usher, Brisa. "Political Progress of Women Impresses Even Men in the GOP." *Akron* (OH) *Beacon Journal.* July 15, 1984. Accessed May 19, 2018, newspapers.com.
Van Oot, Torey. "For Women in Congress, the State of the Union Is a #MeToo Moment." *Glamour.* January 30, 2018. Accessed June 14, 2018, glamour.com.
Vickers, Sarah Pauline. *The Life of Ruth Bryan Owen: Florida's First Congresswoman and America's First Woman Diplomat.* Tallahassee, FL: Sentry Press, 2009.
"Vote My Conscience." Ileana Ros-Lehtinen Interview with the *Human Rights Campaign.* Winter 2013. Accessed March 12, 2017, hrc.org.
Wallace, Patricia Ward. *Politics of Conscience: A Biography of Margaret Chase Smith.* Westport, CT: Praeger, 1995.
Walsh, Kenneth T., and Gloria Borger. "Psst, Bob Dole Beats His Wife." *US News & World Report.* May 31, 1999. Accessed March 18, 2018, Lexis Nexis Academic Universe.
Walter, Dave. *More Montana Campfire Tales: Fifteen Historical Narratives.* Helena, MT: Farcountry Press, 2002.
_____. "Rebel with a Cause." *Montana* 110 (November–December 1991): 66–72.
Wang, Vivian. "Ocasio-Cortez's Next Task: Empowering Other Female Outsiders to Win." *New York Times.* July 6, 2018. Accessed December 23, 2018, nytimes.com.
"War on the Kansas Map." *New York Times.* February 21, 1916. Accessed June 12, 2018, *New York Times* Historical Database.
"Washington Woman Put Up for Congress." *St. Louis Post-Dispatch.* September 14, 1916. Accessed February 27, 2018, newspapers.com.
"Washington's Luckiest Kids: The Children of Congressmen Live in a World of Open Doors, Famous People, and Big Goings-On." *Life* (June 6, 1949): 146–152.
Wasniewski, Matthew A. *Women in Congress, 1917–2006.* Washington: G.P.O., 2006.
Wasson, Don. "Big Foot-Stomping Rally Climaxes Wallace Swing." *Montgomery Advertiser.* October 25, 1966. Accessed March 26, 2018, newspapers.com.
Wayne, Leslie. "Millicent Fenwick: 'Power Has No Charm.'" *Philadelphia Inquirer.* November 24, 1974. Accessed January 3, 2018, newspapers.com.
"We Presume We Must Accept." *Democrat and Chronicle* (Rochester, NY). July 11, 1871. Accessed January 7, 2018, newspapers.com.
Weatherford, Doris. *Women in American Politics: History and Milestones.* Vol. 1. Washington, D.C.: CQ Press, 2012.
"The Week." *Public Opinion* 14, no. 32 (April 3, 1902): 419.
Wertheimer, Molly Meijer, and Nichola D. Gutgold. *Elizabeth Hanford Dole: Speaking from the Heart.* Westport, CT: Praeger Publishers, 2004.
Weston, Chris. "Workman Fails to Get Showdown with Patterson." *Greenville* (SC) *News.* January 30, 1986. Accessed January 14, 2018, newspapers.com.
Whitaker, Lois Duke. "Women Politicians and the Mass Media: Does Gender Influence the News?" In *Women in Politics: Outsiders or Insiders?: A Collection of Readings,* 73–88. Edited by Lois Duke Whitaker. 5th ed. Boston: Longman, 2011.
Whitehouse, Ken. "Annabelle Clement O'Brien Passes Away at 86; Former State Senator Was Stalwart of Tennessee Democratic Politics." *Nashville Post.* September 1, 2009. Accessed March 9, 2018, newspapers.com.

"Who is Jeannette Rankin and What Will She Do?" *Woman's Journal and Suffrage News* (November 18, 1916): 370.

Wickham, DeWayne. "Broaddrick's Back with Old Charges." *Asheville Citizen-Times.* November 1, 2000. Accessed January 12, 2018, newspapers.com.

"The Widow and Familial Connections." History, Art, and Archives, U.S. House of Representatives. Accessed January 23, 2018, history.house.gov.

"Widow of Nolan Is Winner of His Seat in Congress." *St Louis Star and Times.* January 24, 1923. Accessed January 15, 2018, newspapers.com.

Wilgoren, Jodi. "Widows of Bono, Capps Are on Well-Worn Path to Office." *Los Angeles Times.* January 26, 1998. Accessed January 2, 2018, latimes.com.

Willis, Ronald Gary. "The Persuasion of Clare Boothe Luce." Ph.D. diss., Indiana University, 1993.

Wilson, Carol O'Keefe. *In the Governor's Shadow: The True Story of Ma and Pa Ferguson.* Denton: University of North Texas Press, 2014.

Winters, Susan Cramer. "Enlightened Citizen: Frances Payne Bolton and the Nursing Profession." Ph.D. diss., University of Virginia, 1997.

Witt, Linda, Karen M. Paget, and Glenna Matthews. *Running as a Woman: Gender and Power in American Politics.* New York: Free Press, 1994.

"Wolf Blitzer Interview with Cokie Roberts." CNN Politics. April 14, 2008. Accessed February 1, 2018, politicalticker.blogs.cnn.com.

Woloch, Nancy. *Women and the American Experience.* New York: Knopf, 1984.

"Woman Not Nominated." *The Daily Gate City and Constitution-Democrat* (Keokuk, IA). August 12, 1916. Accessed January 21, 2018, newspapers.com.

"Woman Running for Congress: Miss Burkhart Making Canvass on Horseback in Kentucky." *New York Times.* March 30, 1902. Accessed February 6, 2018, *New York Times* Historical Database.

"The Woman's Right Women—The Irrepressible Conflict." *Star Tribune* (Minneapolis). May 18, 1872. Accessed February 23, 2018, newspapers.com.

"Women in the U.S. Congress 2017." CAWP: Center for American Women and Politics. Rutgers Eagleton Institute of Politics. Accessed November 12, 2017, cawp.rutgers. edu.

"Women Office Seekers." *New York Times.* November 1, 1896. Accessed January 20, 2018, *New York Times* Historical Database.

"Women Who Succeeded Their Husbands in Congress." *2013.* CAWP: Center for American Women and Politics. Rutgers Eagleton Institute of Politics. Accessed February 9, 2018, cawp.rutgers.edu.

"Woodhull and Claflin at the Polls." *Harrisburg Telegraph.* November 14, 1871. Accessed March 1, 2018, newspapers.com.

"Woodhull and Claflin on the Tramp." *Burlington Free Press.* December 18, 1871. Accessed March 1, 2018, newspapers.com.

"Woodhull and Claflin Slander." *The Friends of Temperance* (Raleigh, NC). September 6, 1871. Accessed March 1, 2018, newspapers.com.

"Woodhull and Douglass." *Sun* (New York). May 11, 1872. Accessed March 1, 2018, newspapers.com.

Woodhull, Victoria. "Mrs. Woodhull's Own Statement." *The Great Sensation: A Full, Complete and Reliable History of the Beecher-Tilton-Woodhull Scandal, with Biographical Sketches of the Principal Characters,* 82–116. Edited by Leon Oliver. Chicago: Beverly Company, 1873.

_____. "Tried as by Fire: Or, the True and the False, Socially." *The Victoria Woodhull Reader,* 1–44. Edited by Madeleine B. Stern. Weston, MA: M&S Press, 1974.

"The Woodhull-Claflin Family." *Brooklyn Daily Eagle.* May 11, 1871. Accessed March 5, 2018, newspapers.com.

Woodward, Calvin. "On the Road to Denver, St. Paul: Obama Audaciously Overcame Huge Favorite." *Decatur* (IL) *Daily.* August 25, 2008. Accessed January 22, 2018, decatur daily.com.

"The Workingmen's Voice." *Sun* (New York). December 18, 1871. Accessed March 9, 2018, newspapers.com.

Yachnin, Jennifer. "In New Mexico, It's Good to Be a Luján." *E&E Daily.* June 26, 2015. Accessed May 12, 2018, eenews.net.

Youth, Jobs and Defense. Washington, D.C.: National Youth Administration, 1941.

Zernike, Kate, and Denise Lu. "Women Run for Congress in Droves, but Their Path Is Narrowing." *New York Times.* May 15, 2018. Accessed August 11, 2018, nytimes.com.

Index

www.ingramcontent.com/pod-product-compliance
Lightning Source LLC
Chambersburg PA
CBHW020242290326
41929CB00045B/1533